CONTENTS

BED AND BREAKFAST IN BRITAIN 1995

Have you ever wondered whether or not *you* are the perfect guest? We often change personality when we travel, when we're away from home, and behave in ways that are sometimes subtly and at other times violently different from our normal pattern. A man on business who may be a lamb at home, can become a lion when he stays away; children turn into monsters and sweet old ladies develop biting tongues. Anyone who deals with us, the public, at large, knows how difficult we can be and those who cater for our food and accommodation are most especially in the firing line!

The staff in a large hotel or at a busy motorway service area will probably quickly forget the rude and awkward customer but the owners of guest houses or your B&B landladies are often opening up and sharing their homes. They are much more likely to extend the limits of hospitality when they see that their efforts are appreciated and that their own privacy is respected. In Britain we are lucky to have our well-established tradition of informal 'bed & breakfast' overnight stops which offer great value-for-money and friendly service. Visitors from abroad envy our good fortune - but do we ourselves always give praise where it is due?

In *BED & BREAKFAST IN BRITAIN 1995* we have our usual large and varied selection of entries from all over the country. We hope that you'll find what you want and that if it's appropriate, you won't forget to leave a complimentary comment in the Visitors' Book!

More generally, you may find the following notes helpful when you are using *BED AND BREAKFAST IN BRITAIN.* You'll find it easy to book direct from the addresses and telephone numbers shown in our entries. Before you confirm a booking, make sure that price and other details are what you expect. We suggest that whenever possible you book ahead and if you have to cancel, you should let your host know, as far in advance as possible. The information and prices quoted in the entries in this guide are published in good faith but we do go to press early. If you have any problems - and we hear of very few - which cannot be settled on the spot, let us know and we will follow up. We regret, however, that we cannot act as intermediaries and that we cannot accept responsibility for errors, omissions or changes in holiday details - or for accommodation and/or services provided.

Naturally we cannot guarantee to have an address for every holiday or business trip you make and we will be pleased to receive recommendations for any new proprietors we can approach.

Every year we award a small number of FHG Diplomas to advertisers whose services have been specially commended by our readers. We welcome your nominations and the award winners are always proud to display their Diploma as an acknowledgement of their hospitality.

Please mention *BED AND BREAKFAST IN BRITAIN* when you are making enquiries or bookings and don't forget to use our Readers' Offer Voucher/Coupons if you're near any of the attractions which are kindly participating.

Peter Clark ***Publishing Director***

BED AND BREAKFAST IN BRITAIN 1995

Overnight and Short Break Accommodation

With or without Evening Meals

FHG PUBLICATIONS

Other FHG Publications 1995

Recommended Country Hotels of Britain
Recommended Wayside Inns of Britain
Recommended Short-Break Holidays in Britain
Pets Welcome!
The Golf Guide: Where to Play/Where to Stay
Farm Holiday Guide England/Wales
Farm Holiday Guide Scotland
Self-Catering & Furnished Holidays
Britain's Best Holidays
Guide to Caravan and Camping Holidays
Bed and Breakfast Stops
Children Welcome! Family Holiday Guide

1995 Edition
ISBN 1 85055 193 6

Cover design: Sheila Begbie, Glasgow
Cartography by GEO projects, Reading

Set by Image & Print Group, Glasgow
Printed and bound in Great Britain by The Guernsey Press, Guernsey

Distribution: **Book Trade:** WLM, Downing Road,
West Meadows Industrial Estate, Derby, Derbyshire DE21 6HA
(Tel: 01332 343332; Fax: 01332 340408/340464).
News Trade: UMD, 16-28 Tabernacle Street, London EC2A 4BN
(Tel: 0171-638 4666. Fax: 0171-638 4665).

Published by FHG Publications Ltd., Abbey Mill Business Centre,
Seedhill, Paisley PA1 1TJ (0141-887 0428. Fax: 0141-889 7204)

un A United Newspapers publication

FHG

READERS' OFFER 1995

VALID until end 1995

INTERNATIONAL HELICOPTER MUSEUM

Weston Airport, Locking Moor Road, Weston-super-Mare, Avon BS22 8PP Tel: 01934 635227

Admit **ONE CHILD FREE** with full paying adult

NOT TO BE USED IN CONJUNCTION WITH ANY OTHER OFFER

FHG

READERS' OFFER 1995

VALID during 1995 Season

Beale Park

Lower Basildon, Reading, Berkshire RG8 9NH Tel: (01734) 845172

Admit **ONE CHILD FREE** with an accompanying adult

NOT TO BE USED IN CONJUNCTION WITH ANY OTHER OFFER

FHG

READERS' OFFER 1995

VALID during 1995

Sacrewell Farm & Country Centre

Thornhaugh, Peterborough, Cambridgeshire PE8 6HJ Telephone: (01780) 782222

One **FREE** admission with each paid entry of similar age group (adult/child)

NOT TO BE USED IN CONJUNCTION WITH ANY OTHER OFFER

FHG

READERS' OFFER 1995

VALID during 1995 Season

Flambards Village Theme Park

Helston, Cornwall TR13 0GA Telephone: (01326) 574549

£1.00 OFF full admission price

NOT TO BE USED IN CONJUNCTION WITH ANY OTHER OFFER

FHG

READERS' OFFER 1995

VALID during 1995 Season

North Cornwall Museum and Gallery

The Clease, Camelford, Cornwall Telephone: (01840) 212954

One **FREE** adult entry with every paid adult entry

NOT TO BE USED IN CONJUNCTION WITH ANY OTHER OFFER

Britain's only dedicated helicopter museum with over 50 full-size exhibits, models, displays, restoration hangar, ride simulator. Cafeteria.

DIRECTIONS: A371 on east boundary of town; 5 mins from M5 Junction 21. Follow the 'propellor' road signs.

OPEN: 10am-6pm daily (4pm Nov to March). Closed Christmas, Boxing Day & New Year's Day.

FHG PUBLICATIONS, ABBEY MILL BUSINESS CENTRE, PAISLEY PA1 1TJ

Exotic birds, pets' corner, adventure playgrounds, river cruises etc, all set in acres of gardens, lakes and water meadows.

DIRECTIONS: on A329 one mile from Pangbourne.

OPEN: daily February 20th–December 23rd.

FHG PUBLICATIONS, ABBEY MILL BUSINESS CENTRE, PAISLEY PA1 1TJ

The fascinating story of farming and country life with working watermill, gardens, collections of bygones, farm and nature trails. Excellent for young children. Campers and Caravanners welcome.

DIRECTIONS: off A47, 8 miles west of Peterborough.

OPEN: daily all year.

FHG PUBLICATIONS, ABBEY MILL BUSINESS CENTRE, PAISLEY PA1 1TJ

All-weather entertainment for all the family. Victorian Village, Britain in the Blitz, super family rides, entertainment, gardens and much more.

DIRECTIONS: A394 to Helston.

OPEN: Easter to end October.

FHG PUBLICATIONS, ABBEY MILL BUSINESS CENTRE, PAISLEY PA1 1TJ

Life in Cornwall during the past century. Workmen's tools, domestic items, collection of Cornish and Devonshire pottery.

DIRECTIONS: off A39 18 miles south of Bude.

OPEN: Easter to end September daily except Sundays.

FHG PUBLICATIONS, ABBEY MILL BUSINESS CENTRE, PAISLEY PA1 1TJ

FHG

READERS' OFFER 1995

VALID April to end October 1995

South Tynedale Railway

Alston, Cumbria CA9 3JB Telephone (01434) 381696

Reduction of 40p on adult ticket and 20p on child ticket

NOT TO BE USED IN CONJUNCTION WITH ANY OTHER OFFER

FHG

READERS' OFFER 1995

VALID during 1995 season (museum entry only)

Windermere Steamboat Museum

Rayrigg Road, Windermere, Cumbria LA23 1BN Tel: 015394 45565

ONE FREE ENTRY for every paying adult

NOT TO BE USED IN CONJUNCTION WITH ANY OTHER OFFER

FHG

READERS' OFFER 1995

VALID during 1995

The Donington Collection

Donington Park, Castle Donington, Derbyshire DE74 2RP Tel: 01332 810048

ADMIT two for the price of one

NOT TO BE USED IN CONJUNCTION WITH ANY OTHER OFFER

FHG

READERS' OFFER 1995

VALID Spring Bank Holiday to October 1995

Devonshire Collection of Period Costume

43 High Street, Totnes, Devon TQ9 5NP Tel: (01803) 862827

Admit **TWO** for the price of one

NOT TO BE USED IN CONJUNCTION WITH ANY OTHER OFFER

FHG

READERS' OFFER 1995

VALID during 1995

Kents Cavern Showcaves

91 Ilsham Road, Wellswood, Torquay, Devon TQ1 2JF Tel: 01803 294059

One **FREE** guide book per family when purchasing ticket from Kents Cavern office

NOT TO BE USED IN CONJUNCTION WITH ANY OTHER OFFER

England's highest narrow-gauge railway. Steam and diesel engines carry pasengers through the scenic North Pennines.

DIRECTIONS: station is just off A686 Hexham road north of Alston town centre.

OPEN: service operates April to November (daily July and August).

FHG PUBLICATIONS, ABBEY MILL BUSINESS CENTRE, PAISLEY PA1 1TJ

The finest collection of steamboats in the world. Motor boats and other vintage craft are also displayed afloat, under cover.

DIRECTIONS: A591 from Kendal to Rayrigg Road; A592 from Newby Bridge.

OPEN: Easter to October 10am to 5pm daily.

FHG PUBLICATIONS, ABBEY MILL BUSINESS CENTRE, PAISLEY PA1 1TJ

World's largest collection of single seater racing cars, housed in five halls. Fully licensed restaurant. Ample free parking.

DIRECTIONS: 2 miles east of East Midlands Airport; 3 miles from M1 Junction 23a; approach via Birmingham by M42/A42.

OPEN: Daily except Christmas Day, Boxing Day and New Year's Day. 10am to 5pm daily.

FHG PUBLICATIONS, ABBEY MILL BUSINESS CENTRE, PAISLEY PA1 1TJ

A selection of costumes and accessories (changed each year) on show in one of the oldest and most interesting houses in the heart of Totnes.

DIRECTIONS: part of the Butterwalk which is near main town car park.

OPEN: Spring Bank Holiday to October 1st (closed Saturdays).

FHG PUBLICATIONS, ABBEY MILL BUSINESS CENTRE, PAISLEY PA1 1TJ

Underground world packed with secrets of times gone by. One of the most important archaeological sites in Britain.

DIRECTIONS: From Torquay Harbour follow brown tourist signs – Ilsham Road is off Babbacombe Road.

OPEN: April to Sept 10am-5.15pm (plus evenings in July and Aug). Oct to March: 10am-4.15pm.

FHG PUBLICATIONS, ABBEY MILL BUSINESS CENTRE, PAISLEY PA1 1TJ

FHG

READERS' OFFER 1995

VALID during 1995

Tank Museum

Bovington, Wareham, Dorset BH20 6JG Telephone: (01929) 463953

50p Restaurant Voucher to be used in Gauntlet Restaurant

NOT TO BE USED IN CONJUNCTION WITH ANY OTHER OFFER

FHG

READERS' OFFER 1995

VALID during 1995

BERKELEY CASTLE

Berkeley, Gloucestershire GL13 9BQ Telephone: (01453) 810332

Admit one **FAMILY** at group rates

NOT TO BE USED IN CONJUNCTION WITH ANY OTHER OFFER

FHG

READERS' OFFER 1995

VALID during 1995 Season

Cotswold Farm Park

Guiting Power, Cheltenham, Gloucestershire GL54 5UG Tel: (01451) 850307

Admit one child **FREE** with an adult paying full entrance fee

NOT TO BE USED IN CONJUNCTION WITH ANY OTHER OFFER

FHG

READERS' OFFER 1995

VALID April to October 1995

The Cider Museum Centre

Pomona Place, Hereford HR4 0LW Telephone: (01432) 354207

Admit **TWO ADULTS** at group reduction rate

NOT TO BE USED IN CONJUNCTION WITH ANY OTHER OFFER

FHG

READERS' OFFER 1995

VALID during 1995 Season

FRONTIERLAND

Promenade, Morecambe, Lancashire LA4 4DG Telephone: (01524) 410024

Buy one Day Pass and get another **FREE**

NOT TO BE USED IN CONJUNCTION WITH ANY OTHER OFFER

Over 300 armoured fighting vehicles from 25 countries. Drive-a-tank simulators, video theatres, restaurant.

DIRECTIONS: A352 between Dorchester and Wareham.

OPEN: 10am-5pm daily except at Christmas period.

FHG PUBLICATIONS, ABBEY MILL BUSINESS CENTRE, PAISLEY PA1 1TJ

Magnificent home of the Berkeley family for nearly 850 years.
Full of treasures including paintings, tapestries, porcelain.

DIRECTIONS: off A38 midway between Bristol and Gloucester. From M5 use Exit 13 or 14.

OPEN: April to Sept: open daily except Mondays. Oct: open Sunday afternoons only.

FHG PUBLICATIONS, ABBEY MILL BUSINESS CENTRE, PAISLEY PA1 1TJ

The home of rare breeds conservation, with over 50 breeding flocks and herds of rare farm animals. Adventure playground, pets' corners, picnic area, farm nature trail.

DIRECTIONS: M5 Junction 9, off B4077 Stow-on-the-Wold road. 5 miles from Bourton-on-the-Water.

OPEN: daily 10.30am to 5pm – April to September.

FHG PUBLICATIONS, ABBEY MILL BUSINESS CENTRE, PAISLEY PA1 1TJ

Cider Museum and Distillery telling the fascinating story of traditional cider making through the ages. Programme of temporary exhibitions and activities throughout the year.

DIRECTIONS: off A438 from Hereford to Brecon.

OPEN: April to October daily 10am-5.30pm; November to March Mon-Sat 1-5pm.

FHG PUBLICATIONS, ABBEY MILL BUSINESS CENTRE, PAISLEY PA1 1TJ

Western theme park with over 30 rides and attractions for all the family.

DIRECTIONS: on coast 8 miles south of M6 Junction 34.

OPEN: March to October – Main season – May 28th to September 18th.

FHG PUBLICATIONS, ABBEY MILL BUSINESS CENTRE, PAISLEY PA1 1TJ

FHG

READERS' OFFER 1995

VALID Jan-March and Sept-Oct 1995

SNIBSTON DISCOVERY PARK

Ashby Road, Coalville, Leicestershire LE67 3LN Telephone: (01530) 510851

20% DISCOUNT on adult and concessionary tickets

NOT TO BE USED IN CONJUNCTION WITH ANY OTHER OFFER

FHG

READERS' OFFER 1995

VALID during 1995

NATURELAND SEAL SANCTUARY

North Parade, Skegness, Lincolnshire PE25 1DB Telephone: (01754) 764345

FREE entry for one child when accompanied by paying adult

NOT TO BE USED IN CONJUNCTION WITH ANY OTHER OFFER

FHG

READERS' OFFER 1995

VALID during 1995 except Bank Holidays

SOUTHPORT ZOO AND CONSERVATION TRUST

Princes Park, Southport, Merseyside PR8 1RX Telephone: (01704) 538102

One child **FREE** entry with two full paying adults

NOT TO BE USED IN CONJUNCTION WITH ANY OTHER OFFER

FHG

READERS' OFFER 1995

VALID March to October 1995

HEXHAM HERBS

Chesters Walled Garden, Chollerford, Hexham, Northumberland NE46 4BQ Tel: (01434) 681483

One adult FREE with paid adult entry

NOT TO BE USED IN CONJUNCTION WITH ANY OTHER OFFER

FHG

READERS' OFFER 1995

VALID during 1995

White Post Modern Farm Centre

Farnsfield, Near Newark, Nottinghamshire NG22 8HL Tel: (01623) 882977

TWO child admissions for the price of one

NOT TO BE USED IN CONJUNCTION WITH ANY OTHER OFFER

Five main gallery areas tell the story of the county's rich industrial heritage. Hands-on *Science Alive!*, nature trail and picnic areas.

DIRECTIONS: 12 miles north-west of Leicester.

OPEN: daily except Christmas and Boxing Day.

FHG PUBLICATIONS, ABBEY MILL BUSINESS CENTRE, PAISLEY PA1 1TJ

Rescues and rears abandoned seal pups before returnng them to the wild. Specialised collection includes penguins, reptiles etc.

DIRECTIONS: coastal resort 19 miles north-east of Boston.

OPEN: daily except Christmas Day, Boxing Day and New Year's Day.

FHG PUBLICATIONS, ABBEY MILL BUSINESS CENTRE, PAISLEY PA1 1TJ

Lions, snow leopards, chimpanzees, penguins, reptiles, aquarium and lots more set amidst landscaped gardens.

DIRECTIONS: On the coast 16 miles north of Liverpool; follow brown tourist signs.

OPEN: daily except Christmas Day. Summer 10am to 6pm; Winter 10am to 4pm.

FHG PUBLICATIONS, ABBEY MILL BUSINESS CENTRE, PAISLEY PA1 1TJ

Beautiful walled garden with nearly 900 types of herbs, woodland walk, nursery, shop. Guide dogs only.

DIRECTIONS: 6 miles north of Hexham, next to Chesters Roman Fort.

OPEN: daily March to October/November.

FHG PUBLICATIONS, ABBEY MILL BUSINESS CENTRE, PAISLEY PA1 1TJ

A modern working farm with over 3000 animals including ducklings, deer, bees, rheas, piglets, snails, lambs (all year). New pet centre.

DIRECTIONS: off the A614 at Farnsfield, 12 miles north of Nottingham. From M1 Junction 27 follow 'Robin Hood' signs for 10 miles.

OPEN: daily all year round.

FHG PUBLICATIONS, ABBEY MILL BUSINESS CENTRE, PAISLEY PA1 1TJ

FHG

READERS' OFFER 1995

VALID April to end October 1995

Cogges Manor Farm Museum

Church Lane, Witney, Oxfordshire OX8 6LA Tel: (01993) 772602

FREE pot of tea on production of voucher

NOT TO BE USED IN CONJUNCTION WITH ANY OTHER OFFER

FHG

READERS' OFFER 1995

VALID until 26 November 1995

Didcot Railway Centre

Didcot, Oxfordshire Telephone: (01235) 817200

One child **FREE** when accompanied by full paying adult

NOT TO BE USED IN CONJUNCTION WITH ANY OTHER OFFER

FHG

READERS' OFFER 1995

VALID during 1995

PERRY'S CIDER MILLS

Dowlish Wake, Near Ilminster, Somerset TA19 0NY Telephone: (01460) 52681

10% OFF all shop goods excluding cider and cider brandy (free entry to Cider Mills)

NOT TO BE USED IN CONJUNCTION WITH ANY OTHER OFFER

FHG

READERS' OFFER 1995

VALID during 1995

RODE BIRD GARDENS

Rode, Near Bath, Somerset BA3 6QW Telephone: (01373) 830326

One child **FREE** with each full paying adult

NOT TO BE USED IN CONJUNCTION WITH ANY OTHER OFFER

FHG

READERS' OFFER 1995

VALID during 1995

Planet Earth

Garden Paradise, Avis Road, Newhaven, East Sussex BN9 0DH Tel: (01273) 512123

Admit one **FREE** adult or child with one adult paying full entrance price

NOT TO BE USED IN CONJUNCTION WITH ANY OTHER OFFER

A museum of the Oxfordshire countryside, with Manor House, working farm, riverside walks etc, plus daily demonstration of cooking on the kitchen range.

DIRECTIONS: follow signs from A40, close to Witney town centre.

OPEN: 4th April to end October. Closed Mondays except Bank Holidays.

FHG PUBLICATIONS, ABBEY MILL BUSINESS CENTRE, PAISLEY PA1 1TJ

The golden age of the Great Western Railway – steam trains, original equipment; picnic area and refreshment room. Rides on trains all Sundays June to August, Bank Holidays - enquire for other times.

DIRECTIONS: 10 miles south of Oxford, signposted from M4 (Junction 13) and A34. At Didcot Parkway Rail Station.

OPEN: weekends all year; daily April to September.

FHG PUBLICATIONS, ABBEY MILL BUSINESS CENTRE, PAISLEY PA1 1TJ

Traditional cider and cider brandy on sale all year – sample before you buy. Shop, museum of farm tools, country photographs.

DIRECTIONS: approximately 2 miles from Ilminster off A303, 3 miles from Cricket St Thomas.

OPEN: all year except Sunday afternoons.

FHG PUBLICATIONS, ABBEY MILL BUSINESS CENTRE, PAISLEY PA1 1TJ

Hundreds of brilliant exotic birds in 17 acres of woodlands, lakes and flower gardens. Children's play area. Woodland steam railway (summer, weather permitting).

DIRECTIONS: turn off the A36 10 miles south of Bath (follow brown tourist signs).

OPEN: all year except Christmas Day.

FHG PUBLICATIONS, ABBEY MILL BUSINESS CENTRE, PAISLEY PA1 1TJ

World of Natural History including Plantasia Desert and Tropical Gardens, World of Dinosaurs, and Fossil Museum

DIRECTIONS: signposted 'Garden Paradise' off A26 and A259.

OPEN: all year, except Christmas Day and Boxing Day.

FHG PUBLICATIONS, ABBEY MILL BUSINESS CENTRE, PAISLEY PA1 1TJ

FHG

READERS' OFFER 1995

VALID during 1995 Season

Cadeby Steam & Brass Rubbing Centre

Nuneaton, Warwickshire CV13 0AS Telephone: (01455) 290462

Train ride for two, and two cream teas or similar

NOT TO BE USED IN CONJUNCTION WITH ANY OTHER OFFER

FHG

READERS' OFFER 1995

VALID during 1995

Museum of British Road Transport

St Agnes Lane, Hales Street, Coventry, West Midlands CV1 1PN Tel: 01203 832425

45p OFF, full child & adult admission prices

NOT TO BE USED IN CONJUNCTION WITH ANY OTHER OFFER

FHG

READERS' OFFER 1995

VALID until 31st October 1995

Dyson Perrins Museum of Worcester Porcelain

Severn Street, Worcester WR1 2NE Telephone: (01905) 23221

Admit **TWO** Adults for the price of one museum entry

NOT TO BE USED IN CONJUNCTION WITH ANY OTHER OFFER

FHG

READERS' OFFER 1995

VALID during 1995

FRIARGATE WAX MUSEUM

Lower Friargate, York YO1 1SL Telephone: (01904) 658775

One **FREE** admission when one of equal value is purchased

NOT TO BE USED IN CONJUNCTION WITH ANY OTHER OFFER

FHG

READERS' OFFER 1995

VALID Easter to end Sept 1995 (except Bank Holidays)

Flamingo Land Family Fun Park

Kirby Misperton, Malton, North Yorkshire YO17 0UX Tel: 01653 668287

One **FREE** entry when accompanied by two full paying persons

NOT TO BE USED IN CONJUNCTION WITH ANY OTHER OFFER

Working narrow gauge steam railway, railway museum
and over 70 replica brasses to rub

DIRECTIONS: on the A447 six miles north of Hinckley.

OPEN: second Saturday each month.

FHG PUBLICATIONS, ABBEY MILL BUSINESS CENTRE, PAISLEY PA1 1TJ

Largest display of British road transport telling the story of Coventry's motor industry.

DIRECTIONS: in City centre.

OPEN: daily except Christmas Eve and Day plus Boxing Day.

FHG PUBLICATIONS, ABBEY MILL BUSINESS CENTRE, PAISLEY PA1 1TJ

World's largest and most comprehensive collection of Worcester Porcelain, including
magnificent Chicago Exhibition Vase (4ft 6 inches tall). Reg. Charity No. 223753

DIRECTIONS: M5 Junction 7 to city centre, then left at 3rd set of traffic lights.

OPEN: Mon-Fri. 9.30am-5pm – Sat & Bank Holidays 10am-5pm.

FHG PUBLICATIONS, ABBEY MILL BUSINESS CENTRE, PAISLEY PA1 1TJ

As winner of the BTA 'Come to Britain Award', expect something special here.
Educationally entertaining. Black Cave now in 11th year.

DIRECTIONS: off Clifford Street in central York.

OPEN: daily from mid-January to end November.

FHG PUBLICATIONS, ABBEY MILL BUSINESS CENTRE, PAISLEY PA1 1TJ

Over 100 great rides, slides, shows and attractions including
The Bullet, Waikiki Wave, Skyflyer and Corkscrew.

DIRECTIONS: off A169 Malton to Pickering road.

OPEN: daily from Easter to October.

FHG PUBLICATIONS, ABBEY MILL BUSINESS CENTRE, PAISLEY PA1 1TJ

FHG

READERS' OFFER 1995

VALID until 30th June 1995

RHONDDA HERITAGE PARK

Lewis Merthyr, Coed Cae Road, Trehafod, Mid-Glamorgan CF37 7NP Tel: (01443) 682036

Admit one child **FREE** with each full paying adult

NOT TO BE USED IN CONJUNCTION WITH ANY OTHER OFFER

FHG

READERS' OFFER 1995

VALID during 1995

Big Pit Mining Museum

Blaenafon, Gwent NP4 9XP Tel: 01495 790311

Admit one child **FREE** per voucher with a full paying adult

NOT TO BE USED IN CONJUNCTION WITH ANY OTHER OFFER

FHG

READERS' OFFER 1995

VALID during 1995

Sygun Copper Mine

Beddgelert, Gwynedd LL55 4NE Tel: 01766 890595

10% OFF full adult and child admission prices

NOT TO BE USED IN CONJUNCTION WITH ANY OTHER OFFER

FHG

READERS' OFFER 1995

VALID: Phone for details

MUSEUM OF CHILDHOOD

1 Castle Street, Beaumaris, Anglesey LL58 8AP Telephone: (01248) 712498

Admit one child or Senior Citizen **FREE** when accompanied by 2 paying adults

NOT TO BE USED IN CONJUNCTION WITH ANY OTHER OFFER

FHG

READERS' OFFER 1995

VALID April to Oct 1995 on timetabled service trains

Talyllyn Railway

Wharf Station, Tywyn, Gwynedd LL36 9EY Tel: 01654 710472

One child **FREE** with each fare paying adult passenger

NOT TO BE USED IN CONJUNCTION WITH ANY OTHER OFFER

Journey back in time with the new underground tour; 'Black Gold'; audio-visual presentation; artefact exhibitions.

DIRECTIONS: just off A470 between Pontypridd and Porth.

OPEN: April to September: open daily; October to March: Tuesday to Sunday.

FHG PUBLICATIONS, ABBEY MILL BUSINESS CENTRE, PAISLEY PA1 1TJ

Underground tours of original colliery workings guided by experienced miners. On the surface: exhibitions, forge, stables, craft shop and licensed cafeteria.

DIRECTIONS: M4 Junction 26, then A4042/3 to Pontypool and Blaenafon. From M50, A449 to Raglan, then A40 to Abergavenny and A4246 to Blaenafon.

OPEN: daily March to November. Phone for Winter opening times. Last admission 3.30 pm.

FHG PUBLICATIONS, ABBEY MILL BUSINESS CENTRE, PAISLEY PA1 1TJ

Set in the heart of Snowdonia, Prince of Wales Award-winning underground audio-visual tours. Magnificent stalactite and stalagmite formations.

DIRECTIONS: one mile from Beddgelert on A498 towards Capel Curig A5.

OPEN: all year.

FHG PUBLICATIONS, ABBEY MILL BUSINESS CENTRE, PAISLEY PA1 1TJ

Superb collection of over 2000 items illustrating the habits and interests of children and families over the past 150 years. Shop.

DIRECTIONS: 4 miles from Britannia Bridge, opposite Beaumaris Castle.

OPEN: Easter to November 1st.

FHG PUBLICATIONS, ABBEY MILL BUSINESS CENTRE, PAISLEY PA1 1TJ

The world's first preserved railway running from Tywyn to Dolgoch Falls, Abergynolwyn and Nant Gwernol in Snowdonia National Park.

DIRECTIONS: Tywyn is on Mid-Wales coast on A493.

OPEN: from April to October and during Christmas/New Year period.

FHG PUBLICATIONS, ABBEY MILL BUSINESS CENTRE, PAISLEY PA1 1TJ

FHG

READERS' OFFER 1995

VALID January to March 1995

SATROSPHERE

19 Justice Mill Lane, Aberdeen AB1 2EQ Telephone: (01224) 213232

Admit one child **FREE** with full paying adult

NOT TO BE USED IN CONJUNCTION WITH ANY OTHER OFFER

FHG

READERS' OFFER 1995

VALID until March 1996

North East Falconry Visitor Centre

Broadland, Cairnie, Huntly, Aberdeenshire AB54 4UU Telephone: (01466) 87328

50p off entry fee (March to Oct 1995); £10 off tuition course (Oct 1995 to March 1996)

NOT TO BE USED IN CONJUNCTION WITH ANY OTHER OFFER

FHG

READERS' OFFER 1995

VALID April to October 1995

Scottish Maritime Museum

Harbourside, Irvine, Ayrshire KA12 8QE Telephone: (01294) 278283

Admit **ONE CHILD FREE** with adult paying full entry price

NOT TO BE USED IN CONJUNCTION WITH ANY OTHER OFFER

FHG

READERS' OFFER 1995

VALID Easter to end October 1995

KELBURN COUNTRY CENTRE

Fairlie, Ayrshire KA29 0BE Telephone: (01475) 568685

One child admitted **FREE** on family visit

NOT TO BE USED IN CONJUNCTION WITH ANY OTHER OFFER

FHG

READERS' OFFER 1995

VALID during 1995

Myreton Motor Museum

Aberlady, East Lothian EH32 0PZ Telephone: (01875) 870288

One child under 16 **FREE** with full paying adult

NOT TO BE USED IN CONJUNCTION WITH ANY OTHER OFFER

Only interactive 'hands-on' centre in Scotland. Have fun finding out about science. Cafe, shop with scientific gifts.

DIRECTIONS: west end of Aberdeen, off Holborn Junction.

OPEN: daily.

FHG PUBLICATIONS, ABBEY MILL BUSINESS CENTRE, PAISLEY PA1 1TJ

Regular flying displays with full commentary by falconer. Cafeteria, gift shop, picnic area.

DIRECTIONS: follow signs off A96 Aberdeen to Inverness trunk road near Huntly.

OPEN: daily March to October.

FHG PUBLICATIONS, ABBEY MILL BUSINESS CENTRE, PAISLEY PA1 1TJ

Floating collection of historic vessels; special exhibition, shop, tearoom. Guided tours of engine shop and historic fleet; special events and craftsmen's demonstrations.

DIRECTIONS: 400 yards from Irvine rail station. By road follow signs to Irvine Harbourside.

OPEN: 1st April–31st October.

FHG PUBLICATIONS, ABBEY MILL BUSINESS CENTRE, PAISLEY PA1 1TJ

Glen walks, waterfalls, gardens; horse riding, children's adventure play areas, pets' corner. New Secret Forest, nature centre. Licensed cafe, gift shop, picnic areas.

DIRECTIONS: on A78 between Largs and Fairlie. From Glasgow: M8, then A737 to Irvine, then A760 to Largs. From Ayr: A78 north.

OPEN: daily Easter to end October. End October to Easter grounds only open daily.

FHG PUBLICATIONS, ABBEY MILL BUSINESS CENTRE, PAISLEY PA1 1TJ

Motorcars from 1896, motorcycles from 1902, WWII British Military Vehicles; period advertising and motoring ephemera.

DIRECTIONS: near Aberlady between A198 and B1377. A1 two miles.

OPEN: daily.

FHG PUBLICATIONS, ABBEY MILL BUSINESS CENTRE, PAISLEY PA1 1TJ

FHG

READERS' OFFER 1995

VALID during 1995

Edinburgh Crystal Visitor Centre

Eastfield, Penicuik, Midlothian EH26 8HB Telephone: (01968) 675128

TWO adult entry tickets to standard factory tour for the price of one

NOT TO BE USED IN CONJUNCTION WITH ANY OTHER OFFER

FHG

READERS' OFFER 1995

VALID during 1995 Season

BLOWPLAIN OPEN FARM

Balmaclellan, Kirkcudbrightshire Telephone: (0164-42) 206

One **FREE** entry with each paid entry

NOT TO BE USED IN CONJUNCTION WITH ANY OTHER OFFER

FHG

READERS' OFFER 1995

VALID during 1995

New Lanark Visitor Centre

Lanark, Lanarkshire ML11 9DB Telephone: (01555) 661345

One **FREE** child entry with each full paying adult

NOT TO BE USED IN CONJUNCTION WITH ANY OTHER OFFER

FHG

READERS' OFFER 1995

VALID April to June & Sept to Oct

Museum of Lead Mining

Wanlockhead, By Biggar, Lanarkshire ML12 6UT Tel: 01659 74387

One child **FREE** with each full paying adult

NOT TO BE USED IN CONJUNCTION WITH ANY OTHER OFFER

FHG

READERS' OFFER 1995

VALID May & June Sept & Oct

Jedforest Deer and Farm Park

Mervinslaw, Camptown, Jedburgh, Roxburghshire TD8 6PL Tel: 01835 840364

One **FREE** child with every two full paying adults

NOT TO BE USED IN CONJUNCTION WITH ANY OTHER OFFER

Guided tour showing glassblowing, cutting and engraving; world's largest collection of Edinburgh Crystal; historic crystal exhibition. Factory shop, coffee shop.

DIRECTIONS: 10 miles south of Edinburgh on A701 Peebles road.

OPEN: daily; tours until 3pm Monday to Friday, plus weekends May to September. No children under 8 allowed on tour.

FHG PUBLICATIONS, ABBEY MILL BUSINESS CENTRE, PAISLEY PA1 1TJ

Award-winning open farm with cattle, sheep, poultry; pets' corner and lambs. Conducted tours daily except Saturday.

DIRECTIONS: 2 miles from Balmaclellan off A712 between Dumfries and New Galloway.

OPEN: daily except Saturday until end October.

FHG PUBLICATIONS, ABBEY MILL BUSINESS CENTRE, PAISLEY PA1 1TJ

Award-winning 200-year-old conservation village with Disney-style 'dark' ride, exhibition, gift and coffee shop. Play area and riverside walks.

DIRECTIONS: off A73 south-east of Glasgow.

OPEN: daily all year round (except 25/26 December and 1/2 January).

FHG PUBLICATIONS, ABBEY MILL BUSINESS CENTRE, PAISLEY PA1 1TJ

Explore the underground world of Lochnell Mine; step back in time at Straisteps Cottages. Guided tours, gift shop, visitor centre, licensed restaurant.

DIRECTIONS: signposted from M74 Abingdon and A76 Mennock.

OPEN: daily April to October. Winter bookings.

FHG PUBLICATIONS, ABBEY MILL BUSINESS CENTRE, PAISLEY PA1 1TJ

Working farm with rare breeds of sheep, cattle, pigs, poultry etc. Adventure play area, marked and guided walks, fishing. Shop, cafe, interpretive barn.

DIRECTIONS: 5 miles south of Jedburgh on A68, signposted 'Deer and Farm Park'.

OPEN: daily from May to end October.

FHG PUBLICATIONS, ABBEY MILL BUSINESS CENTRE, PAISLEY PA1 1TJ

AVON

Bath, Weston-Super-Mare

HORSESHOE HOUSE ♛♛ Commended

51 Sydney Buildings, Bath, Avon
BA2 6DB Tel: (01225) 466354

Georgian house in quiet residential area facing green fields, yet overlooking Abbey/City Centre 10 minute walk away. Run as 'living home', only five guests ensures personal attention and very high standard cuisine.
Single B&B £24, twin/double £48, en suite £56; 4 course dinner £18. Details of breaks, both B&B and Dinner, B&B on request.

ABBEY RISE

97 WELLS ROAD
BATH BA2 3AN
Tel: 01225 316177

Modernised Victorian town house. Very attractively decorated rooms offering panoramic views over the city, all with tea/coffee facilities and TV. Few minutes' walk to city centre, bus and rail station. From £17 per person.
Proprietor Jill Heath.

The Perfect Venue - for that Riviera Touch!

The Old Mill Hotel
Revolving Waterwheel Restaurant

Idyllic riverside location on the banks of the River Avon, beside the **Historic Tollbridge,** overlooking breathtaking panoramic views and the weir – yet only 15 miles from Bath City centre!

* **Unique Revolving Restaurant** with floor turning with the huge waterwheel – showing the diners varied river views.
* **Accommodation** – All en suite rooms with colour TV, telephones etc. Most rooms offer river views. **Honeymooners' Paradise** – four-poster beds and river views.

• Car Park • Riverside Bar • Fishing • Also Budget Accommodation Hotel:
Singles from £35; Doubles from £50; De Luxe from £60.
Lodge: Singles from £25; Doubles from £35; Family from £50.
Conferences, Wedding Receptions, Private Parties Our Speciality!

Tollbridge Road, Bath BA1 7DE Tel: 01225 858476 Fax: 01225 852600

ETB ♛♛♛ Highly Commended **** RAC Comfort Award**

SIENA HOTEL

25 Pulteney Road, BATH BA2 4EZ

A family-run hotel, renovated to provide spacious, well-appointed, en suite rooms. The Hotel is a few minutes' level walk from the Roman Baths; Bath Abbey and a county cricket ground are viewed from the rear. Gardens. Car parking. Licensed.

Tel: (01225) 425495

BAILBROOK LODGE

35/37 London Road West
BATH BA1 7HZ

Splendid Georgian house overlooking the Avon Valley. All rooms are en suite with TV and tea/coffee making facilities. From £24 p.p. Some antique four-posters. Parking.

RAC Highly Acclaimed
ETB ♛♛♛ AA QQQ
Tel: 01225 859090

VAYNOR GUEST HOUSE

Bed and Breakfast (Evening Dinner optional)

• H & C in rooms • TV in rooms
• Central heating • Car space • Good food
• Weston-Super-Mare is the largest family resort in the West Country, the centre of the famous touring areas of Bath, Bristol, Cheddar etc.

From £11.00

Mrs G. Monk, 346 Locking Road
Weston-Super-Mare BS22 8PD

Tel: 01934 632332 RAC Listed

Stoneycroft House

Stock Lane, Langford, Bristol, Avon BS18 7EX. Tel: (01934) 852624
Proprietor: Mrs Griffin

Stoneycroft House is situated in the Wrington Valley, set in 20 acres of farmland, close to the Mendip Hills and only 10 minutes from Bristol Airport. Superb four poster/family room with ensuite, twin room with ensuite and double room with adjacent bathroom. All rooms have colour TV, tea/coffee making facilities and excellent views. Enjoy your choice of breakfast in the beamed dining room with its Minster stone fireplace. Unlimited parking. Nearby attractions are the Cheddar Gorge, Wells Cathedral and the historic cities of Bath and Bristol. Sporting facilities and seaside nearby. Open all year. Brochure available. Highly Commended.

Avon — Classified Advertisements

BATH

BRIAN AND JOSIE SURRY, 'DENE VILLA', 5 NEWBRIDGE HILL, BATH BA1 3PW (01225 427676). 2 double rooms en suite, one double with shower, 1 single room; colour TV in all rooms. Central heating. Parking. Full English Breakfast from £15.00. Open all year. Two Crowns.

JILL AND BUNNY HARVEY, DELLA ROSA, 59 NORTH ROAD, COMBE DOWN, BATH BA2 5DF (01225 837193). What are you looking for? Comfort? Yes. Good food? Yes. Value for money? Yes. Plenty of off-street parking? Yes. Why not try us then? Bed and Breakfast from £14. 2 Crowns.

MRS D. STRONG, WELLSWAY GUEST HOUSE, 51 WELLSWAY, BATH BA2 4RS (01225 423434). Warm, comfortable Edwardian house, city 8 minutes' walk. Washbasins, colour television in bedrooms. Tea to welcome you. Full English Breakfast. From £12. Parking available. One Crown.

JANE AND JOHN SHEPHERD, 21 NEWBRIDGE ROAD, BATH BA1 3HE (01225 314694). B&B for non-smokers. Victorian house, family atmosphere. Convenient for exploring Bath and environs. Superb traditional, vegetarian, vegan, special diet breakfasts. From £15. WCTB 1 Crown.

M. A. COOPER, FLAXLEY VILLA, 9 NEW BRIDGE HILL, BATH BA1 3PW (01225 313237). Comfortable Victorian house. 5 minutes town centre. All rooms with colour televisions, also showers, tea/coffee making in all rooms. Full English Breakfast. Parking. ETB One Crown.

JUDITH GODDARD, CHERRY TREE VILLA, 7 NEWBRIDGE HILL, BATH BA1 3PW (01225 331671). Friendly Victorian home approximately one mile from city centre. Bright comfortable bedrooms, all with washbasin, colour TV, tea/coffee making facilities. Shower. Full central heating. Off-street parking. Bed and full English Breakfast from £14 per person. 1 Crown. FHG Diploma winner.

BRISTOL

CAMELEY LODGE, CAMELEY, TEMPLE CLOUD, BRISTOL BS18 5AH (01761 452790) .Centrally positioned, 10 miles from Bristol, Bath and Wells. Cameley Lodge is situated one mile off the A37 in a peaceful hamlet. Overlooking trout lakes and open countryside. An ideal base to explore the West Country.

CLEVEDON

MRS E. POTTER, 5 SUNNYSIDE ROAD, CLEVEDON BS21 7TE (01275 873315), Bed and Breakfast from £15.00. H&C in all rooms. Double and family rooms. Car parking. M5 one mile.

FALFIELD

MR AND MRS B.C. BURRELL, GREEN FARM GUEST HOUSE, FALFIELD, GLOS, GL12 8DL (01454 260319). 16th century Farmhouse, 2 minutes J14 M5. Easy access M4, 10 minutes AZTEC Business Park. Ample parking. Good selection of home cooked food available. Ensuite available. B & B from £15. Open all year. In winter log fires and candlelit dinners feature. A warm welcome assured at Green Farm.

BEDFORDSHIRE

Pulloxhill

POND FARM
7 HIGH STREET,
PULLOXHILL
BEDFORD MK45 5HA
Phil & Judy Tookey
Tel: 01525 712316

Arable farm opposite village green. Ideal for Woburn Abbey & Safari Park, Whipsnade Zoo, The Shuttleworth Collection of Historic Aircraft & Luton Airport. Flitwick mainline station and A6 3 miles; 5 miles M1 Junc. 12. Resident Great Dane. Rooms have colour TV, H&C, tea/coffee facilities. Terms from £14. ETB Listed.

BERKSHIRE

Berkshire — Classified Advertisements

HENLEY-ON-THAMES

MRS H. CARVER, WINDY BROW, 204 VICTORIA ROAD, WARGRAVE, NEAR HENLEY-ON-THAMES RG10 8AJ (01734 403336). Detached Victorian House. Ideal for Windsor/Oxford. Heathrow half-hour. London bus/train service one mile. Tourist Board Listed and Graded. Excellent food locally. Colour TV and tea/coffee facilities in all rooms.

WINDSOR

KAREN JACKSON AND LYNETTE MOORE, TRINITY GUEST HOUSE, 18 TRINITY PLACE, WINDSOR SL4 3AT (01753 864186; Fax: 01753 862640). Comfortable Guest House in the heart of Windsor. Close to Castle, river and stations. Run by traditional English family and Highly Recommended worldwide. ETB 2 Crowns.

CLARENCE HOTEL, 9 CLARENCE ROAD, WINDSOR SL4 5AE (01753 864436); Fax: (01753 857060). Town centre location. Licensed bar. High quality accommodation at guest house prices. All rooms have en suite bathrooms, TV, tea/coffee making facilities, radio alarms and hairdryers. ETB 2 Crowns, AA and RAC Listed. Heathrow Airport 25 minutes by car.

BUCKINGHAMSHIRE

Buckinghamshire — Classified Advertisements

MARLOW

MRS CORINNE BERRY, 2 HYDE GREEN, MARLOW SL7 1QL (01628 483526). Comfortable family house close shops, river, station (Paddington 1 hour). Two twin, one double rooms; CTV, tea/coffee facilities. Two rooms en-suite. Parking. Heathrow 30 minutes. ETB Listed.

MILTON KEYNES

MRS S. CLITHEROE, 5 WALNUT CLOSE, NEWPORT PAGNELL MK16 8JH (Tel & Fax: 01908 611643). Friendly, comfortable B&B with two twin-bedded rooms and two singles. Two bathrooms solely for guests' use and a small comfortable lounge with TV and coffee making facilities. Ample off-road parking. ETB Listed. Twin £28, single £16.

CAMBRIDGESHIRE

Cambridge

DORSET HOUSE

**35 Newton Road,
Little Shelford,
Cambridge CB2 5QJ
Tel: 01223 844440**

Just 3 miles from the historic city of Cambridge, **DORSET HOUSE** is situated in its own extensive grounds. The house has open fireplaces and wooden beams, and each luxury bedroom is individually decorated. The rooms have colour TV and tea/coffee facilities. Breakfast is served in our lovely dining room and dinner is available midweek by request.

If you are looking for the best: Bed and Breakfast £28 single, £42 double.

The Old Bricklayers Arms
Ermine Street, Caxton CB3 9PQ
Tel: 01954 719228

16th century Grade II Listed Cottage offers comfortable accommodation in double, twin & single rooms. Dining and sitting rooms with inglenook, oak beams, log fires. Home cooking. Dogs by arrangement. Convenient for M11, A10, A45. B&B from £35 double, £25 single; Dinner from £11 (Vegetarian £10). Longer stay terms on request.

ETB ♛♛♛ Commended Mrs P. BENSON

THE LAURELS
104 Victoria Street, Littleport, Ely CB6 1LZ
Tel: 01353 861972; 0850 199299

We offer a high standard of accommodation in our large attractive Victorian house 200 yards from riverside pub. All rooms have colour TV, radio, tea/coffee, locks, parking. Non-smoking.
Double and Twin en suite from £15 per person. Families and disabled persons welcome.

Cambridgeshire — Classified Advertisements

CAMBRIDGE

CRISTINA'S GUEST HOUSE, 47 ST ANDREW'S ROAD, CAMBRIDGE CB4 1DL (01223 65855/327700). Guests are assured of a warm welcome at this quietly located Guest House, only 15 minutes' walk from city centre. All rooms with colour TV and tea/coffee facilities; en suite available. Central heating, comfortable TV lounge. Private car park. AA QQQ. RAC Listed, Les Routiers, ETB 2 Crowns.

MRS D. J. WYATT, THE WILLOWS, 102 HIGH STREET, LANDBEACH, NEAR MILTON, CAMBRIDGE CB4 4DT (01223 860332). Georgian farmhouse off A10, three miles north of Cambridge. Family room and twin room, up to six persons accommodated. Washbasins. Tea/coffee. No smoking. From £15.00.

MRS B. GRAY, WORSTED BARROWS, BABRAHAM, CAMBRIDGE CB2 4AX (01223 833298). Seven miles from Cambridge, close to Duxford Air Museum and within easy reach of attractive Suffolk/Essex villages. The house is in its own grounds, offers centrally heated en suite rooms with TV and beverage facilities. Prices from £16 per person. ETB 3 Crowns.

CHESHIRE

Kettleshulme

Mr & Mrs J. Bradshaw
The Tea Cosy
PADDOCK LODGE
Kettleshulme
SK12 7RD

Lovely Grade II Listed building set in picturesque village in Peak District National Park; 6 miles from Macclesfield, Wilmslow or Buxton. Guests' own dining room, bathroom. Lovely bedrooms - one double, two twin - with central heating and TV. Licensed. Car Park. Open from February to December. Bed and Breakfast £15.00.

ETB Registered **Tel: 01663 732116**

Cheshire — Classified Advertisements

CHESTER

MITCHELL'S OF CHESTER, GREEN GABLES, 28 HOUGH GREEN CH4 8JQ (01244 679004). Relax in this elegantly restored Victorian Gentleman's Residence. All rooms en-suite, equipped with full facilitiies. Close to City Centre on A5104, on bus route. Also off street parking. Bed & Breakfast from £18. ETB 2 Crown Highly Commended.

THE GABLES GUEST HOUSE, 5 VICARAGE ROAD, HOOLE, CHESTER CH2 3HZ (01244 323969). Situated in quiet road, ideal touring base. One mile city centre. All rooms teamaking facilities, colour TV. Bath/shower room. Lounge/diningroom. Remote Control TV in each room. AA, RAC; Tourist Board one crown. Bed and Breakfast from £14 per person.

CORNWALL

Bodmin, Bude

Mrs D. Treweeke

LOWER WOON FARM

Lanivet, Bodmin PL30 5JE

Centrally situated for both north and south coast beaches. Small, friendly and comfortable. Private parking. Bed and Breakfast - Evening Meal optional. Cornwall Tourist Board registered.

Telephone: 01208 831756

Fax: 01208 831024

The
MORNISH
SUMMERLEAZE CRESCENT Hotel
BUDE • EX23 8HJ
(01288) 352972
Bookings/enquiries FREEPHONE
0500 131239
• All rooms en-suite and well furnished with colour T.V. and tea/coffee making facilities
• Special rates for Short Breaks
• Full Central Heating
• Residents Bar
• Dinner, Bed & Breakfast £171.50 per week
MORNISH HOTEL
Ideally situated - only 2 minutes walk away from the Town Centre, Golf Course & Open Air Swimming Pool

Stamford Hill Hotel

"A Country House Hotel"

Set in five acres of gardens and woodland overlooking open countryside yet only a mile from the sandy beaches of Bude, our spacious Georgian Manor House with 15 en suite bedrooms with TV and tea/coffee making facilities, outdoor heated pool, tennis court, badminton court, games room and sauna is the ideal place for a relaxing holiday or short break. Daily B&B from £21.00. Three Day Break DB&B from £90. Pets welcome.

Ian and Joy McFeat, Stamford Hill Hotel, Stratton, Bude, Cornwall EX23 9AY (01288) 352709

TRENARTH

Friendly Comfortable Quiet

Large cottage in beautiful countryside, central for touring coast and moors. Three bedrooms, all with washbasins; two with own shower. TV lounge. Parking. Singles and partially disabled welcome. NO SMOKING. Well behaved dogs welcome.

Tel: 01840 213295

Mrs. E. A. Hopkins, Trenarth, Camelford, Cornwall PL32 9XE

CARTUTHER BARTON

LISKEARD
CORNWALL PL14 3PS
Tel: 01579 343244

Pleasant Cornish manor farmhouse about one mile from Liskeard. Within easy reach of Looe, Polperro and many other coastal resorts; ideal for touring. Golf course approx. 4 miles. Lounge with TV; dining-room with separate tables. Wash-basins in bedrooms. Bed and Breakfast; Dinner if required. Further details from Mrs A. R. Hawke.

LITTLE LARNICK FARM

PELYNT LOOE PL13 2NB
Telephone: Looe (01503) 262837

Family room, twin room and double room;
all with en suite facilities. Open February to November
Bed and Breakfast from £14.00
Tea/coffee making facilities.
Optional Evening Meal.
Reg. Cornwall Tourist Board. ETB

STEEP HOUSE Portmellon Cove, Mevagissey

Steep House stands in an acre of ground by the sea, in a natural cove with a safe sandy beach twenty yards from the large garden. Comfortable, centrally heated double bedrooms with wash basins and sea or beach views, colour TV and tea/coffee maker; some are en suite. Generous English breakfast and imaginative home cooked dinners which are served in a wood panelled diningroom overlooking Portmellon Cove. All meals include as much home grown produce as possible. Covered summertime swimming pool. Guests welcome all year. Modest prices, special weekly and winter break rates. Children over 10 years welcome. Christmas celebrations. Licensed. Free private parking. Fire certificate.

Jane Youlden. Tel: 01726 843732

TREGURRIAN HOTEL

AA**
ETB

WATERGATE BAY,
NR. NEWQUAY TR8 4AB
Tel: St. Mawgan (01637) 860280
Les Routiers

* 27 rooms, most en suite, with heaters, tea makers, colour TV
* Heated pool, sun patio, solarium
* Licensed bar, games room
* Central for touring all of Cornwall, own car park
* Parties and coaches by arrangement
* Family-run, children welcome at reduced rates (some free offers)
* Open Easter to November
* Spring and Autumn breaks
* Dinner, Bed and Breakfast £144 to £230 (inclusive of VAT)
* Bed and Breakfast £17.00 to £28.00 inc

BROCHURE FROM RESIDENT PROPRIETORS,
MARIAN AND DERRICK MOLLOY

The Old Mill Country House

Little Petherick, Near Padstow PL27 7QT Tel: 01841 540388

This 16th century converted corn mill retains its character and charm whilst providing guests with modern amenities. Situated close to Padstow and sandy beaches. Traditional cuisine is served in the Mill Room and there are six well appointed bedrooms which have views of the countryside (most en suite).

RAC Acclaimed   AA QQQ   ETB Commended   Ashley Courtenay

PENALVA PRIVATE HOTEL

Well-positioned imposing late Victorian hotel in wide tree-lined boulevard. Ample parking. Close to promenade and shops. Perfect centre for enjoying the wealth of beautiful sandy coves, historic remains and magnificent walks. A Non-Smokers' Haven offering full central heating, immaculate interior, en-suite facilities, excellent food and a real welcome with courteous service. Large Guest lounge and separate dining room. Colour TV and coffee/tea making facilities in bedrooms. Open all year. No pets. Bed and Breakfast from £10.00 to £16.00 per person; Dinner £8.00 extra. Children 6-12 years half price if sharing family rooms. Highly recommended. AA QQQ.

Brochure (SAE please): Mr and Mrs G. W. Buswell, Penalva Private Hotel, Alexandra Road, Penzance TR18 4LZ (01736 69060).

CARNSON HOUSE HOTEL

ETB

RAC LISTED

East Terrace, Penzance TR18 2TD.
Tel: 01736-65589 (24 hr Ansafone)

A warm and friendly welcome always awaits you at Carnson. Centrally located and ideal for rail and coach travellers. A super centre for touring all the Land's End Peninsula. Eight comfortable bedrooms all with heating, tea-makers and colour television and some with en suite facilities. Pleasant lounge. Residential licence. Attractive dining room with separate tables. Excellent varied food.

Write or phone for free brochure to: Mr & Mrs R.H. Hilder

Cornwall — Classified Advertisements

BUDE

SEAVIEW, 51 KILLERTON ROAD, BUDE EX23 8EN (01288 352665). Central for all amenities. It is with some pride that we welcome back many familiar faces every year. Homely atmosphere, good English food. Washbasins, tea-making facilities. TV lounge. Car parking. Garden. B&B £15.00.

LAUNCESTON

MRS KATHRYN BROAD, LOWER DUTSON FARM, LAUNCESTON PL15 9SP (01566 776456). AA QQ. Welcome to our 17th century farmhouse. Central for touring Devon/Cornwall. Some en suite; tea/coffee facilities. TV lounge. B&B from £91 per week, £13.50 per night. Self catering and fishing available.

MARY RICH, "NATHANIA", ALTARNUN, LAUNCESTON. PL15 7SL (01566 86426). Christian couple offer B & B & EM. Small farm on Bodmin Moors. Near Coast. Double and twin rooms, en-suite, bathroom, tea making facilities. Write or telephone for terms.

THE LIZARD

MRS JO LYNE, CAERTHILLIAN FARM, THE LIZARD TR12 7NX (01326 290596). Friendly farmhouse B&B. Beautiful bedrooms with sea views, Washbasins, tea, coffee. Wonderful walled garden. Lovely lazy lounge. Flower-filled conservatory. Big breakfast, endless cups of tea. Veggies well catered for. Animals galore. Footpaths and coves in abundance. Just Perfick! £14.00

LOOE

MR J. R. A. STORER, KANTARA LICENSED GUEST HOUSE, 7 TRELAWNEY TERRACE, WEST LOOE PL13 2AG (01503 262093). A family-run Guest House noted for its warm and informal atmosphere. Convenient for amenities and beach. All rooms 24-hour access, with washbasins, Sky TV and videolink, tea/coffee. Bar lounge with 28" TV. Children and pets welcome. Many additional facilities available. AA Q, ETB One Crown Approved.

MEVAGISSEY

MRS BARBARA HOWSON, TREVELLION, POLSTREATH HILL, MEVAGISSEY PL26 6TH (01726 844158). This bustling fishing village is an ideal setting from which to explore Cornwall. Our family home offers two double rooms with washbasins, tea/coffee facilities. Guest bathroom, luxurious lounge, lovely garden. Bed and full English breakfast £15. Sorry no smoking.

LAVORRICK ORCHARD HOTEL, VICARAGE HILL, MEVAGISSEY PL26 6SZ (01726 842265). Family run licensed hotel. Private parking. En-suite rooms with colour television and tea making facilities. Excellent cuisine and service. Children and pets welcome. WCTB 2 Crowns.

PENZANCE

WOODSTOCK GUEST HOUSE, 29 MORRAB ROAD, PENZANCE TR18 4EZ (01736 69049). A well appointed Guest House in central Penzance. Ideal for touring the Land's End Peninsula and as an overnight stop to the Isles of Scilly. Some en suite rooms available. All major credit cards accepted. ETB 2 Crowns, RAC Listed.

GLORIA AND JOHN GOWER, TREVENTON GUEST HOUSE, ALEXANDRA PLACE, PENZANCE TR18 4NE (01736 63521). All rooms with washbasins, shaver/dryer points, tea/coffee making facilities and colour TV. Central heating. Easy parking. Full breakfast arranged for all sailings/flights. Bed and Breakfast from £13. Evening Meal optional. Well-behaved pets welcome. Highly recommended.

CUMBRIA

Ambleside

Bracken Fell

PETER AND ANNE HART, BRACKEN FELL, OUTGATE, AMBLESIDE, CUMBRIA LA22 0NH HAWKSHEAD 015394 36289

Bracken Fell is situated in beautiful open countryside between Ambleside and Hawkshead, in the picturesque hamlet of Outgate. Ideally positioned for exploring the Lake District and within easy reach of Coniston, Windermere, Ambleside, Grasmere and Keswick. All major outdoor activities are catered for nearby including wind-surfing, sailing, fishing, pony trekking, etc. All six bedrooms have private facilities, complimentary tea/coffee and outstanding views. There is central heating throughout, a comfortable lounge and dining room, together with ample parking and two acres of gardens. Fire Certificate. Open all year. Bed and Breakfast from £18.50. Non-smoking. Self catering accommodation also available. Write or phone for brochure and tariff.

Commended

THE ANCHORAGE

Rydal Road, Ambleside
LA22 9AY Tel: 015394 32046
ETB 2 Crowns Commended,
RAC Acclaimed

Modern Guest House with private car park. All rooms with colour TV and tea/coffee making. En suite rooms available. 300 metres from centre of Ambleside. Warm welcome and excellent breakfast assured. £17 to £22.50. Reductions for three or more nights.

KINGSWOOD
OLD LAKE ROAD, AMBLESIDE
Tel: 015394 34081

Near town centre yet off main road. Ample car parking. Comfortable well equipped bedrooms with washbasins, tea/coffee making facilities. Colour TV, central heating. Non-smoking. Pets welcome. Bargain Breaks off season. Phone for rates.

FISHERBECK FARMHOUSE

Old Lake Road, Ambleside LA22 0DH
Tel: 015394 32523

Bed and Breakfast in 16th century farmhouse, not a working farm, situated a few minutes' level walk to Ambleside town centre. Single, double and twin rooms; family room; all with hot and cold washbasins and central heating. There is a TV lounge and separate breakfast room. A car is not essential, but there is parking. Dogs allowed.

Storrs Gate House

Longtail Hill, Bowness-on-Windermere, Cumbria LA23 3JD Tel: 015394 43272

A detached villa in secluded gardens 100 yards from Lake and Marina, close to Hawkshead car ferry and a short walk from Bowness centre.

All five bedrooms are C/H and have washbasins, TV and tea making facilities. We have double, twin and family rooms, some en suite. There is an attractive lounge (with TV) and dining room. There is also ample parking.

Bed and Breakfast (English) from £15-£20. Reductions for children and longer stays. We are situated on the junction of the A592 with the B5284 opposite the Marina.

NEWPALLYARDS COUNTRY FARMHOUSE

HETHERSGILL, CARLISLE CA6 6HZ
Tel: 01228 577308
FILMED FOR BBC TV

Relax and see beautiful North Cumbria and Scottish Borders, Hadrian's Wall and the Lakes. A warm welcome awaits you. Easily accessible from M6. Accommodation in 2 double, 2 family rooms (all en suite); 1 twin/single. All with tea/coffee facilities. Bed & Breakfast from £18; Dinner, Bed and Breakfast from £26.50 daily. Half board from £150 to £170 weekly. Menu choice. Best Breakfast in Britain Winner. Commended

COUNTY HOTEL

Commended
*** RAC

9 Botchergate
Carlisle, Cumbria CA1 1QS

84 en suite rooms in a City Centre location, adjacent to Carlisle's Citadel Station. Parking on the premises for 100 cars. Two restaurants, two bars, one traditional ale Inn. Built in Georgian times, this beautiful Listed building is extensively renovated with all in-room modern facilities.

Single from £37.00, Double £48.00. Mini Breaks from £66.00 (2 nights, 2 people).

Tel 01228 31316

THE HORSE SHOE INN

HUTTON ROOF, NEAR MUNGRISDALE CA11 0XS
Tel: 017684 84354

The Skiddaw range of fells makes an ideal background to the well apppointed Inn, near to Ullswater Lake. Comfortable rooms with TV. Home cooking. Real ale.

Bed and Breakfast from £12.50.

GARNETT HOUSE FARM

Burneside, Kendal LA9 5SF Tel: 01539 724542

AA/RAC Acclaimed 15th century farmhouse situated half mile from the A591 Kendal-Windermere Road. Accommodation comprises doubles, twins and family rooms – most en suite. All with washbasins, colour TV and tea making facilities. Full English Breakfast and 5-course dinners. Children welcome at reduced rates if sharing with two adults. Special offer during January, February and March – 3 nights B&B £39, en suite £45.

BERKELEY GUEST HOUSE

The Heads, Keswick, Cumbria CA12 5ER
Mrs Barbara Crompton Tel: 017687 74222

Berkeley is situated in a quiet road overlooking Crow Park and mini-golf course. The south-facing bedrooms have beautiful views of Walla Crag, Derwentwater and Derwent Fells; to the rear there are views of Skiddaw Mountain. Close to Keswick town centre, with restaurants, shops and swimming spa; five minutes' walk from the Lake.
Double, twin and family bedrooms, each with washbasin, colour TV, tea/coffee making facilities; two rooms en suite. No smoking. Bed and Breakfast from £14.50 per person.
From Keswick centre, take Borrowdale/Lakeside road;
The Heads is the third road on the right.
PLEASE SEND FOR BROCHURE.

THE CARTWHEEL KESWICK

5 Blencathra Street, Keswick CA12 4HW
Tel: 017687 73182

The Cartwheel is situated in a quiet area yet close to the town centre and within easy walking distance of Derwentwater. Comfortable accommodation is offered with excellent traditional home cooking. Full English breakfast. Tea/coffee making facilities. Central heating. TV in all rooms. Children welcome. Non-smoking.

ETB Listed

GOODWIN HOUSE

29 SOUTHEY STREET, KESWICK CA12 4EE
Tel: 017687 74634 Mrs F.J.M. Dawson

Goodwin House is an imposing three-storey residence. All rooms have central heating, washbasin, tea making facilities and colour T.V. There are en suite rooms and guests have own front door keys. Guests can enjoy delicious home cooking. Evening meal optional. B&B from £12.00, Evening Meal £8.00. Weekly Bed and Breakfast terms by arrangement. Reduced rates for children. Sorry no dogs. Open all year. AA QQQ Recommended.

Carmel House
GUEST HOUSE

Mount Pleasant, Tebay, Cumbria CA10 3TH
(015396 24651)

Ideally situated between the beautiful Lune and Eden Valleys, 1/4 mile from M6 Junction 38. Ideal stopover or base for touring – midway between Lakes and Yorkshire Dales – or fishing the River Lune and walking the lovely surrounding countryside. Three double, one twin and two singles, all en suite, with colour TV, central heating and tea/coffee facilities. Full Fire Certificate. Private Parking.

ETB 2 Crowns, AA QQQ, RAC Acclaimed.
Bed and Breakfast from £15.50

Fair Place

Watermillock-on-Ullswater
Wholefood Country Guest House
Bed and Breakfast NO SMOKING

Once the village school, now beautifully converted, with all rooms en suite, electric fires, tea makers and colour TV. We are only 7 miles from Junction 40 M6, 200 yards past Watermillock Church. B & B from £20.00.

Details from Mrs D. Bewley, Fair Place, Watermillock, Penrith, Cumbria CA11 0LR. Tel: (017684) 86235

TRANTHWAITE HALL

Underbarrow, Nr. Kendal LA8 8HG
Mrs D. M. Swindlehurst. Tel: 015395 68285

This magnificent old world Farmhouse is said to date back to 1186. One of the oldest in the district, with oak beams and original Black Iron fire grate. Peaceful setting half a mile up an unspoilt country lane, where deer and other wildlife can be seen. Kendal 3 miles. Windermere 5 miles. Many good country pubs in easy reach. Two double, one twin, one family room, all with tea/coffee making facilities and central heating. En suite available. Lounge, dining room, bathroom and shower. A warm welcome awaits guests; we want you to enjoy our home as much as we do. This is a real working farm.

Excellent Bed and Breakfast is offered from £16-£19 *in clean, comfortable surroundings and furnishings.*
Open all year round.
A.A. and Cumbria Tourist Board Commended.

GLENCREE Lake Road, Windermere, Cumbria LA23 2EQ

A warm welcome to our elegantly furnished and decorated small Hotel will enhance your enjoyment of your stay in the Most Beautiful Corner of England.

☆ Lovely spacious en suite rooms ☆ Colour TV

☆ Tea/Coffee Trays ☆ Comfortable Beds – Some Kingsize

☆ A pretty woodland outlook from most rooms

A traditional English Breakfast cooked to perfection will fortify your exploration of Lakes & Fells. QQQ Recommended by AA; Highly Acclaimed award by RAC and other prestigious guides. Access/Visa. Call us now for reservation. Tel: 015394 45822 Prop: Mrs Julie P. Butler.

Commended AA QQQ RAC Acclaimed

HAISTHORPE

GUEST HOUSE

Holly Road, Windermere

LA23 2AF

Tel: (015394) 43445

Mick & Angela Brown

Family-run guest house situated in a quiet location yet close to the centre of Windermere. Within 10 mins walk of Station and coach park, complimentary transport by arrangement. Colour TV with satellite channel and tea/coffee facilities in all rooms. Most rooms en suite. Children welcome at reduced rates up to 14 years. Car park. B&B from £13-£18. 3 course EM from £6.50. Phone for further details.

Beechwood Private Hotel

Beresford Rd., Bowness on Windermere
Cumbria LA23 2JG Tel & Fax: 015394 43403

Beechwood is superbly situated as all the bedrooms overlook delightful rose gardens, with splendid mountain, fell and some with lake views. We offer a charming variety of bedrooms from standard en-suites with king-size beds and pretty lace canopies to spacious deluxe suites with sofas, remote control colour TV and king-size four-posters. Special occasions - complimentary bubbly and arrangements made for chocolates or flowers for your arrival. Three minutes' stroll to restaurants, shops and esplanade. Large private car park. 5% discount for immediate bookings (4 nights min). B&B from £18 to £36 pp. SAE for details. OPEN ALL YEAR. ETB 3 Crowns.

AA RAC Highly Acclaimed **Commended**

GLENVILLE

Lake Road, Windermere LA23 2EQ
Tel: (015394) 43371

Glenville stands comfortably within its own grounds perfectly positioned for access to all amenities and within walking distance of the Lake. Retaining a host of original features, full of character, with a friendly country house atmosphere and high standards of comfort and cleanliness. En suite bedrooms with colour TV and tea/coffee making facilities. Licensed, with comfortable lounge. Superb car park. Mid week and short stays welcome. Please telephone for room availability.

DENE CREST GUEST HOUSE

Woodland Road, Windermere LA23 2AE
Tel: 015394 44979

OPEN ALL YEAR-SHORT BREAK TERMS

Close to Town Centre, yet quiet; only 2 minutes bus/rail stations, complimentary transport to/from Guest House. Drying room for walkers & fishermen. Pets welcome. Discounts on longer stays. Accommodation in choice of en suite rooms, tastefully decorated, all with central heating, colour TV, shaver points and hospitality trays. Excellent Breakfast. From £11.50 per night.

Miss J. Glover **ETB Listed**

HILTON HOUSE HOTEL

A charming stone-built Edwardian residence, retaining its original wood carving and panelling. All bedrooms have en suite showers and toilets. New ground floor non-smoking rooms. Additional guests' bathroom and toilets. Full central heating and licensed lounge. Children and dogs welcomed. Car and boat park. *Free use of swimming pool and leisure facilities.*

Please write or telephone:

Patricia and Andrew Barnicott
New Road, Windermere,
Cumbria LA23 2EE
Telephone: 015394 43934

English Lake District Hotels & Caterers Association · Member ·

ETB

Irene & George Eastwood

Sandown

Lake Road, Windermere LA23 2JF
Tel: 015394 45272

Open all year

Superb bed and breakfast accommodation. All rooms en suite with colour television and tea/coffee making facilities. Situated two minutes from Lake Windermere, shops and cafes. Many lovely walks. Open all year. From £18.00-£27.00 per person (excluding Bank Holidays.) Well behaved dogs welcome. Each room has own safe private car parking. SAE or telephone for further details.

HOLLY LODGE *'A Lakeland Guest House'*

Holly Lodge is one of the oldest houses in Windermere and is run by the resident proprietors who give a personal and friendly service. A full English Breakfast is provided and Evening Meal if required. There is central heating, a comfortable lounge with open fire, and a pleasant dining room. Each bedroom has hot and cold water, tea and coffee making facilities and colour TV. Some rooms en suite. No pets except guide dogs. Children welcome; up to 12 years at reduced rates. Open all year. Bed and Breakfast from £16; Evening Meal £10.00.

AA Listed ETB Commended

Licensed. Parking.

Tony and Lindy Priestley, Holly Lodge, 6 College Road, Windermere, Cumbria LA23 1BX. Telephone or Fax: 015394 43873.

The Beaumont Hotel

Holly Road, Windermere, Cumbria LA23 2AF
Tel: 015394 47075

Opened Easter 1992, this elegant Victorian House Hotel lends itself to all the grace and charm of its time combined with all the comforts of today.

Ideally situated for Windermere and Bowness and perfect location for touring the Lakes.

The Beaumont has very quickly gained a reputation for quality.

All 12 luxury bedrooms are en suite with tea making facilities, TV, hair dryers. Four-poster bedrooms are available for that special occasion and a 'Romantic Presentation' of wine, chocolates, fruit and flowers may be ordered. The standards are high, breakfasts are hearty and the hospitality is warm and sincere. Private parking. Leisure facilities available. Terms from £20.

Highly Commended RAC Highly Acclaimed AA Selected QQQQ

ST JOHN'S LODGE

Lake Road, Windermere LA23 2EQ
Tel: 015394 43078

A private hotel situated midway between Windermere and the Lake, close to all amenities. The 14 bedrooms have en suite facilities and are comfortably furnished, with colour TV and tea/coffee making facilities. Centrally heated throughout. There is a comfortable lounge for residents, and a friendly bar. Four course dinners personally prepared by Chef/Proprietor. £55 for 2 nights Dinner, Bed and Breakfast, £75 for 3 nights D, B&B, November to June inclusive. Facilities of private Leisure Club available to guests.

Commended AA RAC Highly Acclaimed

Oldfield House

BED & BREAKFAST

Bob and Maureen Theobald,
Oldfield House, Oldfield Road,
Windermere, Cumbria LA23 2BY

Telephone: (015394) 88445
Fax: (015394) 43250

We would like to welcome you to Oldfield House, which has a friendly, informal atmosphere within a traditionally-built Lakeland stone residence.
8 Bedrooms, most en-suite, four poster room, all with Colour TV, Radio, Telephone & Tea/Coffee making facilities ● Quiet central location ● Free use of Leisure Club facilities ● Reductions for 3 nights/children

AA QQQ COMMENDED RAC

ROCKSIDE

Ambleside Road, Windermere LA23 1AQ

A Lakeland Guest House full of character, Rockside is situated 2 minutes from the railway station and the shops and restaurants of Windermere. Parking for 12 cars. All bedrooms have washbasins, central heating, colour TV, clock radio and telephone. Most rooms have private bathroom and tea/coffee making facilities. Breakfast choice served from 8.30 to 9.15 am. Open all year for single, twins, doubles and families to enjoy the most beautiful corner of England. Bed and Breakfast from £14.50 to £22.50. RAC Acclaimed. BTA 2 Crowns. Car routes and walks arranged if required.

Mrs M. Fowles Tel: 015394 45343

Mr and Mrs Sandwell

HOLLY PARK HOUSE

1 Park Road
Windermere LA23 2AW
Tel: 015394 42107

COMMENDED

Victorian house of character but offering modern comforts. Convenient for shops, restaurants and train and bus services. Spacious en-suite rooms with colour TV and tea and coffee making facilities. A warm welcome assured from Ian and Doreen Sandwell. Bed and Breakfast from £16.00.

AA QQQ, RAC Highly Acclaimed

AA QQ

"FANTASTIC BREAKFAST - WONDERFUL ROOM"

LATIMER HOUSE

Lake Road, Bowness-on-Windermere, Cumbria
LA23 2JJ Tel: (015394) 46888

EXCLUSIVELY FOR NON-SMOKERS

* Beautiful feature rooms, mostly en suite
* Our famous traditional full English Breakfast served in your room
* Colour TVs and tea/coffee facilities
* Car park and garaging
* Large secluded garden to relax in
* Short stroll to lake
* Many walks and car tours (we provide maps and routes)

"Excellent again - We just can't stay away" "Luxurious" "Great Hospitality!"

Just a few comments from our visitors' book. If you are looking for somewhere just a little special, pay us a visit and sample our hospitality. Major credit cards accepted.
For reservations (advisable for weekends, Bank Holidays and school holidays) or a colour brochure please call.

Cumbria— Classified Advertisements

AMBLESIDE

MR AND MRS P. HART, BRACKEN FELL, OUTGATE, NEAR HAWKSHEAD, AMBLESIDE LA22 0NH (015394 36289). Comfortable bed and breakfast accommodation between Ambleside and Hawkshead in the picturesque hamlet of Outgate. All rooms have private facilities, complimentary tea/coffee and outstanding views. Central heating. Ample parking. Non-smoking. Bed and breakfast from £18.50. Two Crowns Commended.

APPLEBY-IN-WESTMORLAND

MRS E. PIGNEY, HOWGILL HOUSE, APPLEBY-IN-WESTMORLAND CA16 6UW (017683 51574/51240). Beautiful scenic area only 10 minutes' walk from town centre. All rooms have washbasins, tea-making, electric fires. Cot and TV available. Separate sitting and dining rooms. Parking. Bed and breakfast from £12.50 nightly, from £65.00 weekly. One Crown Commended. Send SAE for further details.

BOWNESS-ON-WINDERMERE

MRS C. A. STEVENSON, NEW HALL BANK, FALLBARROW ROAD, BOWNESS-ON-WINDERMERE LA23 3DJ (015394 43558). Situated in a quiet area within two minutes' walking distance of town centre and Lake. Ample parking space. Lake views. Bed and Breakfast. ETB Listed.

BRAMPTON

MRS JANET HEMPSTEAD, COURTYARD COTTAGES, WARREN BANK, STATION ROAD, BRAMPTON CA8 1EX (016977 41818). Unique concept of B&B providing independence and privacy. Detached luxury cottage in the courtyard of a Victorian Mansion, breakfast served in your room. Come and be pampered. Disabled facilities. From £25 per person.

BUTTERMERE

DALEGARTH, HASSNESS ESTATE, BUTTERMERE CA13 9XA (017687 70233). Dalegarth Guest House, close to the Lake shore, 1¼ miles south of village. Bed and Breakfast from £17.00 including VAT.

CARLISLE

MRS DOROTHY NICHOLSON, GILL FARM, BLACKFORD, CARLISLE (0122 875 326). Georgian-style farmhouse offers friendly welcome to all guests. Near Hadrian's Wall, Borders and Lake District. All bedrooms with washbasins, tea/coffee facilities. Open all year. ETB One Crown. Telephone for further details.

CROSTHWAITE

MR & MRS M. D. NEVETT, HIGH TOWN YEAT, CROSTHWAITE, KENDAL LA8 8BW (015395 68251). Peaceful 16th century farmhouse with panoramic views of Lyth Valley. Double and twin bedded rooms with tea/coffee. Comfortable oak-beamed TV lounge. B&B £15.00 per person.

ESKDALE

MR & MRS A. FOSTER, BURNMOOR INN, BOOT, ESKDALE CA19 1TG (019467 23224). No crowns or stars, just warm en suite rooms, magnificent scenery, plus Heidi's superb cooking in restaurant or bar. Enquire for special Winter Break terms.

HAWKSHEAD

MR AND MRS P. HART, BRACKEN FELL, OUTGATE, NEAR HAWKSHEAD, AMBLESIDE LA22 0NH (015394 36289). Comfortable bed and breakfast accommodation between Ambleside and Hawkshead in the picturesque hamlet of Outgate. All rooms have private facilities, complimentary tea/coffee and outstanding views. Central heating. Ample parking. Non-smoking. Bed and breakfast from £18.50. Two Crowns Commended.

KESWICK

LYDNHURST GUEST HOUSE, 22 SOUTHEY STREET, KESWICK CA12 4EF (017687 72303). Family run guest house near shops, parks, lake. Rooms centrally heated; washbasins, razor points, beverage makers. Own keys. Evening meal optional. Home cooking. Open all year. B&B £13-£14 per person, DB&B £21-£22.50. ETB One Crown.

MRS J. HUTTON, 'WOODLANDS', THE HAWTHORNS, KESWICK CA12 4LL (017687 74010). Set in the picturesque Lake District, a warm welcome awaits you at 'Woodlands'. Full English Breakfast. Lounge with colour TV; full central heating; all rooms with washbasins. Private parking. Bed and Breakfast from £13.50 according to season.

PENRITH

THE LIMES COUNTRY HOTEL, REDHILLS, PENRITH CA11 0DT (01768 63343). Spacious Victorian house in peaceful countryside. Large garden. Convenient Lake District, Ullswater 4 miles. Ideal for motorway travellers, M6 two minutes. All rooms ensuite. Residential licence. Excellent home-cooked food, please pre-book for Dinner. Bargain Breaks October to Easter: brochure available. AA, RAC Listed; ETB 2 Crowns.

WINDERMERE

VILLA LODGE, CROSS STREET, WINDERMERE LA23 1AE. Friendliness and cleanliness guaranteed. Peaceful situation, two minutes railway station. Seven lovely bedrooms, mostly en suite, some four-posters, all with colour TV, tea/coffee facilities. Most with magnificent views. Private safe parking for six cars. Special offers November -March. Open all year. Ring JOHN & LIZ CHRISTOPHERSON (Tel and Fax: 015394 43318).

CAMBRIDGE HOUSE, 9 OAK STREET, WINDERMERE LA23 1EN (015394 43846). Village centre location convenient for all amenities including buses and trains. Modern, comfortable rooms with en suite facilities. Full English, Continental or vegetarian breakfast. ETB Listed 'Commended'.

JENNIFER WRIGLEY, UPPER OAKMERE, 3 UPPER OAK STREET, WINDERMERE LA23 2LB (015394 45649 and 0831 845547). Built in traditional Lakeland stone, situated approximately 100 yards from village. Single people welcome. Warm, clean and very friendly. The price is the same throughout the year. B&B £14.50; optional Dinner. Pets and children welcome.

THE DOG AND PARTRIDGE COUNTRY INN

Swinscoe, Ashbourne, Derbyshire DE6 2HS
Tel: 01335 343183 Fax: 01335 342742

Mary and Martin Stelfox welcome you to a family run seventeenth century inn and motel set in five acres, five miles from Alton Towers and close to Dovedale and Ashbourne. We specialise in family breaks, and special diets and vegetarians are catered for. All rooms have private bathrooms, colour TV, direct dial telephone, tea making facilities and baby listening service. It is ideally situated for touring Stoke Potteries, Derbyshire Dales and Staffordshire moorlands. The restaurant is open all day, and non residents are welcome.

Sheldon House

Chapel Street,
Monyash, Nr Bakewell
Derbyshire DE45 1JJ
Tel: 01629 813067

An 18th century Listed building in the picturesque village of Monyash (5 miles from Bakewell) in the heart of the Peak National Park and at the head of beautiful Lathkill Dale. Recently renovated to a high standard, we offer comfortable accommodation in a friendly atmosphere. 3 double rooms with en suite facilities (2 with TV). All rooms have central heating and tea/coffee making facilities. Ideal base for visits to Chatsworth House, Haddon and Hardwick Halls. Excellent for cycling and walking. Open all year except Christmas and New Year. **No smoking**. ETB. ♛♛Highly Commended

B & B from £17.50 per person.

Kelseys

Swiss House Hotel & Restaurant
How Lane, Castleton,
Near Sheffield S30 2WJ

Situated in historic village in heart of Peak District, ideal centre for all beauty spots. Family-run licensed restaurant and guest house with clean, comfortable accommodation. All rooms en suite with colour TV and tea-making facilities. Excellent and interesting food, all diets catered for. ♛♛♛ Commended.

B&B £22.50 per person sharing double room; Single supplement £7 *Tel: 01433 621098*

YE OLDE CHESHIRE CHEESE INN

How Lane, Castleton, Derbyshire S30 2WJ
Tel: 01433 620330

The **"Cheshire Cheese Inn"** is a delightful 17th century free house situated in Castleton, Derbyshire - the heart of the Peak District National Park. An ideal base for walkers and climbers, and sporting activities in the area include cycling, golf, swimming, gliding, hang-gliding, horse riding and fishing. Castleton itself holds many a treat in store, with its caves and mines including the world famous "Blue John" mine. There are six pretty bedrooms with colour TV and en suite shower facilities. Our village fayre menu is available lunchtimes and evenings, all dishes home cooked in traditional manner. Home made pies, lasagne, chilli, etc. Also game menu in Winter. Daily specials include roast wild boar, smoked chicken and roast hock. No juke box, no pool, no machines, just a traditional 17th century Inn. Full Fire Certificate. **Les Routiers**

Derbyshire — Classified Advertisements

ASHFORD-IN-THE-WATER

WHEEL COTTAGE, FENNEL STREET, ASHFORD-IN-THE-WATER, NEAR BAKEWELL (0162-981 4339). Two double and one single room with colour TV and tea/coffee making facilities. Special diets catered for. Bed and Breakfast from £13. Evening Meal by arrangement. Open all year.

CASTLETON

MR & MRS T.E. SKELTON, CRYER HOUSE, CASTLETON, NEAR SHEFFIELD S30 2WG (01433 620244). 17th century Rectory, opposite church, in Peak District village. Two double rooms, one family room. Beautiful cottage garden. Ideal for walking, pot-holing, visits to Chatsworth, etc. Tourist Board Listed.

HATHERSAGE

MRS MELANIE J.A. JENNINGS, HILLCOTE, 7 PARK EDGE, HATHERSAGE, SHEFFIELD S30 1BS (01433 651110). Bed and Breakfast in family house surrounded by beautiful countryside of Derbyshire Peak District. Ideal situation for walking and climbing. Double/family/twin 'no smoking' bedroom with private shower. Sorry, no pets. Terms from £14.50.

MATLOCK

MRS OVSANNA ALLEN, "EDGEMOUNT" 16 EDEG ROAD, MATLOCK DE4 3NH (01629 584787). Comfortable homely Bed and Breakfast accommodation in pleasant central location near public transport. Ideal for exploring historic stately houses, e.g. Chatsworth, Roman caves, Heights of Abraham. In the heart of the beautiful Derbyshire Dales' holiday attractions. Open all year. B&B £13-£14 per person.

MRS CLAYTON, WOODLANDS VIEW, 226 DALE ROAD, MATLOCK BATH DE4 3RT (01629 55762). Bed and Breakfast from £10.00. Ideal for tourists. Situated on level ground. Close to shops, restaurants, railway station, Heights of Abraham Cable Car. Beautiful scenery. Telephone for details. EMTB One Crown.

MRS S. ELLIOTT, 'GLENDON', KNOWLESTON PLACE, MATLOCK DE4 3BU (01629 584732). Large Georgian House. Own car park. Excellent touring base for Derbyshire Dales and the beautiful Peak District. Bed and Breakfast from £15.

TIDESWELL

PAT HARRIS, LAUREL HOUSE, THE GREEN, LITTON, NR BUXTON SK17 8QP (01298 871971). Our Victorian house overlooks the green in this pretty farming village. Ideal for walking and touring. Pubs and Restaurants ½ mile. One double en suite, one twin with washbasin, both with tea making facilities. Non smoking. From £15.00. Reductions for one week.

DEVON

Barnstaple

MRS. V. M. CHUGG Tel: 01271 43458

"VALLEY VIEW"

Guineaford, Marwood, Near Barnstaple, Devon

Friendly Bed and Breakfast accommodation in bungalow situated on 300 acre farm. Near Marwood Hill Gardens and Arlington Court. Colour TV and video. Children most welcome, free baby-sitting. Evening Meal available if required. Bedtime drink at no extra charge. Open all year round. Dogs by arrangement.

Terms from £12

The Pines at Eastleigh

Near Bideford, Devon EX39 4PA Tel & Fax: 01271 860561

AA "QQQ" RAC Acclaimed. A Georgian House in seven acres with glorious views overlooking Bideford and the sea at Hartland Point and Lundy Island. 5 en suite bedrooms with colour TV, direct dial telephones and tea/coffee making facilities. Full central heating. The beach, Exmoor and Torridge valley are minutes away. Enjoy beautifully prepared food, a quiet drink in the bar, or curl up in front of our log fires. We arrange golfing, riding, painting and watersports holidays. Bed & Breakfast from £17, weekly from £90. Dinner by arrangement. Short Breaks available.

Richmond House Hotel

Higher Manor Road, Brixham TQ5 8HA Tel: 01803 882391

Commended

Victorian Hotel of Character central to historic harbour, shop and restaurants yet quietly located with residents' car park and south-facing sun terrace. Spacious rooms with pleasant views, en suite and family rooms available. Well appointed lounge with colour television, video and games. Bed and full English Breakfast from £16.00 per person per night. Visa and Access accepted.

The Globe Inn

High Street, Chagford, Devon TQ13 8AJ

Built in the XVI Century this historic coaching inn is situated in the centre of the delightful country town of Chagford within the Dartmoor National Park.

Established in the shadow of Meldon Hill close to the beautiful River Teign and amid the breathtaking countryside of mid Devon. Chagford is a superb centre for touring or walking, being within easy reach of all the moorland beauty spots.

We have a limited number of spacious en suite bedrooms, all with colour television and tea & coffee making facilities.

Phone: 01647 433485 or write for a brochure.

DARTMOOR LADYMEDE

Throwleigh, Nr Okehampton EX20 2HU

Tel: (01647) 231492

Delightful detached bungalow situated on the edge of the very popular village of Throwleigh, which nestles in the tranquillity of the Dartmoor foothills. Good area for walking and riding. Friendly atmosphere, children and pets welcome. Tea-making. Local pub serves Evening Meals. B&B: £13 one night, £12.50 for more than one night.

ETB Registered **MRS PIPER**

A379 turn off from main A38 Exeter to Plymouth road.

MARRIDGE FARM

Ugborough, Nr Ivybridge PL21 0HR

Traditional family run dairy farm in the heart of peaceful countryside, with beautiful garden and meadow views. Local unspoilt sandy beaches. Good home cooked food, cream and fresh home grown vegetables. One double room with washbasin, one en suite family room. Children welcome. Cot, highchair, babysitting available. Open all year.

Bed and breakfast from £14. Optional evening meal.

Mrs Susan Winzer

Telephone: Gara Bridge (01548) 821560

TREBLES COTTAGE HOTEL

Kingston, Near Kingsbridge
South Devon TQ7 4PT
Tel: 01548 810268

This pretty cottage stands at the top of a quaint and tranquil village, yet is only 12 miles from Plymouth. The cottage style bedrooms are well equipped and there is a comfortable lounge with a dining room adjoining a cosy bar which leads out to a tiny flower-filled patio. Resident proprietors Georgiana and David Kinder are jolly hosts and Georgiana provides enjoyable meals using fresh produce.

MOOR VIEW HOTEL

Vale Down, Lydford, Devon
EX20 4BB Tel: 0182 282 220
AA QQQQQ RAC Acclaimed
ETB ♛♛♛ Commended

Small peaceful Victorian Country House. En suite accommodation. English Breakfast, Dinner. Reputation for good food, sound wine. No smoking. Midway between Okehampton, Tavistock on A386 Plymouth Road. Open all year.

GLENVILLE HOUSE

2 Tors Road, Lynmouth
North Devon EX35 6ET

Comfortable, licensed Victorian house in sunny riverside position. Ideal for touring/walking Exmoor and coast. Rooms with en suite shower available. Tea/coffee making. A warm welcome, good food and friendly hospitality assured.

Tel: 01598 752202

IRVINE'S
Bed & Breakfast

50 Grand Parade, West Hoe, Plymouth, Devon PL1 3DJ
Telephone: 01752 227739

Victorian Town House overlooking Drake's Island and Plymouth Sound offering comfortable B&B. Accommodation comprises one double and one twin bedroom with colour TV, washbasins, tea/coffee facilities, central heating and double glazing. Bathroom, separate shower room and private parking. All amenities within easy walking distance. B&B from £13 per person.

Lyme Bay House Hotel

Den Promenade, Teignmouth TQ14 8SZ
Tel: (01626) 772953

On the sea front close to rail/coach stations, shops. En suite facilities. Lift – no steps! Bed and Breakfast. Clean, groomed pets very welcome.

WAYFARER HOUSE

Small Guest House four minutes' walk from town centre, leading to harbour and beaches. Open all year. Bed and Breakfast only. Traditional or vegetarian Breakfast. Tea-making facilities available. Dieters welcome. Health-conscious household.

Discount for over-50s.

Mr & Mrs R.L. Buckmaster,
51 Chatsworth Road, Torquay TQ1 3BJ
Tel: (01803) 294663

BRADDON HALL HOTEL

70 BRADDONS HILL ROAD EAST
TORQUAY TQ1 1HF
TEL: 01803 293908 ETB♛♛♛

AA QQQ. Delightful licensed hotel of character * 500 yards from harbour and entertainments * All tastefully decorated rooms en suite with remote-control colour TV's and teamakers * Romantic four-poster bed * Superb traditional food * Ground floor bedroom * Full central heating for those early and late breaks * Parking * Bed and Breakfast from £16 to £20 per person.

ROSE MARIE

2 BRIDGE ROAD, TORQUAY
TQ2 5AX Tel: 01803 297975

Centrally situated for railway/coach stations, all amenities, leisure/conference centre. All bedrooms satellite TV/video link, tea/coffee making and central heating. Own keys, en suite available. Bed and full English Breakfast from £10; optional Evening Dinner available. Special weekly prices. Children half price if sharing family room with parents. Open all year. SAE for brochure.

Mrs Joan Davey.

CLAVER GUEST HOUSE

A WARM WELCOME AWAITS YOU!

Only a few minutes' walk to sea, shops, and all entertainments. Small car park. En suite room available. TV lounge. Tea making facilities in all rooms. Good English cooking. Bed and Breakfast from £12.00. Evening Meal available. Reduced weekly rates for children. Families most welcome.

Write or phone: Nigel and Angela Pearce, 119 Abbey Road, Torquay, Devon TQ2 5NP. Tel: (01803) 297118

OPEN ALL YEAR

KE'THLA HOTEL

Belgrave Road, Torquay TQ2 5HX Devon **Tel: 01803 294995**

All rooms completely refurbished to a high standard. All are en suite and have colour TV, satellite channels, tea-making facilities and central heating. Studios also available for B&B or S/C. Central to all amenities, seafront and Riviera Leisure Centre. Discount for Senior Citizens early or late season. Tariff from £11 to £20. Phone for brochure. **Mr & Mrs T Wilson.**

CLEVEDON HOTEL

Meadfoot Sea Road, TORQUAY TQ1 2LQ
Tel: 01803 294260

Ideally situated in peaceful wooded suburb half mile from harbour and town, 300 yards from the beach. Delicious food and a genuine home from home atmosphere suits both business and holiday guests. All rooms en suite with TV and tea-making. Dogs by arrangement. Ample parking. Evening Meal optional. **B&B from £18.**

EMMETT FARM

Umberleigh,
North Devon EX37 9AG
Tel: 01769 540243

Situated in quiet countryside, approximately seven miles from South Molton and Barnstaple. 165 acre beef and sheep farm which visitors are welcome to explore. Free-range eggs, fresh garden produce. Lovely sandy beaches of North Devon within easy reach. Spacious dining room and warm comfortable lounge with open fire and colour TV. All bedrooms equipped with tea/coffee facilities. B&B from £13; Evening Meal if required from £8.

Devon — Classified Advertisements

BAMPTON

THE OLD FORGE, PETTON CROSS, SHILLINGFORD, BAMPTON, NEAR TIVERTON EX16 9BG (013986 202). A warm welcome to the Old Forge on the B3227 (formerly the A361). Take Junction 27 from Taunton. Ideal stop on the way to Cornwall, Exmoor, Dartmoor and North Devon. One family room or twin en suite, one double room. Bathroom and shower. B&B from £13.50.

BIDEFORD

MRS S. WADE, COLLABERIE FARM, WELCOMBE, BIDEFORD EX39 6HF (Morwenstow ([01288 331] 391). Modern farmhouse in beautiful unspoilt countryside overlooking wooded valley and sea. Excellent touring centre for North Devon and North Cornwall. Open all year except Christmas. Children welcome. Fire Certificate held. Bed, Breakfast, Evening Meal optional.

CHAGFORD

I. SATOW, WEEKE BROOK, CHAGFORD TQ13 8JQ (01647 433345). Away from the tumult of the world. One mile charming small Dartmoor town. Lovely ancient thatched house. Pets welcome. Bed and Breakfast £11.00 to £15.00.

CLOVELLY

MRS P. VANSTONE, THE OLD SMITHY, SLERRA HILL, CLOVELLY, BIDEFORD EX39 5ST (01237 431202). Comfortable cottage accommodation - easy reach Exmoor, Dartmoor and Cornwall. Standard and en suite rooms, all with TV and tea/coffee. Dogs allowed. Open all year.

EXETER

MR DEREK SERCOMBE, "RHONA" GUEST HOUSE, 15 BLACKALL ROAD, EXETER EX4 4HE (01392 77791). Small family Guest House 7 minutes' walk from centre of historic Exeter. Ideal base for touring Exmoor and Dartmoor. All rooms with colour TV and tea/coffee facilities. Luxury en-suite accommodation. Open all year. Single rooms from £11, twin/family rooms from £21. Full English breakfast; Dinner on request.

MRS K. WILLIAMS, CHIVERSTONE FARM, KENTON, EXETER EX6 8NL (01626 890268). Bed and Breakfast (Evening Meal optional) on working farm. Beautiful countryside, peaceful setting. Sandy beach 4 miles, moors 20 miles. B & B £14 p.n.; £85 p.w., Full English breakfast. Separate dining room, lounge with colour TV. Opens Easter.

MRS DOROTHY GLANVILL, "LOCHINVAR", SHEPHERDS PARK FARM, WOODBURY, NEAR EXETER EX5 1LA (01395 232185). Three miles from M5 motorway in quiet country position. One double & one twin bedrooms en-suite. Family room with private bathroom. All have radio alarms, hairdryers, tea/coffee making facilities, colour TV and central heating. Open all year. Brochure available. B&B from £15. ETB 2 Crowns.

CLOCK TOWER HOTEL, 16 NEW NORTH ROAD, EXETER EX4 4HF (01392 424545). Listed building of character in city centre, 10 minutes level walk stations, shops and Cathedral. All modern facilities including en suite rooms with baths and satellite TV. Licensed. Credit cards. Rates from £12.50 B&B. Colour brochure. Two Crowns.

HONITON

ANN AND DOUG RICKSON, SUNNYSIDE FARM, COMBE RALEIGH, HONITON EX14 0UJ (01404 43489). Comfortable accommodation in Devon countryside. Superb views. Just 25 minutes from coast. TV in bedrooms. Tea/coffee facilities. Children and pets welcome. Bed and Breakfast £11.

HOPE COVE

MRS VAL HEWITT, 'ROCKCLIFFE', OUTER HOPE COVE, NEAR KINGSBRIDGE TQ7 3HG (01548 560061). First class en suite B&B accommodation £16.50 per person, £112 weekly. Village and beaches 100 yards. All rooms have lovely sea views, colour TV and tea/coffee facilities. Full English Breakfast. Parking. Pets by arrangement.

KINGSBRIDGE

THE GLOBE INN, FROGMORE, NEAR KINGSBRIDGE TQ7 2NR (01548 531351). Attractive 18th century village inn. Six well appointed bedrooms (three en suite). Atmospheric bars and restaurant; extensive menu of home-cooked fare. Gardens overlook creek. Parking. Pets and children welcome. 2 Crowns, AA QQ Recommended.

MRS J. CROCKER, ESTUARY VIEW FARM, WEST ALVINGTON, KINGSBRIDGE TQ7 1EF (01548 856487). Spacious luxury farm bungalow. One bedroom with en suite facilities, others with own private bathrooms. All rooms colour TV & tea/coffee facilities. Situated on the Old Salcombe Coach Road. Friendly and peaceful atmosphere. £14-£16 per person.

KING'S NYMPTON

BETTY AND RALPH COLE, GREAT OAKWELL FARM, KING'S NYMPTON, UMBERLEIGH EX37 9TE (01769 572810). Join us in our lovely old farmhouse near South Molton. Exmoor/Devon coast within easy reach. Two double (with TV) and single rooms all have tea/coffee facilities. Evening Meals from £7.50. Bed and Breakfast from £14.00. ETB Listed.

LYDFORD

MRS A. CROCKER, HEATHERGATE, LYDFORD, OKEHAMPTON EX20 4BP (0182282 486). Friendly farming atmosphere with beautiful views of Dartmoor. One double, one twin with bathroom. Sitting/dining room. Tea/coffee facilities. Good home cooking. B&B £13.00

LYNMOUTH

MRS P. PILE, 'OAKLEIGH', 4 TORS ROAD, LYNMOUTH EX35 6ET (Lynton [01598] 752220). Comfortable Guest House. Washbasins and shaving points, tea/coffee making facilities in all bedrooms. Convenient sea and Exmoor. Free car park. Dinner optional. SAE for details, or telephone.

NORTH TAWTON

MR AND MRS J. RUSSELL, KAYDEN HOUSE HOTEL, HIGH STREET, NORTH TAWTON EX20 2HF (01837 82242). Family run hotel five miles from Okehampton. Ideal base for touring countryside and coast. A la carte restaurant. Bed and Breakfast from £17. Please send for brochure.

OKEHAMPTON

MRS I. COURTNEY, IFOLD HOUSE, 27 NEW ROAD, OKEHAMPTION EX20 1JE (01837 52712). Ideal touring centre. Bed and Breakfast from £12.50. Evening Meal optional. All bedrooms have washbasins and shaver points. Central heating. TV lounge. Parking. Open all year.

PLYMOUTH

STELLA BUDZIAK, ALLINGTON HOUSE, 6 ST. JAMES PLACE EAST, THE HOE, PLYMOUTH PL1 3AS (01752 221435). Close to shopping centre, seafront, theatres, ferries, stations. Our aim is good food, cleanliness and comfort. Street parking. Bed and Breakfast from £14.

THE BREAKAWAY GUEST HOUSE, 28 NORTH ROAD EAST, PLYMOUTH PL4 6AS (01752 227767). Situated very close to city centre, rail and coach stations. All rooms with TV, tea/coffee making facilities. Car parking. Single room £13, double £25.

SIDMOUTH

MRS J. A. SHENFIELD, SIDLING FIELD, 105 PEASLANDS ROAD, SIDMOUTH EX10 8XE (01395 513859). Large centrally heated bungalow. Two acres of ground. Outskirts of town, 400 yards from seafront. One double, one twin; sitting/dining room, colour TV. Ample parking. Bed and Breakfast £12.50. Sidmouth is delightfully unspoilt with plenty to do within easy reach.

SOUTH MOLTON

MRS MARY YENDELL, CRANGS HEASLEIGH, HEASLEY MILL, NORTH MOLTON, SOUTH MOLTON EX36 3LE (015984 268). Bed and substantial Breakfast offered in Farmhouse, Exmoor National Park area. Good food and comfortable accommodation. Good road. Convenient for coast and market towns. Open all year. 2 Crowns.

TAVISTOCK

MRS S. DAWE, LANGFORD FARM, LAMERTON, TAVISTOCK (01822 612202). Tranquil 500 year old farmhouse. Homely atmosphere. Many places of interest, National Trust properties, golf courses, Dartmoor and beaches close by. Tavistock one and a half miles B3362.

TIVERTON

MR AND MRS A. EVANS, ANGEL GUEST HOUSE, 13 ST PETER STREET, TIVERTON EX16 6NU (01884 253392). Comfortable, Licensed Georgian Guest House in town centre. Central heating and hot drink facilities in rooms. Lounge. Parking. Ensuite available. Bed and Breakfast from £14.00

MRS S. M. KERSLAKE, LANDRAKE FARM, CHEVITHORNE, TIVERTON EX16 7QN (01398 331221). Situated four miles north of Tiverton. N.T. House and Gardens nearby. Home produced food served. Room and Breakfast from £13. Evening Meal available. ETB Listed.

TORQUAY

NIGEL AND ANGELA PEARCE, CLAVER GUEST HOUSE, 119 ABBEY ROAD, TORQUAY TQ2 5NP (01803 297118). A real home from home, close to sea, shops and all entertainments. Good English cooking. En suite room available. Tea-making facilities, all rooms. Reduced weekly rates and for children. We are here to make sure you enjoy your holiday. B&B from £12.00. Write or phone for brochure.

MRS B. HURREN, 'TREANDER', 10 MORGAN AVENUE, TORQUAY TQ2 5RS (01803 296906). Enjoy a first-class informal holiday at a comfortable establishment ideally situated for beaches and all amenities. All rooms colour TV, tea making, some with sea views. Children welcome. Central heating. Car park. Own keys, access at all times. WCTB and Hotel Association Listed. (Pets welcome by arrangement).

DORSET

Bournemouth

Denewood Hotel

1 Percy Road, Boscombe
Bournemouth BH5 1JE
Tel: 01202 394493

Denewood is situated midway between golden beaches and the Sovereign Centre, adjacent to Marguerite Thorpe Health and Beauty Salon. Comfortably furnished bedrooms offer central heating, tea/coffee facilities, colour TV. Double and twin suites available. Convenient for ferries, coach tours, golf courses, first-class fishing, and all water sports *OR* let us arrange for you a flying lesson for as little as £29.00

Terms per person
Bed & Breakfast with vegetarian alternative from £15.00

Open all year * Private car park
Special diets * Bar snacks
Packed lunches * Pets by arrangement

Readers are requested to mention this guidebook when seeking accommodation (and please enclose a stamped addressed envelope).

SEACREST LODGE

63 Alum Chine Road, Bournemouth BH4 8DU
Tel: 01202 767438

A warm welcome awaits you whether you are here on business or for leisure. We are ideally situated at the head of beautiful Alum Chine, leading to miles of golden beaches. Also close to shops, restaurants and entertainments and within easy reach of the New Forest, Poole Harbour and many other attractions.

Good accommodation en suite, tea/coffee making facilities, colour TV all rooms.

Full English Breakfast • Ample car parking • Large garden for guests' use

---

AA ETB

Mayfield PRIVATE HOTEL

46 Frances Road, Bournemouth BH1 3SA
Tel: (01202) 551839

Central coach/rail stations, sea and shops
* Residential Licence * Parking * First class food and accommodation * Some rooms en suite
* Colour TV & tea making facilities all rooms

Bed & Breakfast £14-£16 daily, £90-£105 weekly
Dinner, Bed & Breakfast £19-£21 daily, £106-£124 weekly

BARGAIN BREAKS OCTOBER-APRIL

Westbrook

64 Alum Chine Road, Bournemouth BH4 8DZ
Tel: (01202) 761081

Westbrook is ideally situated for your Bed and Breakfast holiday at the top of wooded Alum Chine which leads to a beautiful sandy beach and just a few minutes' walk away are Westbourne shops where you will find a variety of restaurants and shops.

☆ Full English Breakfast ☆ Tea making
En suite WC available ☆ Parking
☆ Full Fire Certificate

Bed and Breakfast from £14 per night.

BOURNEMOUTH ENTERTAINS ALL YEAR ROUND

SWEET BRIAR Tel: (01202) 553028

...is a traditional English Guest House overlooking Gardens with Bowls, Putting and Tennis–short walk to sea

- ☆Full English Breakfast
- ☆Comfortable TV lounge
- ☆Comfortable bedrooms with tea/coffee making
- ☆En suite available
- ☆Access & Visa accepted
- ☆Easy Parking
- ☆Toilets & showers on both floors
- ☆Linen sheets
- ☆Senior Citizen and
- ☆Child Discounts
- ☆Access at all times
- ☆Short Breaks & Holidays
- ☆Convenient coach/rail stations

BED AND BREAKFAST FROM £13 DAILY

Write or phone for terms and brochure to:

Sue and Bob Overall, 12 Derby Road Bournemouth BH1 3QA

Overnight Guests Welcome

Florence Hotel

8 Boscombe Spa Road, Bournemouth BH5 1AU
Tel: 01202 393485

- ☆ 30 bedrooms
- ☆ All rooms radio, colour TV, teamaking facilities
- ☆ En suites available
- ☆ Ground floor rooms
- ☆ Close sea/shops
- ☆ Full English Breakfast
- ☆ Garden
- ☆ Large car park
- ☆ Evening meal optional

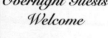

Bed & Breakfast from £12.50 Daily

Freshfields Hotel

55 CHRISTCHURCH ROAD, BOURNEMOUTH
DORSET BH1 3PA TEL: 01202 394023

Small Licensed Hotel, short walk to sandy beach through Boscombe Chine. Close to town and all Bournemouth's attractions, shops and theatres. Golf, tennis, putting and bowling are all nearby. All rooms have colour TV and tea/coffee. Most are en suite. Access at all times with own keys. Frontal car park.

B&B from £12.50, reductions for Senior Citizens.
BARGAIN BREAKS SEPTEMBER TO JUNE

AA Listed **BOURNEMOUTH** *RAC Listed*

Joan & John Adams welcome you to the newly modernised Valberg Hotel

*All rooms have colour TV, also private shower and toilet en suite *Superb quiet position * One minute from cliff top * Full central heating * Licensed bar *Garden and ample parking.

Bed and Breakfast £90-£120 weekly incl.
£15-£20 daily incl.
Dinner optional – £7 daily
***Brochure* VALBERG HOTEL**
1A Wollstonecraft Road, Boscombe
Bournemouth BH5 1JQ Tel: 01202 394644

Bayview Hotel

Southbourne Overcliff Drive
Bournemouth, Dorset BH6 3QP
Tel: 01202 429315 or 0585 488150

* 14 en-suite bedrooms with colour TV & Teasmaid
* Car parking
* Panoramic sea views from most rooms
* Sandy beaches. Level cliff top walks
* Personal service with maximum attention to comfort and fine food
* Special Christmas programme
* For brochure please write or phone Resident Proprietors Alison & Adrian Homa

Terms: B&B from £17 per night.
Dinner also available.

Commended

CHERRY VIEW HOTEL

66 Alum Chine Road,
Bournemouth BH4 8DZ
Tel: 01202 760910

AA Listed
Quality Award
RAC Acclaimed
ETB

Family-run. Ideally situated between shops and beaches.

★ 11 en suite rooms with TV, radio, teamaking, Central Heating - non-smoking available.
★ Excellent food - choice of menu.
★ Residents' bar ★ Private parking

CHRISTMAS & NEW YEAR PROGRAMME
OPEN ALL YEAR
2 to 5 day bargain breaks early/late season; special tariff on request

***Terms:** Daily from £15 to £30; Weekly from £90 to £180*

Sandy Beach Hotel

ETB Licensed

Family-run hotel in superb position overlooking sea.

Easy access to safe, sandy beach. Near to shops and buses. Convenient for Bournemouth, New Forest and day trips . Most rooms en suite. All rooms colour TV and tea/coffee facilities. Access to hotel at all times. Licensed bar. Ample parking. B&B from £17 per night. Special weekly rates. Brochure from Resident Proprietors,

Bryan and Caroline Channing, Sandy Beach Hotel, Southbourne Overcliff Drive, Southbourne, Bournemouth BH6 3QB Tel: 01202 424385

De-Luxe English Tourist Board & QQQQQ Premier Selected AA, BOTH TOP QUALITY AWARDS

Friendly informal atmosphere & extremely comfortable & relaxing in an unusual colonial ambience. Carefully furnished en-suite rooms with easy chairs, col TV. Tea/coffee. C/H. Set in 'National Garden Scheme' feature gardens with many unusual plants. Award winning traditional English home cooking. B&B £23 pppd. Dinner £12. Stay a while and explore varied & contrasting places, NT gardens, houses, moors, quaint old villages, Dorset coast & Hardy country. List provided 50 places. A no smoking house. Open all year.

Mrs Swann, Broadview, East Street, Crewkerne, Dorset Border, Somerset TA18 7AG
Phone 01460 73424.

LULWORTH COVE
Cromwell House Hotel

Lulworth Cove, Dorset BH20 5RJ
Tel: 01929 400253
Fax: 01929 400566

CATRIONA AND ALISTAIR MILLER welcome guests to their comfortable family-run Hotel, set in secluded gardens with spectacular sea views. Direct access to Dorset Coast Path. Heated swimming pool May to October. Accommodation in 14 double bedrooms, all en suite, with tea/coffee facilities, radio, TV and telephone. Restaurant and bar. Cottage annexe also available, 300 yards.

LULWORTH COVE

Val & Barry Burrill
GRAYBANK GUEST HOUSE
Main Road, West Lulworth,
Dorset BH20 5RL
Tel: 01929 400256.

Tourist Board registered-Listed. Victorian Guest House situated in beautiful country surroundings five minutes' walk from Lulworth Cove. This central location is an excellent base for walking the Coastal Path and surrounding countryside and touring the many places of interest in Dorset. Come and enjoy excellent hospitality in this comfortable Guesthouse. All rooms have H&C water, heating, tea/coffee making facilities. Most rooms have remote control colour TV's. Car Park. B&B from £17.

The Old Barn

Mr & Mrs M. Else
The Old Barn, West Lulworth
Wareham BH20 5RL
Tel: 0192 9400 305

The Old Barn is situated in a superb position with a glorious view of the rolling Dorset hills, yet only a few hundred yards from the famous beauty spot of Lulworth Cove. Choice of Bed and Breakfast and/or "Please-Yourself" rooms (equipped for self-catering). Central heating. Fire Certificate. Large garden; parking. Shops and sea nearby, and wide choice of restaurants offering local specialities. Entertainment at Bournemouth (22 miles) and Weymouth (15 miles). Daily/weekly terms and details on request with SAE. Southern Tourist Board and ETB listed.

Dorset — Classified Advertisements

BRIDPORT

MRS K. E. TAIT, 179 ST ANDREW'S ROAD, BRIDPORT (01308 22038). Bed and Breakfast from £12.50. Two miles from coast. Lyme Regis 10 miles, Weymouth 20. Washbasins. Tea-making facilities. Parking space.

DORCHESTER

MRS ROSEMARY DUKE, GROVE HILL HOUSE, MARTINSTOWN, DORCHESTER DT2 9JP (01305 889555). Spacious, modern farmhouse with extensive views in rolling Dorset Downland setting. Ideal walking country. Dorchester 4 miles, Weymouth 7 miles. Twin room, private bathroom, own sitting room. Colour TV, tea/coffee making facilities. From £15.

MR & MRS MICHAEL EATON, THE DOWER HOUSE, BRADFORD PEVERELL, DORCHESTER DT2 9SF (01305 266125). 2 Crowns Commended. Warm welcome in our relaxing village house set in 4½ acres of garden and woodland. 3 miles from Dorchester. Home made cakes on arrival. Breakfast a speciality. Comfortable bedrooms with cotton sheets and private bathrooms from £16 B&B.

LULWORTH COVE

MRS C. MILLER, 5 BINDON ROAD, WEST LULWORTH, NEAR WAREHAM BH20 5RU (01929 400253). Sunnyside Cottages. Cottage accommodation in quiet rural surroundings run in conjunction with CROMWELL HOUSE HOTEL. Dorset Coast path 50 yards. Lulworth Cove 600 yards. One double, one twin, washbasins, private bathroom. TV Lounge. Meals in Hotel 300 yards. B&B from £15.

LYME REGIS

JENNY AND IVAN HARDING, COVERDALE, WOODMEAD ROAD, LYME REGIS DT7 3AB (01297 442882). Comfortable guest house in residential area of Lyme. Short walk from sea and town centre. En suite available. Good home cooking. Private parking. Scenic area for touring and walking. Walkers welcome. No smoking. B&B from £12. Dinner optional. ETB 2 Crowns, AA Recommended QQ.

STUDLAND

MRS R. VINE, MANOR FARM COTTAGE, NEAR SWANAGE BH19 3AT (0192 944254). Bed and breakfast in 17th century National Trust farmhouse. Colour TV and tea/coffee facilities in all rooms. Lovely coastal and country walks; five minutes from beaches.2

WAREHAM

L.S. BARNES, LUCKFORD WOOD FARMHOUSE, EAST STOKE, WAREHAM BH20 6AW (01929 463098). Bed and breakfast, comfortable, spacious farmhouse; private bath, shower, colour TV most rooms, central heating. Near Lulworth, Tank Museum and Corfe Castle. Quiet and peaceful, most picturesque surroundings. £15-£22. AA QQ Recommended. Tourist Board Listed.

WEYMOUTH

MRS MARGARET JOHNSON, 'FAIRLIGHT', 50 LITTLEMOOR ROAD, PRESTON, WEYMOUTH DT3 6AA (01305 832293). Bed and Breakfast. Evening Meals optional. Ground floor rooms; colour TV; handbasins, shaver points; refreshment trays. Central heating. Open all year. Separate bathroom and toilet. Non-smokers preferred. Car parking. Own keys. Beautiful Boleaze Cove half a mile, Weymouth two and a half miles. Many satisfied customers. ETB Listed. B & B from £13.50-£15. Evening Meal £7.

GREENACRE, 83 PRESTON ROAD, WEYMOUTH DT3 6PY (01305 832047). Close to Bowteaze Cove. 5 minutes' drive town centre & harbour. Colour TV/teamaking all rooms. Friendly atmosphere, hearty breakfast, ample parking. Ideal bird-watchers & coastal walkers. Bed & Breakfast from £14.50 per person.

DURHAM

Durham

DURHAM

St Aidan's College, University of Durham
Windmill Hill, Durham DH1 3LJ
Tel: 0191-374 3269

Modern College in landscaped gardens overlooking Cathedral. Comfortable standard and en suite single and twin-bedded rooms. Good food. Fine base to explore North East or break your journey for a day. Available during University vacations - December, January, March, April, July-September. ETB Listed.

Durham — Classified Advertisements

STANLEY

MRS P. GIBSON, BUSHBLADES FARM, HARPERLEY, STANLEY DH9 9UA (01207 232722). Comfortable Georgian farmhouse in rural setting. All rooms tea/coffee facilities, colour TV, easy chairs. En suite available. Easy access to A1(M), Metro Centre (15 minutes), Hadrian's Wall; Northumberland coast under an hour; Beamish Museum 2 miles, Durham City 20 minutes. B&B from £16.

WESTGATE-IN-WEARDALE

MRS L. SAY, BRECKON HILL, WESTGATE-IN-WEARDALE DL13 1PD (01388 517228). Breckon Hill, with its breathtaking views across Weardale, offers high class accommodation for your enjoyment in a no-smoking environment. All bedrooms have en-suite facilities, welcome tray, TV and central heating. We serve home cooked food. B&B £20, DB&B £32.50. 3 Crowns Highly Commended.

ESSEX

Colchester

40 miles from Stansted
20 miles from Harwich
Directions from A12/A120
Follow signs for Rollerworld

ETB ♛♛♛♛
Commended
AA/RAC ***

ROSE & CROWN HOTEL
COLCHESTER

The Oldest Inn in England's oldest recorded town, recently modernised and refurbished yet retaining the character of its heritage. 30 en suite bedrooms all with free satellite TV. 70 seater restaurant, Tudor Bar. Close to town centre. Free off-street parking. Singles £40-£45/Doubles £50-£55 depending on season.

ROSE & CROWN HOTEL, EAST STREET
Colchester, Essex CO1 2TZ
Tel: 01206 866677 Fax: 01206 866616

ETB ♛ Commended

Rurally situated farmhouse, ideal touring stopover for London, ferries from Harwich and Felixstowe, also Stansted Airport. Twin and double bedded rooms, all with washbasins, tea/coffee making and colour TV.

Bed & Breakfast from £16.00

Mr and Mrs Richard Smith

TEL: 01371 820510

Potash Farm

Causeway End Road,
Cobblers Green, Felsted
Dunmow, Essex CM6 3LX

Essex — Classified Advertisements

CLACTON-ON-SEA

MRS B. SMITH, LAXFIELD PRIVATE HOTEL, 3 BEACH ROAD, CLACTON-ON-SEA CO15 1UG (01255 422822). Bed and Breakfast, Evening Meal optional. Only a few yards from pier, promenade and town centre. Residential licence. Friendly atmosphere, children welcome.

ONGAR

MRS BERYL MARTIN, NEWHOUSE FARM, STANFORD RIVERS, ONGAR CM5 9QH (01277 362132). Tudor farmhouse in unspoilt countryside. Ten acres of grass and lakes around house. Disabled unit in yard. Within easy reach of East Anglia and Cambridge. One Crown.

GLOUCESTERSHIRE

Birdlip, Bourton-on-the-Water

MRS. P. M. CARTER
BEECHMOUNT
Birdlip, Gloucestershire
Tel: Gloucester (01452) 862262.

Small friendly guest house between Gloucester and Cirencester. Central heating. Some bedrooms en-suite, all with washbasins. Colour TV. Garden. Car Park. Close to many places of interest. Good views and walks. Key for unrestricted access. Fire Certificate. Evening meal by arrangement. Home grown produce when available. Highly recommended.
Competitive rates, details on request.
ETB ♛♛ Commended

FARNCOMBE

Clapton-on-the-Hill
Bourton-on-the-Water
Gloucestershire GL54 2LG
Tel: 01451 820120

Farncombe offers quiet comfortable accommodation for non-smokers. Superb views of Windrush Valley, 2.5 miles from Bourton-on-the-Water. Large peaceful garden. Ideally situated for touring the Cotswolds, Oxford, Stratford and for walking. Special diets. Parking for three cars. 2 double bedrooms with showers; 1 twin; 1 en suite bathroom and 2 public bathrooms. Prices from £17.00

MRS SANDRA SPARREY

4 PITTVILLE CRESCENT, PITTVILLE,
CHELTENHAM GL52 2QZ
TELEPHONE: 01242 575567

Excellent accommodation in fine Regency house overlooking parkland in lovely area of Cheltenham.
Centrally placed for touring all Cotswolds.
Colour TV in rooms. Tea making facilities.
Bed and Breakfast from £15.50 - £16.50

Commended

The Old School House

Whittles Lane, Frampton on Severn
Gloucestershire GL2 7EB
Tel: 01452 740457

The Old School House is over 200 years old and has recently been renovated to a high standard. Situated at the end of a quiet lane, we are ideal for touring the Cotswolds or visiting the Wildlife and Wetlands Trust at Slimbridge. Cheltenham, Bath and Bristol are all within easy driving distance. We are only a few minutes' drive from Junction 13 on the M5 motorway and an ideal stopover for tourists.

CLAREMONT GUEST HOUSE

135 Stroud Road, Gloucester GL1 5JL
Tel: 01452 529270 or 529540

AA Listed ETB Listed

Small friendly Guest House situated one mile from city and leisure centre near historic docks. Near Railway/Coach Station (bus every 12 minutes). Car parking. Six bedrooms with washbasins, TV/SKY TV. Tea making facilities. Open all year, reasonable rates.

Under personal supervision of Proprietor, Mrs C. E. Powell

TYMS HOLM COUNTRY GUEST HOUSE

Apperley, Gloucester
GL19 4DW
Tel: 01452 780386

Situated in open countryside in the Severn Vale, Tyms Holm - now an attractive guest house - was originally a thatched cottage which now provides the dining room. Situated close to Tewkesbury Abbey, Gloucester Cathedral and The Cotswolds.
ETB 2 Crowns Commended

SEVERN BANK

MINSTERWORTH Nr GLOUCESTER

A fine country house set in 6 acres of riverside grounds 4 miles west of Gloucester. Large en-suite, non-smoking bedrooms with superb views. Colour TV, tea-making facilities and central heating. Ideal for touring Cotswolds, Forest of Dean, Wye Valley and Severn Vale, and for viewing the Severn Bore tidal wave.
Bed and full English Breakfast £17.00-£19.50.
Reduced rates for children. Restaurants nearby.
ETB

Apply Mrs. S. Carter, Severn Bank,
Minsterworth GL2 8JH Tel: 01452 750357

South Cotswolds, Mrs P. Strong, **THE VICARAGE,** Nailsworth, Gloucester

GL6 0BS Tel: 01453 832181

Stay in quality accommodation in small market town 40 minutes from Bath, Cheltenham and Bourton-on-the-Water. EN SUITE AND PRIVATE BATHROOMS, one ground floor room. Dinner by arrangement. Easy access to historic houses, Slimbridge, Gloucester and other attractions. Good walking country. 10% discount for a week's stay. Pets and children welcome.

Mrs Pauline Loving *Tel: 01451 860427*

NORTHFIELD BED AND BREAKFAST

Cirencester Road (A429)
Northleach, Cheltenham GL54 3JL

Detached family house in the country, set in large gardens with own garden produce to complement home cooked dishes. All rooms en suite. Close to all local services in market town of Northleach. Excellent centre for visiting Cotswolds, Stratford and Oxford. BED & BREAKFAST from £15; EVENING MEAL optional.

Non-smoking establishment

Brochure on request

Sheila J. Barnfield Tel: (01452) 840224

"KILMORIE HOLDINGS"

Gloucester Road, Corse, Staunton, Near Gloucester
Holiday on a working smallholding keeping livestock/fruit.
GOOD HOME COOKING. *Open all year.*
With own produce when available. Ideal for touring West Country. Many places of natural and historical beauty. Central heating. Fire certificate. 4 double rooms, 1 family, 1 twin, all with washbasins; some rooms with private facilities available. 2 bathrooms, 3 toilets.
Colour TV. Children over six and pets welcome. Tea making facilities in rooms.
DINNER, BED AND BREAKFAST FROM £19.00
BED AND BREAKFAST FROM £12.50

Rose & Crown Inn

Access **Nympsfield, Stonehouse** *Visa*
Tel: Dursley (01453) 860240

- ☆ 300 year-old Inn set in quiet Cotswold village halfway between Dursley and Stroud and half a mile from Cotswold Way.
- ☆ Evening meal together with vegetarian dishes from our extensive home-prepared menu.
- ☆ Accommodation includes centrally heated en suite twin or double rooms.

Ideal location for touring and rambling.

ETB ♛♛♛ Commended, AA & RAC Listed

ETB

OLDENDS FARM

WELSH PONIES A&B — BED & BREAKFAST

Oldends Lane, Stonehouse, Gloucestershire

Two miles from M5, Junction 13, off A419 and within walking distance of Stonehouse. Grade II Listed farmhouse surrounded by orchards and open fields. A working farm supporting suckler cows and Welsh ponies. Comfortable accommodation with Family room (en suite), Double twin (hb) and two singles. B&B from £13.50. Pub food 100 yds.

Proprietor: Mrs J. Nicholls Tel: 01453 822135

♛ ♛

SOUTH HILL FARM HOUSE

Bed and Breakfast

Telephone and Fax: 01451 831219

Enjoy a visit to our Victorian Farmhouse built of the honey-coloured Cotswold stone and set along an avenue of beech trees on the outskirts of beautiful Stow-on-the-Wold. An ideal base for touring the Cotswold beauty spots and historic towns: Gloucester and Oxford 30 miles, Cheltenham 20 miles, Stratford 18. All rooms (twin, double and family) are traditionally furnished, with TV and central heating, and most have full en suite facilities. Spacious Guests' Lounge with TV and log fire. Laundry service. Ample parking. A satisfying Breakfast is served in our oak-beamed dining room. Daily or weekly terms, competitive off-season rates. Write/ring for details.

Mrs G. Kenneally, South Hill Farm House, Fosseway, Stow-On-The-Wold GL54 1JU

THE LIMES
EVESHAM ROAD,
STOW-ON-THE-WOLD GL54 1EN
TEL: 01451 830034 AA & RAC Listed

Established over 20 years. Large country house with attractive garden, overlooking fields. Four minutes town centre. Two en suite rooms, one four-poster and one twin bedroom. Tea/coffee making facilities, colour TV all rooms. TV lounge. Central heating. Children welcome. Bed and full English Breakfast from £15.50 - £18.50 per night. Open all year except Christmas. Les Routiers Recommended.

DOWNFIELD HOTEL
Cainscross Road, Stroud GL5 4HN
Tel: Stroud (01453) 764496

Bed and Breakfast: Evening Meal optional. Washbasins all rooms, some private baths. central heating. Colour TV lounge. Residents' bar. Ideal centre for touring Cotswolds. Personal supervision by owners. 5 miles from M5 motorway. Ideal stopover for travel to Devon/Cornwall from the north. Ample parking. Children and pets welcome. Access/Visa.
AA QQQ, RAC Acclaimed.

Lower Lode Hotel
FORTHAMPTON
NR. TEWKESBURY, GLOUCESTERSHIRE GL19 4RE
TEL: (01684) 293224

15th century, family run riverside Inn with 3½ acres of river front lawn at the end of a country lane. Two double, one twin and one single room. Bed and Breakfast (en suite room) £16.50pp; sharing bathroom £13. Dogs welcome. Slipway.
Bar meals available. Touring caravans site.

INSCHDENE
Atcombe Road, South Woodchester, Stroud GL5 5EW Tel: 01453 873254

Comfortable family house with magnificent views across the valley, set in an acre of garden near centre of quiet village. A twin and a double room are available with washbasin and tea/coffee making facilities. Colour TV available. An ideal centre for the Cotswolds. Bed and Breakfast from £12 to £17.50. Guests requested not to smoke in the house.

Gloucestershire — Classified Advertisements

CHELTENHAM

MR & MRS A. E. HUGHES, HAM HILL FARM, WHITTINGTON, CHELTENHAM GL54 4EZ (01242 584415). 160 acre farm with new farmhouse built in true Cotswold style. Many leisure activities nearby. Terms: Family Room £36 per room, Double Room £33 per room, Ensuites £35 per room, Chalets £34 per room. Open all year. Children over 7 welcome. Brochure on request.

BRENNAN GUEST HOUSE, 21 ST LUKES ROAD, CHELTENHAM GL53 7JF (01242 525904). Quiet residential area three minutes from town centre. All bedrooms have TV, washbasins, heating, and beverages. Full Fire Certificate. Bed and Breakfast £16.50 to £18.00. AA; ETB One Crown.

MRS A. SEKULIC, 'KIELDER', 222 LONDON ROAD, CHARLTON KINGS, CHELTENHAM GL52 6HW (01242 237138). Kielder is a late Victorian suburban house one mile from Cheltenham town centre. Tea/coffee facilities, colour TV in all rooms. Stair chair lift available. Non smoking. On A40. Cheltenham-Oxford road near junction with A435 to Cirencester. Single £16-£17, double £30-£32. One Crown Commended.

STOW-ON-THE-WOLD

ROBERT AND DAWN SMITH, CORSHAM FIELD FARMHOUSE, BLEDINGTON ROAD, STOW-ON-THE-WOLD GL54 1JH (01451 831750). Homely farmhouse with traditional features and breathtaking views, one mile from Stow-on-the-Wold. Ideally situated for exploring picturesque Cotswold villages, historic castles, places of interest. Pets and children welcome. AA, ETB 2 Crowns. Twin, double and family rooms, some en suite. Good pub food 5 minutes' walk. Terms from £12 to £17.50 per person.

MRS F. J. ADAMS, BANKS FARM, UPPER ODDINGTON, MORETON-IN-MARSH GL56 0XG (01451 830475). Double and twin-bedded rooms, both with washbasins, tea/coffee making facilities and electric blankets. Sitting-room with TV. Open March to October. No smoking in public areas. B&B from £16.75; weekly from £112. (1994 prices held for advance bookings). Pubs, good food nearby. ETB Listed Commended.

WITCOMBE

MISS B. BICKELL, SPRINGFIELDS FARM, WITCOMBE, NEAR GLOUCESTER GL3 4TU (01452 863532). Bed and breakfast in farmhouse - home produce. Guests' TV lounge. Near Cotswold Way and ideal for touring Cotswolds. Double room £26, single £14, family £30.

WOTTON-UNDER-EDGE

CHRIS AND KATE ROUTLEDGE, COOMBE HOUSE, COOMBE, WOTTON-UNDER-EDGE GL12 7NF (01453 842732). 17th century family home. Superb views. Excellent walking. Double and twin bedrooms with washbasins, TV, coffee/tea making facilities. Very friendly and welcoming.

HAMPSHIRE

Eastleigh, East Meon

TWYFORD LODGE GUEST HOUSE
104-106 Twyford Road
Eastleigh, Hampshire
Tel: 01703 612245
Family run Guest House.
Residential licence. En suite facility.
Television lounge.
Southampton Airport 7 mins.
Main line station 5 mins.
Bed and Breakfast from £17.00.
Proprietors: Pat & Colin Morris

DUNVEGAN COTTAGE
Frogmore Lane, East Meon,
Petersfield GU32 1QJ
Tel: 01730 823213
Comfortable, centrally heated, mainly en-suite accommodation, some ground floor. Set in tranquil 3-acre garden, the house overlooks the South Downs. Guest lounge with colour TV. Ample off-road parking. Full Fire Certificate. Superb walking country. Chichester, Winchester, Portsmouth 30 minutes. Children welcome. Brochure on request.
ETB

Our Bench

Commended
AA QQQQ RAC Acclaimed

A warm welcome awaits you in our large bungalow situated between the New Forest and the coast. Large garden with indoor heated swimming pool, jacuzzi and sauna. Some rooms en suite. Dining room, separate lounge with colour TV. Evening Meals available. For non-smokers only and sorry, no children. From £17 pp per night.

Our Bench, 9 Lodge Road, Pennington, Lymington, Hampshire SO41 8HH
Tel and Fax: 01590 673141

GORSE MEADOW

Sway Road, Lymington, Hampshire SO41 8LR

Set in 13½ acres with charming gardens; horses graze the paddocks; heated swimming pool. Lymington 1½ miles; New Forest one mile; beaches 5 miles. Golf courses, riding stables, tennis and many charming country pubs all nearby. *Self-contained flat* - B&B or self catering from £350 per week, high season - £220 per week, low season. *Family room:* room and full breakfast from £50. *Doubles*: room and full breakfast from £40-£46 (en suite). All with central heating, washbasins, TV, coffee/tea makers etc. Excellent home cooked Dinners £12. Accommodation and food prices reduced for children.

Mrs B. Tee ***Tel: 01590 673354***

THE PENNY FARTHING HOTEL *"In the heart of the New Forest"*

ROMSEY ROAD, LYNDHURST, HAMPSHIRE, SO43 7AA

AA RAC Commended

This family run hotel offers single, double, twin and family rooms tastefully refurbished with en suite, colour TV and tea/coffee facilities. Also car parking and a Licensed Bar. Our position a moment's walk from Lyndhurst High Street makes this the ideal choice for a break in some of the most beautiful countryside in England. Large car park to rear. Residents' bar with satellite TV. Call for a brochure.

Tel: 01703 284422 **Fax: 01703 284488**

THE NEW FOREST

Near Beaulieu

B&B bungalow on fringe of New Forest near Lepe beach, opposite Isle of Wight

Good windsurfing beaches. Comfortable bedrooms: wash basins, central heating, tea making facilities, colour TV, shower room; wc. Large breakfast. Parking. Non- smokers only. 11 miles Lymington for Isle of Wight Ferries. 3 miles Exbury Azalea Gardens (Rothschild's collection). From £14.00 per person per night. Contact:

MRS M STONE, Heathlands, Lepe Road, Langley, near Beaulieu, New Forest, SO45 1YT
(01703) 892517

Carbery Guest House

Stockbridge SO20 6EZ Tel: 01264 810771

Commended **RAC Acclaimed** **AA Listed**

Ann and Philip Hooper welcome you to Carbery Guest House situated just outside the village of Stockbridge. This Georgian House has one acre of landscaped gardens, with swimming pool. Accommodation includes double, twin, family and single rooms, available with private facilities. Centrally heated with colour TV, tea and coffee making. Cots, high chairs. Car essential. Open January to December for D, B&B or B&B. Terms on application.

Hampshire— Classified Advertisements

HOOK

MRS P. JENNIONS, CEDAR COURT, READING ROAD, HOOK, NEAR BASINGSTOKE RG27 9DB (01256 762178). Family/twin/double rooms, washbasins or private bathroom. TV lounge. Delightful gardens in secluded woodland setting. ETB 2 Crowns, RAC and AA Listed.

PETERSFIELD

MRS B. WEST, 'RIDGEFIELD', STATION ROAD, PETERSFIELD GU32 3DE (01730 261402). Family atmosphere in lovely market town near end of South Downs Way and a short walk from the railway station. £16.00 per person, £32.00 double.

PORTSMOUTH

MRS S. TUBB, 'HAMILTON HOUSE', 95 VICTORIA ROAD NORTH, SOUTHSEA, PORTSMOUTH PO5 1PS (Tel/Fax: 01705 823502). Delightful AA Listed/RAC Acclaimed family-run Guest House. Pleasant centrally-heated rooms, all with colour TVs and tea-making facilities, some en suite. 5 minutes by car to Continental Ferryport and local tourist attractions. Ideal touring base for Southern England. Nightly/weekly stays welcome all year. STB Member; ETB 2 Crowns Commended.

MRS J. COLLICK, ST ANN'S GUEST HOUSE, 17 MALVERN ROAD, SOUTHSEA PO5 2LZ (01705 827173). Close to seafront, shops and all amenities. Near Portsmouth, HMS Victory, Mary Rose and Warrior. Own keys. Licensed. Convenient to Continental Ferry Terminals. Short Breaks welcome. 2 Crowns.

CRANBOURNE HOUSE, 6 HERBERT ROAD, SOUTHSEA, PORTSMOUTH PO4 0QA (01705 824981). En-suite accommodation just 10 minutes from Ferry Terminals and five minutes' walk from Seafront, in a QUIET area close to Theatre, Shops etc.

SOUTHAMPTON

MRS PAT WARD, ASHELEE LODGE, 36 ATHERLEY ROAD, SHIRLEY, SOUTHAMPTON S01 5DQ (01703 222095). Guest House with friendly atmosphere, varied menus, TV lounge, Garden Dip Pool. Central to Southampton Town, train/coach Station, M27 and Sealink Ferries. Good touring area, New Forest, Salisbury, Stonehenge and many beauty spots. Bed & Breakfast £14-£15 (STB Listed Commended)

SWAY

MRS THELMA ROWE, 9 CRUSE CLOSE, SWAY, HANTS SO41 6AY (01590 683092). Ground floor accommodation. Bedroom, private bathroom and sitting room. Tea-making, TV. New Forest village, 3 minutes open forest, 4 miles coast. B & B from £14.50 per person.

WINCHESTER

MRS ANN REGAN, 'LECKHAMPTON', 62 KILHAM LANE, WINCHESTER SO22 5QD (01962 852831). Fine peaceful accommodation in large country home; garden; drive-in parking; close to all major roads. Good for Cathedral, Stonehenge, New Forest. Twin, double, family rooms, private facilities. No smoking. Bed and Breakfast from £15 per person. Two Crowns Commended. AA QQQQ Selected.

HEREFORDSHIRE

Hereford, Ross-on-Wye

AA **

DORMINGTON COURT

Highly Commended

Country House

Hereford HR1 4DA Tel/Fax: 01432 850370

Two acres of lovely gardens. A place to relax in quiet country luxury. Singles from £30, Doubles from £25 for Bed and Full English Breakfast

All bedrooms en suite with colour TV, tea/coffee making facilities, hairdryers and lovely country views

A small elegant Georgian/Elizabethan Country Manor House quietly situated yet only 5 miles from the centre of historic Hereford. A perfect base to explore the Malvern Hills, Wye Valley, Brecon Beacons, Cotswolds, Black Mountains. Surrounded by hop fields and apple orchards.

CWM CRAIG FARM

Little Dewchurch, Hereford

HR2 6PS Tel: 01432 840250

Commended

Spacious Georgian Farmhouse surrounded by superb unspoilt countryside midway between Ross-on-Wye and Hereford. Twin/Double and Family rooms. En suite available. Tea/coffee facilities. TV Lounge. Full farmhouse breakfast. Inns within 3 miles for evening meals. Double from £14 per person.

Geoffrey and Josephine Baker

BROOKFIELD HOUSE

Ledbury Road, Ross-on-Wye HR9 7AT

Tel: 01989 562188

Large Georgian House close to town centre on M50 entrance into town. All rooms with TV, hot & cold, central heating, tea & coffee facilities and some with bath/shower amd WC.

A good choice of breakfast (diets catered for). A large private car park. Ideal for overnight stop-offs.

B&B from £18 per person.

AA & RAC Listed, Travellers Britain Recommended

ETB

Herefordshire — Classified Advertisements

HEREFORDSHIRE/HEREFORD

MRS R. T. ANDREWS, WEBTON COURT FARMHOUSE, KINGSTONE HR2 9NF (01981 250220). Georgian farmhouse. Beautiful setting. Ideal touring country. Accommodation ideal for large parties. Licensed. B&B from £14. Many reductions available. Evening meals and packed lunches on request.

ISLE OF WIGHT

Isle of Wight — Classified Advertisements

SHANKLIN

DENISE & MARTIN NICKLESS, KEATS COTTAGE HOTEL & TEA ROOMS, 76 HIGH STREET, SHANKLIN OLD VILLAGE PO37 6NJ (01983 866351). A small, family-run, licensed hotel * Centrally heated * TV lounge with log fire * 18-jet aqua spa bath * En suite family rooms * Open all year * "One night or more - that's what we're here for" * 1992 prices held * B&B from £13.50 * Credit cards accepted * Tourist Board Listed *

KENT

Biddenden, Canterbury, Dover

BISHOPDALE OAST
Biddenden, Kent TN27 8DR
Tel: 01580 291027/292065
Fax: 01580 292321
Iain and Jane Drysdale

18th century oast house of historical interest. Set in four acres with magnificent views in a peaceful setting. The large bedrooms are en suite with King Size beds, colour TV, radio, tea/coffee facilities. Excellent dinners served in our private dining room. Bed and Breakfast from £20.00, reductions for children. Dinner from £13.50. Open all year.
Highly Commended

Bower Farmhouse
Stelling Minnis
Near Canterbury
Kent CT4 6BB

Ann and Nick Hunt welcome you to this traditional 17th century farmhouse situated 7 miles south of Canterbury and 9 miles from the coast. A double and a twin bedded room each with private facilities. Full English breakfast with home-made bread, marmalade and free-range eggs. Children welcome, pets by arrangement. Car essential. Bed and Breakfast from £17.50. Tourist Board Listed and Commended.

Tel: 01227 709430

Crockshard Farmhouse
Tel: 01227 720464
Fax: 01227 721125

Exceptionally attractive farmhouse in beautiful gardens and farmland. Ideally situated for visiting any part of Kent. Canterbury 15 minutes, Dover 20 minutes, Folkestone 30 minutes.

Prices from £17.50

N.J. Ellen, Crockshard Farmhouse, Wingham, Canterbury, Kent CT3 1NY

RESTOVER GUESTHOUSE
69 Folkestone Road, Dover
Kent CT17 9RZ
Tel: 01304 206031

A warm welcome awaits you at this family run establishment. Conveniently situated - closest guesthouse to Dover Priory Railway Station and 3 minutes from ports, (Channel Tunnel 10 minutes away). All rooms with washbasin, TV and tea/coffee makers. Private parking and early breakfast available. Member of Dover Hotel & Guesthouse Group. B&B rates £13-£17 (low-high season). Reduced rates for children and 'room only'. **ETB**

BLERIOT'S

47 Park Avenue, Dover, Kent CT16 1HE
Tel: (01304) 211394

A Victorian Guest House situated in a quiet residential area, in the lee of Dover Castle. Within easy reach of trains, bus station, town centre, Hoverport & docks. Channel Tunnel terminus only 10 minutes' drive. Off-road parking. We specialise in one night 'stop-overs' & Mini-breaks. Single, Double, Twin & Family rooms with shower or full en-suite available. All rooms have: Colour TVs, tea & coffee making facilities, washbasins with shaver points/lights and are fully centrally heated. Full English Breakfast from 7.00am, earlier Continental available on request. Evening snacks and meals available in our licensed dining room. Open all year. Tourist Board rating.

Rates: Bed & Breakfast: £14.00 to £16.00 per person per night Mini-Breaks: January - April £12.00, October-December £13.00 per person per night. Small en-suite & single surcharge.

ST ALBANS GUESTHOUSE

71 Folkestone Road, Dover, Kent CT17 9RZ
Tel: 01304 206308

A family run guesthouse, situated opposite Dover Priory Railway Station and 3 minutes to docks, (Channel Tunnel 10 minutes away). Clean, comfortable rooms, early breakfast served. Member of Dover Hotel & Guesthouse Group.

ETB

B&B Rates £13-£17pp (low to high season)

Castle House

For clean, comfortable, non-smoking accommodation, close to Castle, port and all Dover's amenities. All rooms have private shower and toilet, colour TV, tea-making facilities, central heating.

ETB AA QQQ

Contact Rodney and Elizabeth Dimech,
Castle House, 10 Castle Hill Road,
Dover CT16 1QW
(01304 201656; Fax: 01304 210197)

CLEVELAND GUEST HOUSE

Betty and Alastair Dimech
Within walking distance of Ferries, Town Centre and Castle

Beautiful Victorian guest house offers high standards with a homely atmosphere. All rooms have en suite/private facilities, colour TV, tea/coffee making. Full English Breakfast; early departures catered for. B&B from £12.

2 Laureston Place, Off Castle Hill Road, Dover, Kent CT16 1QX Tel: 01304 204622

Mrs Y. Packham

215 Bredhurst Road, Wigmore,
Gillingham, Kent ME8 0QX
Tel: 01634 363275

Friendly, comfortable Bed and Breakfast accommodation close to M2 and M20. Midway between Channel ports and London. Children welcome * Open all year * Full facilities * Good rates

Access Visa Amex Diners

MALVERN HOTEL

Eastern Esplanade, Cliftonville,
MARGATE, KENT CT9 2HL
'Phone: Thanet (01843) 290192

Small licensed Private Hotel overlooking the sea.
Close Margate Winter Gardens, Indoor Bowls etc.

- ☆Ensuite shower & toilet
- ☆Colour Television
- ☆Tea/coffee making facilities
- ☆Short Breaks
- ☆Weekends/Midweek
- ☆French/Belgian Day Trips

ACCESS & VISA–Telephone bookings accepted

TERMS: B&B from £17 per person per night. Stamp only for details.

SPENCER COURT HOTEL

37 SPENCER SQUARE, RAMSGATE CT11 9LD

Tel: 01843 594582 **Commended**

- Private licensed, family-run Hotel, overlooking gardens, sea and tennis courts, directly above RAMSGATE/DUNKIRK /OSTEND Ferry Terminal
- Colour TV lounge ● Open all year ● Bed & Breakfast from £13.00
- Tea/coffee making facilities and TV in all rooms ● En suite available
- Reductions for children sharing parents' room ● Unrestricted parking. We maintain the highest standards of cleanliness and hygiene. SALLY LINE passengers most welcome.

Details forwarded on request.

SEALAN PRIVATE HOTEL

6 Avenue Road, Ramsgate, Kent CT11 8ET

Tel: 01843 593044

Mr and Mrs Saville invite you to their family run hotel. Home cooked food. Licensed Bar. TV and tea facilities in rooms. TV lounge; children welcome; Sally Line trips arranged. Near seafront and town centre. Large garden and private car park.

Please send for free brochure **Tariff on application**

Children Half Price

CLIFFTOPS HOTEL

2 Paragon

RAMSGATE-KENT CT11 9JX

Family run hotel, overlooking sea and harbour.

Bed & English Breakfast from £13.50

Evening Meal Optional

* Bar * TV Lounge * Central heating

*Tea and coffee facilities * Colour TV in all rooms

*Children welcome

Dunkirk ferries opposite hotel.

HOME FROM HOME

Terry Hammond

Tel: Thanet (01843) 591836

MOUNT EDGECUMBE HOUSE HOTEL

The Common, Tunbridge Wells, Kent TN4 8BX

Tel: 01892 526823 Fax: 01892 513851

A fine period hotel built in 1728 on an outcrop of sandstone and set on the edge of Tunbridge Wells Common. Within minutes' walk of the town centre. The Hotel has five en suite bedrooms, one with four-poster bed. All the rooms are equipped to luxury standard, with delightful views.

We also have a Restaurant and a Brasserie/Wine Bar.

Kent — Classified Advertisements

ASHFORD

MRS JENNIFER DENNY, HIGH LODGE, ELMSTEAD, ASHFORD TN25 5JL (012337 50234) ***"The cottage with the view."*** Comfortably modernised 250-year-old Kent cottage with outstanding views over unspoiled downland countryside. Double room with bathroom; 2 single/doubles and second bath.

CANTERBURY

MRS JOY WRIGHT, MILTON HOUSE, 9 SOUTH CANTERBURY ROAD, CANTERBURY CT1 3LH (01227 765531). One double, one twin bedded room, H&C, television. Family home near bus, East railway station, old Dover road. Full English breakfast. Open all year. £14-£16 per person.

MR AND MRS R. D. LINCH, UPPER ANSDORE, DUCKPIT LANE, PETHAM, CANTERBURY CT4 5QB (01227 700672). Secluded Tudor farmhouse five miles from Canterbury, overlooking Nature Reserve. Double rooms and twin/family room en-suite, all with tea/coffee-making facilities. From £18. SAE for further details. ETB listed. AA Listed QQQ.

DOVER

MR N. KYRIACOU, ELMO GUEST HOUSE, 120 FOLKESTONE ROAD, DOVER CT17 9SP (01304 206236). An attractive Victorian house offering a warm welcome to travellers to and from Continent. Single, double, twin and family rooms with TV and tea/coffee making facilities. Private car park, lock-up or garage. Early breakfast catered for. Prices £12.00 to £18.00 per person.

HAWKHURST

SOUTHGATE, - LITTLE FOWLERS, RYE ROAD, HAWKHURST, NEAR CRANBROOK TN18 5DA (01580 752526). Situated on Kent/Sussex borders. 300-year old country house. Near Sissinghurst, Battle, Rye, Bodiam, Hastings. London 47 miles, Dover/Folkestone 30 miles. Period bedrooms - all magnificent views. Private bathrooms. Large gardens. Evening meals arranged. Friendly family. Non-smoking. B&B £18-£20 (child reductions)

RAMSGATE

MRS JANET RHODES, YORK HOUSE, 7 AUGUSTA ROAD, RAMSGATE CT11 8JP (01843 596775). Guest House near sea and shops. Bed and Breakfast from £11.00 per night each. Weekly rates. Good home cooking. Children, Senior Citizens welcome. Fire Certificate.

SEVENOAKS

MRS D. L. KNOOPS, GREEN TILES, 46 THE RISE, SEVENOAKS TN13 1RJ (Tel and Fax: 01732 451522). Quiet ground floor annexe, lovely garden, sleeps 1-5 (single bed, sofa and chair beds). TV, bathroom with shower. Own entrance, off-street parking. Children welcome.

LANCASHIRE

Blackburn

THE BROWN LEAVES HOTEL

LONGSIGHT ROAD,
COPSTER GREEN,
BLACKBURN,
LANCASHIRE BB1 9EU

Conveniently situated on the A59 about half-way between Preston and Clitheroe, five miles from Junction 31 of the M6. All rooms ground floor, have en suite facilities, TV, tea-making and hairdryer. Most credit cards are welcome.

Tel: 01254 249523 Fax: 01254 245240

COME TO BLACKPOOL AND STAY AT THE

ARANDORA STAR HOTEL

559 New South Promenade, Blackpool FY4 INF

20 Bedroom Licensed Seafront Hotel. Some rooms ensuite. Restaurant Meals. Evening Dinner. Lunchtime and Evening Bar Meals. Ample car parking and garage facilities. Colour TV in all rooms. Special weekend and mid-week Mini-Breaks. BED AND BREAKFAST from £12 per person per night.

Special Weekly Terms Reductions for Children

Write or phone for colour brochure

Tel: (01253 41528)

IT'S SERVICE WITH A SMILE AT THE

New Osborne Private Hotel

9 Pleasant Street, North Shore (off Dickson Road), Blackpool FY1 2JA

Tel: 01253 24578 Residential Licence ETB Registered

★ Open all year ★ Bar Lounge ★ Television lounge (colour)
★ Excellent central position only one minute walk to promenade
★ Few minutes' delightful walk along sea-front to North Pier, town centre, railways and bus station
★ Close to local clubs and entertainment
★ Families welcome. Children all ages. Special rates for children and O.A.P.s early season.
★ Central heating ★ Free showers ★ All bedrooms have colour TV and tea/coffee making facilities
★ Bed and breakfast from £10.50 Low Season; Evening Meal, Bed and Breakfast from £13.50

Home cooking our speciality

* Bar lunches and packed lunches always available ★ Pets also very welcome.

WHY NOT JOIN US FOR A MEMORABLE CHRISTMAS?

Please write or telephone Resident Proprietress: **MRS B. READ**

ASH LEA

76 Lord Street, North Shore, Blackpool FY1 2DG Tel: (01253) 28161

All rooms have TV and tea making facilities. Toilets en suite available. Free showers. Large comfortable TV lounge. Friendly welcome and good food. Near bus and railway stations, town centre, theatres and amenities. Open all year, early season B&B from £11.00. Evening meal optional extra.

The Old Coach House

50 Dean Street, Blackpool FY4 1BP

Tel: (01253) 344330 ♛♛♛

An historic detached house set in its own gardens in the heart of Blackpool, one minute from sea and South Pier. All bedrooms en-suite with central heating, colour TV, phone, radio, hairdryer, coffee/tea facilities etc. Sun lounge. Free Parking. Open all year. B&B from £19.95. Choice of breakfast Menu. Licensed restaurant.

Contact: Elaine Smith and Mark Smith

CASTLEMERE HOTEL

13 Shaftesbury Avenue, North Shore Blackpool. Tel: 01253 352430

PROPRIETORS: DAVE & SUE HAYWARD

FHG DIPLOMA WINNER

Castlemere is a licensed private hotel, family run and conveniently situated off Queen's Promenade in the very pleasant North Shore area of Blackpool. The busy town centre, bus and train stations are convenient and a range of entertainment opportunities for all ages and tastes are within an easy walk or a short tram ride, including golf course. Ideal for touring the Lakes and Dales, "Bronte" Country and Fylde Coast. Easy access to M55. En suite rooms; and all rooms have central heating, colour TV with Sky, and tea-making facilities. The Castlemere has a bar and evening snacks are available. Open all year. Car Park.

FROM £18.00 per day for bed and breakfast. Dinner is optional. Winter Break Terms on application. ACCESS AND VISA ACCEPTED

ROYALS HOTEL

34 bedroom mock-Tudor Hotel near Manchester Airport

Offers you a relaxed and pleasant stay, with en suite facilities, television, telephone, tea/coffee in all rooms. Free car parking for the duration of your holiday with courtesy transport to/from Manchester Airport. Rates start from £30.00.

Tel: 0161-998 9011
Royals Hotel, Altrincham Road, Manchester M33 4BJ

Lancashire — Classified Advertisements

GREAT ECCLESTON

MRS B. BROWN, WALL MILL FARM, GREAT ECCLESTON, BLACKPOOL ROAD, NEAR PRESTON PR3 0ZQ (01995 670334). Comfortable accommodation in farmhouse on 46-acre dairy farm. Blackpool 8 miles. Two Double Bedrooms and 1 Single Bedroom. Bed and Breakfast from £13.00.

PRESTON

J. AND L. LOCKWOOD, BROOK HOUSE HOTEL, 662 PRESTON ROAD, CLAYTON-LE-WOODS, NEAR CHORLEY (01772 36403). Set in half-acre. Personally supervised by resident owners. 19 bedrooms offering en-suite facilities for the businessman and tourist. Quality rooms with satellite TV, radio, telephone and tea-making. Private parking. On A6 to Chorley - half mile M6 (J29), M61 (J9). AA Selected QQQQ, RAC Highly Acclaimed.

ANVIL GUEST HOUSE, 321 STATION ROAD, BAMBER BRIDGE, PRESTON PR5 6EE (01772 39022). Situated off Junction 29 M6. On route to lakes and Scotland. Washbasins all rooms. Central heating. TV lounge. ETB Listed. Bed and Breakfast from £12 per person.

LEICESTERSHIRE

Leicestershire — Classified Advertisements

LEICESTER

01664 454 225

MRS D.N. MELLOWS, SOMERBY HOUSE FARM, SOMERBY, NEAR MELTON MOWBRAY LE14 2PZ (0166-477 225). Bed and Breakfast in 18th century farmhouse. Single and double rooms and bath. Family room with bath, WC. TV. Central heating. Children and dogs welcome. Heated swimming pool June to September. Open all year. Stabling for horses May to August. Inns and riding school in village.

MEDBOURNE

MRS M. J. ROBERTS, MEDBOURNE LODGE, MEDBOURNE, MARKET HARBOROUGH LE16 8DD (0185 883 755). Double room with washbasin, twin room with colour TV, and single room, in comfortable, centrally heated farmhouse. Bed and Breakfast from £15. Open all year. 4 star rating "Farmhouse Tours in Great Britain"

MELTON MOWBRAY

MRS H. DOWSON, SULNEY FIELDS, COLONEL'S LANE, UPPER BROUGHTON, MELTON MOWBRAY LE14 3BD (01664 822204). Notts/Leics border. Large country house in quiet position on the edge of the village, with magnificent views over the Vale of Belvoir. Spacious accommodation in one double and two twin rooms. Private facilities usually available.

LINCOLNSHIRE

Lincoln, Swinderby

Lincolnshire — Classified Advertisements

HOLBEACH

WHAPLODE MANOR, SARACENS HEAD, HOLBEACH (01406 22837). Eighteenth century Manor House located just off A17 road between Sleaford and King's Lynn. All rooms ensuite. Colour television lounge. Car Park. Dinner optional. Bed and Breakfast from £15. Open all year.

MABLETHORPE

MRS J. HARVEY, "WHITE HEATHER", 114 VICTORIA ROAD, MABLETHORPE LN12 2AJ (01507 472626). Comfortable, homely accommodation with washbasins, shaver points, tea-making facilities and colour TV. Centrally heated. Shower facilities. Car parking. Licensed. Full English Breakfast.

Hampton Court, Hayes, London

holiday hosts accommodation service

WELCOME TO LONDON

We specialise in good quality accommodation in friendly private homes - South and West London. Near public transport, restaurants and convenient Central London/Wimbledon Tennis and airports. All homes are known to us and regularly inspected. An economical alternative to hotel life for business people and tourists. TV/Tea/Coffee making facilities. From £12.50-£19.50 ea.per night

Anne Scott: HOLIDAY HOSTS 59 Cromwell Road, Wimbledon, London, SW19 8LF.
Tel: 0181-540 7942; FAX:0181-540 2827

SHEPISTON LODGE

31 Shepiston Lane, Hayes UB3 1LJ
Tel/Fax: 0181-569 2536 or Tel: 0181-573 0266

SHEPISTON LODGE is a character house where the emphasis is on comfort and friendliness. All rooms carpeted with washbasins, razor points, central heating and colour TV. Most with showers, all with tea/coffee making facilities. Satellite TV lounge. Payphone. Bar facility; evening meals available. Spacious garden. Car park. Convenient for Heathrow, Uxbridge and Stockley Park, with easy access to A/M4, A/M40, M25. Choice of English or Continental Breakfast.

ETB ♛ Approved RAC Listed AA Listed

Bushy Park Lodge

Sandy Lane, Teddington
Middx TW11 0DR
Tel: 0181-943 5428 Fax: 0181-943 1917

♛♛ Location: Overlooking Bushy Park, close to Kingston town centre and the bridge over the River Thames. Hampton Court can be reached with a direct walk of 20 minutes through the park. Hampton Wick railway station is a 7 minute walk; central London can be reached via Waterloo in 30 minutes. BUSHY PARK LODGE is a purpose-built 6 double bedroom lodge. All bedrooms have bathrooms en suite, remote-control colour TV, tea and coffee making facilities, hair dryers, trouser presses, mini bars and direct-dial telephones. Parking. Single £45.00, double £55.00 including VAT and Continental Breakfast.

EUROPA HOUSE HOTEL

151 Sussex Gardens, Hyde Park, LONDON W2

Europa House Hotel is a small, privately owned Hotel which aims to give personalised service of the highest standard. Full central heating. All rooms en suite. Within easy reach of the West End and situated close to Paddington Station. Singles, doubles and twins; family rooms available. Special rates for children under 10 years. Full English Breakfast.

Terms available on request.

Tel: 0171 723 7343; Fax: 0171-224 9331

BUDGET PRICES * CENTRAL LOCATION * FAMILY RUN

KERWIN HOTEL

Tel: 0171-834 1595 (Reservations)
Tel: 0171-834 8351 (Guests)

20 St George's Drive, Victoria, London SW1V 4BN

Budget price, family-run, friendly hotel. Close to Victoria Rail and Coach stations and convenient for central London. Ideal for sightseeing and shopping. Single rooms from £18-£20; Doubles from £26-£28. Discount for triple and family rooms. Full central heating, hot & cold water in all rooms.

HOLIDAY ACCOMMODATION Classification Schemes in England, Scotland and Wales

The National Tourist Board for England, Scotland and Wales have agreed a common 'Crown Classification' Scheme for serviced (Board) accommodation. All establishments are inspected regularly and are given a classification indicating their level of facilities and services.

There are six grades ranging from 'Listed' to Five Crowns '♛♛♛♛♛'. The higher the classification, the more facilities and services offered. Crown classification is a measure of *facilities* not *quality*. A common quality grading scheme grades the quality of establishments as 'Approved', 'Commended', 'Highly Commended' or 'Deluxe' according to the accommodation, welcome and service they provide.

For Self-Catering , holiday homes in England are awarded 'Keys' after inspection and can also be 'Approved', 'Commended', 'Highly Commended' or 'Deluxe' according to the facilities available. In Scotland the Crown scheme includes self-catering accommodation and Wales also has a voluntary inspection scheme for self-catering grading from '1 (Standard) to '5 (Excellent)'.

Caravan and Camping Parks can participate in the British Holiday Parks grading scheme from 'Approved (✓) to 'Excellent (✓✓✓✓✓)'. In addition, each National Tourist Board has an annual award for high-quality caravan accommodation in England - Rose Awards; in Scotland - Thistle Commendations; in Wales - Dragon Awards.

When advertisers supply us with the information, FHG Publications show Crowns and other awards or gradings, including AA, RAC, Egon Ronay etc. We also award a small number of Farm Holiday Guide Diplomas every year, based on readers' recommendations.

CENTRAL LONDON **BUDGET ACCOMMODATION**

WESTPOINT HOTEL

170-172 SUSSEX GARDENS, HYDE PARK, LONDON W2 1TP
Telephone: 0171-402 0281 (Reservations) Fax: 0171-224 9114

Open all year, Central heating. MOST ROOMS WITH PRIVATE SHOWER AND TOILET. Radio/Intercom & colour TV. Children welcome. TV lounge.

This hotel has long been a popular choice amongst tourists because of its central location, being near to Hyde Park and only two minutes from Paddington and Lancaster Gate tube stations. The West End's tourist attractions, including theatres, museums and Oxford Street stores are within easy reach. Individuals and families welcome.

PRIVATE CAR PARK

	LOW SEASON PER PERSON	**HIGH SEASON PER PERSON**
Rates:-	**Singles from £16**	**Singles from £22**
	Doubles from £13	**Doubles from £17**
	Family Rooms from £12	**Family Rooms from £14**

Low season: For rooms with shower/toilet: add from £5 for Doubles and £8 for Singles, per person

High season: For rooms with shower/toilet: add from £5 for Doubles

Central London **Special Budget Prices**

ABBEY COURT HOTEL

174 Sussex Gardens, Hyde Park, London W2 1TP. Tel: 0171-402 0704 Fax: 0171-262 2055

Open all year. All rooms with private showers and toilets. Access at all times. Colour television lounge. Radio/Intercom in every room. GLC Fire Certificate granted. Car Park. Central heating. Children welcome.

This Hotel has long been popular with tourists because of its central location near to Hyde Park and two minutes from Paddington and Lancaster Gate tube stations. The tourist attractions of the West End including theatres, museums and Oxford Street are within easy reach. Individuals, families and school parties are all welcome.

TERMS PER PERSON: High season: Single from £39, double from £24, family £18. Low season: Single from £29, double from £20, family from £17.
BED AND BREAKFAST

SASS HOUSE HOTEL

11 Craven Terrace
Hyde Park
London W2 3QD

Telephone: 0171 262 2325
Fax: 0171 262 0889

SPECIAL PRICES

☆ Centrally located close to Hyde Park and within easy reach of London's most famous tourist attractions ☆ Centrally heated ☆ Radio and intercom in all rooms ☆ Colour television lounge ☆ Special group and party booking rates, ☆ Served by a network of bus routes ☆ Nearest underground Paddington and Lancaster Gate–no car worries

BED AND BREAKFAST RATES PER PERSON
LOW SEASON: Single from £15; Double from £12; Family room from £11
HIGH SEASON: Single from £20; Double from £15; Family room from £12

West Central London

Reasonable High Quality Accommodation

PHILBEACH INN

17 Longridge Road, London SW5 9SB

Located near the Exhibition Centre, in the Earl's Court area of Chelsea, 200 metres from the Underground (Piccadilly and District lines), only 50 metres from bus stop which connects Kensington High Street, Knightsbridge, Oxford Circus and Piccadilly.

- Cable/Sky TV in every room
- Most rooms with private bath/shower and toilet
- 24 hour staff for guests' security and care
- Credit/debit cards accepted
- Full English Breakfast included
- Kitchen available for cooking by guests
- Special rates for extended stay
- Ladies' safety rooms

Tariff per day: Singles £30 Doubles £40 Doubles (en suite) £50 En suite Triple/Family £60

For Reservations please call: 0171-370 5213/5220 or Fax: 0171-370 0734

Dalmacia Hotel

71 Shepherds Bush Road, Hammersmith,
London W6 7LS
Tel: 0171 603 2887
Fax: 0171 602 9226

We offer comfortable and value for money accommodation

- All rooms ensuite
- Listed by Les Routiers & L.T.B.
- Direct dial telephones
- All major credit cards accepted
- Satellite TV & Remote
- Send for brochure

THE ELYSEE HOTEL

25/26 CRAVEN TERRACE, LONDON W2 3EL
Fax: 0171 402 4193 Tel: 0171 402 7633

Inexpensive stay in the *HEART OF LONDON: HOTEL FACING HYDE PARK.* Near London's famous tourist and shopping areas. Rooms with attached bath/shower and toilets.Tea/coffee making facilities. Limited car parking, at only £5 per day, arranged nearby.

Single £30 Twin/Double £40 (for room) Family £50 (up to 5 persons)

"Ringelblume"

89 Somerton Road, London NW2
Tel: 0181 830 6589 Fax: 0181 830 7589

Personal and complimentary collection by taxi upon arrival. In a quiet Edwardian Street (close to Hampstead Heath, the poet Keats' house and Kenwood House) find our green garden and wild rose porch. See the colourful light reflected through leaded windows onto a terracotta hallway floor. Enter by the grand oak staircase to our private rooms, some with four-posters and real fires. En suite available. A short tube ride takes you to Baker Street, Oxford Street, Wembley Stadium, theatre and opera. Free parking. From £20. Access, Visa.

FALCON HOTEL

Situated in central London, two minutes from Paddington Station, Hyde Park, Oxford Street and Madame Tussaud's. Central for all shopping. Quiet road, surrounded by Norfolk Square. All rooms have private facilities, colour TV and tea/coffee free of charge. Hotel is newly refurbished. Children welcome. Single room from £25 to £30; Double room from £37 to £44; Family room from £15 to £18 per person. All prices inclusive of VAT and full English Breakfast. Family business.

Mr M. Stavrou, Falcon Hotel,
11 Norfolk Square, London W2 1RU
Tel: 0171-723 8603

R.A.C listed **ENJOY** luxury in friendly atmosphere at S.R.A.C. listed

Elliot's

"HAZELWOOD HOUSE"

865 Finchley Road, Golders Green,
London NW11 8LX
Tel: 0181-458 8884

Whether on holiday or business, this Hotel is famous for its 'Home-from-Home' atmosphere in London's exclusive district of Golders Green.

Private forecourt parking
5/6 cars.
Children welcome: animals accepted
Single room with Breakfast £27.50 per night
Double room with Breakfast £38.00 per night
Overnight stay accepted.

BOKA HOTEL

35 EARDLEY CRESCENT,
LONDON SW5 9JT
Tel: 0171-370 1388

A medium sized, smart family-style hotel situated a few minutes' walk from Earls Court tube. We offer budget accommodation for tourists and students.

Single from £14-£20
Double from £20-£29
Sharing from £7-£10.

GOWER HOTEL

129 Sussex Gardens, Hyde Park,
London W2 2RX
Tel: 0171-262 2262/3/4 Fax: 0171-262 2006

Small, family-run hotel, centrally located within easy reach of Paddington Station. Excellent base for sightseeing and shopping, close to Madame Tussauds, Oxford Street and many other attractions. Centrally heated throughout, all bedrooms en suite, tea/coffee making, radio, TV (video and satellite) and direct-dial telephone. Singles from £24 to £34, doubles from £36 to £48. Family rooms can be arranged. Prices include breakfast and VAT.

London — Classified Advertisements

CHISWICK

ELLIOTT PRIVATE HOTEL, 62 ELLIOTT ROAD, CHISWICK, LONDON W4 1PE (0181-995 9794). Bed and Breakfast (13 rooms) run by Spanish lady. 120 metres from Turnham Green Underground Station; frequent buses. Adjoining park with 7 tennis courts. Single £20, Double/Twin £30.

CROYDON

MRS J. DIXON, 17 OSMOND GARDENS, WALLINGTON SM6 8SX (0181-647 1943). Double/family room (maximum 4) with colour TV, en-suite shower, tea/coffee making facilities. London approximately 30 minutes from local station (few minutes' walk). Bed and Breakfast from £18.00. Unrestricted parking.

HARROW

MRS M. FITZGERALD, 47 HINDES ROAD, HARROW HA1 1SQ (0181-861 1248). Private family guest house offering clean, comfortable accommodation, 5 minutes from town centre, bus and train stations. Central London 17 minutes. Single, double, twin and family rooms, all with central heating, washbasins, tea/coffee facilities and colour TV. Sorry, no pets. £16 per night.

KING'S CROSS

CENTRAL HOTEL, 13-18 ARGYLE STREET, KING'S CROSS WC1H 8EQ (0171-278 8682/0171-837 9008). Family-run newly renovated Bed and Breakfast Hotel, conveniently located for all major tourist attractions. Clean rooms with washbasins, shaver points, central heating, colour TV. Recommended. From £12. One Crown.

LONDON

PHILBEACH INN, 17 LONGRIDGE ROAD, LONDON SW5 9SB (0171-370 5213/5220; Fax: 0171-370 0734). Located near the Exhibition Centre, 200 metres from Underground and 50 metres from bus stop. Most rooms with private bath/shower and toilet. Full English breakfast. Singles £25, Double £35 (£40 en suite).

MONARCH HOTEL, 181-183 CROMWELL ROAD, LONDON SW5 0SF (0171-370 6262; Fax: 0171-370 6176). Centrally located, one minute from Earls Court Station. 40 en suite bedrooms (from one to four beds), all with central heating, colour TV and access to kitchen. From £15 single, £25 double including full breakfast.

HOTEL ONE O FOUR, 104 TURNHAM GREEN TERRACE, CHISWICK, LONDON W4 1QN (0181-995 3158 OR 994 9926). Close to Turnham Green Station, minutes from the West End, Airport, M4 North Circular. Central heating, double glazing, showers, tea/coffee making facilities, colour TV in rooms. Easy parking. ETB 2 crowns Approved. Professionally managed. Friendly. Modern day charm. Telephone for details.

EASTON HOTEL, 36-46 BELGRAVE ROAD, VICTORIA, LONDON SW1V 4BJ (0171-834 5938) Fax (0171-976 6560). Comfortable Bed and Breakfast near Victoria, British Rail and coach station, Tube and buses. 55 tastefully furnished rooms with central heating and telephone, many with private facilities. Ideal for travellers needing affordable accommodation near all major attractions.

ARDEN HOTEL, 10-12 ST. GEORGES DRIVE, VICTORIA, LONDON SW1V 4BJ (0171-834 2988; Fax: 0171-976 6560). Comfortable, modern Bed and Breakfast near Victoria, British Rail and Coach Stations, Tube and London buses. 35 tastefully furnished rooms with central heating and telephone, many with private facilities. Ideal for travellers needing affordable accommodation near all major attractions.

THE GLYNNE COURT HOTEL, 41 GREAT CUMBERLAND PLACE, LONDON W1H 7LG (0171-262 4344; Fax: 0171-724 2071). In a prime position in London's West End; easy access to public transport. All rooms have colour TV, washbasins, hospitality tray and telephone. From £20 including Continental breakfast.

KIRNESS HOUSE, 29 BELGRAVE ROAD, VICTORIA, LONDON SW1V 1RB (0171 834 0030). Small, clean. Satisfaction guaranteed. From £18 singles, £30 doubles. Near Victoria Station. All European languages spoken.

UXBRIDGE

CLEVELAND HOTEL, 4 CLEVELAND ROAD, UXBRIDGE UB8 2DW (01895 257618). Easy access to London and Heathrow. All rooms with washbasins, colour TV, coffee/tea facilities; some rooms en suite. Central heating. Off-street parking.

NORFOLK

Great Yarmouth

Swiss Cottage Hotel

31 North Drive, Great Yarmouth NR30 4EW Tel: 01493 855742

Sea front - quiet area.

Highly recommended. Most rooms en suite, TV and tea/coffee making facilities. Seasonal opening. Parking. Bed and Breakfast only. Terms from £15.00 per person.

***Spindrift* Private Hotel**

36 Wellesley Road Great Yarmouth NR30 1EU

AA QQ

Tel: (01493) 858674

APPROVED

'Spindrift' is a small Private Hotel attractively situated adjacent to the sea front, Golden Mile, bowling greens, tennis courts and the waterways. Front bedrooms enjoy excellent sea views. Colour TV and tea/coffee facilities in all bedrooms. En-suite rooms available with toilet and bath/shower. Open all year. Double room, bed and breakfast from £25, en-suite £30.

Nofolk — Classified Advertisements

GREAT YARMOUTH

MR & MRS B. KIMBER, ANGLIA HOUSE, 56 WELLESLEY ROAD, GREAT YARMOUTH NR30 1EX (01493 844395). Welcome to Anglia House, 3 minutes from beach, pier and town centre. Radio, intercom, colour TV and teamaking facilities in all bedrooms. En suite available. Good food with choice of menu. Licensed Bar. Children welcome. B&B from £12. BB&EM from £89 weekly. Open all year.

NORTH WALSHAM

BEECHWOOD HOTEL, CROMER ROAD, NORTH WALSHAM NR28 0HD (01692 403231). The Beechwood is a Georgian hotel with a warm and friendly atmosphere, set in mature grounds and yet only three minutes' walk from the town square. Ten well appointed en-suite bedrooms. Licensed bar, cosy residents' lounge. Johansens Recommended. We look forward to welcoming you.

NORWICH

NORWICH YMCA, 48 ST GILES STREET, NORWICH NR2 1LP (01603 620269). Comfortable, reasonably priced accommodation, in city centre with extensive ancillary facilities. Small groups welcome - booked well in advance. Ideal for long or short stays.

SWAFFHAM

MRS C. WEBSTER, PURBECK GUEST HOUSE, WHITSANDS ROAD, SWAFFHAM PE37 7BJ (01760 721805/725345). Bed and full English Breakfast £16 pp. Colour TV, tea and coffee facilities all rooms. Ideal for touring Sandringham and the Broads. Highly recommended.

WELNEY

MRS S. GERRARD-WRIGHT, WELNEY HOUSE, WELNEY, WISBECH, CAMBRIDGESHIRE PE14 9QA (01354 71207). Georgian farmhouse in beautiful Fen country on border of Norfolk and Cambridgeshire. Two twin bedrooms with washbasins, TV and tea making. Several restaurants within easy reach. B&B from £17.

NORTHAMPTONSHIRE

Weedon

The Countryside Inn

THE GLOBE HOTEL

Conveniently located three miles west of Junction 16 of the M1, this eighteenth century coaching inn offers attractively furnished and well-equipped rooms, all with private bathrooms, colour TV, radio, telephones and tea/coffee making facilities. A comprehensive food operation, OPEN ALL DAY, features home fayre bar meals and value for money à la carte menus. Pies are our speciality. Weedon is centrally located for visiting the many historic places and fascinating market towns in the area, also Silverstone Racing Circuit; leisure activities include golf and walking. AA** Weekend Giveaway Breaks - bed and breakfast £19.95 per person per night sharing a double/twin room.

WATLING STREET, WEEDON, NORTHANTS NN7 4QD
Tel: 01327 340336 Fax: 01327 349058

Commended

Northumberland — Classified Advertisements

CORBRIDGE

MRS MARGARET WEIGHTMAN, THE COURTYARD, MOUNT PLEASANT, SANDHOE, CORBRIDGE NE46 4LX (01434 606850). A traditional range of farm buildings recently converted into a lovely family home, designed around a pretty courtyard. Superb panoramic views south over Corbridge (1½ miles), Corstopitum Roman Fort and the Tyne Valley. All rooms are en suite with TV and central heating. Supper available by arrangement.

CRASTER

MRS FOSTER, KEEPERS COTTAGE, CRASTER SOUTH FARM, CRATER, NEAR ALNWICK (01665 576640). Family bedroom and shower. In mini-farmhouse atmosphere. Views of sea. Near beaches, bird reserves, golf courses, castles. Bed and Breakfast from £16.00 per night, per person. Evening Meal optional. Apply in writing with SAE.

ROMAN WALL

MRS MARY DAWSON, PARK BURNFOOT FARM, HALTWHISTLE NE49 0JP (01434 320378). 18th century farmhouse (log fires). Ideal for exploring the Roman Wall; approx. one hour's drive Ullswater; Gretna Green 25 miles. River and woodland walks from farm. Two rooms with TV and washbasin. ETB Listed. From £14. Also self catering cottage (ETB 3 Keys Commended) from £99.

ROTHBURY

MRS HELEN FARR, LORBOTTLE WEST STEADS, THROPTON, MORPETH NE65 7JT (01665 574672). Spacious farmhouse on working farm five miles from Rothbury. Rooms have TV/tea facilities. Ideal centre for sightseeing Northumberland's natural beauty and historic interests. ETB Listed.

WARKWORTH

MRS SHEILA PERCIVAL, ROXBRO HOUSE, 5 CASTLE TERRACE, WARKWORTH NE65 0UP (01665 711416). Small family guest house in centre of village, half mile from beach. Family and double rooms, all with showers. Open all year. B&B from £15.00. Non-smokers only.

FREE and REDUCED RATE Holiday Visits!
Don't miss our Reader's Offer Vouchers on pages 5 to 22

NOTTINGHAMSHIRE

Nottingham

YEW TREE GRANGE

2 Nethergate, Clifton Village, Nottingham NG11 8NL

Tel: 0115 984 7562

Yew Tree Grange is a Georgian residence of great charm and character located five miles from the M1 Junction 24. The house is situated in the quiet rural setting of Clifton Village, only 10 minutes from the City Centre. Accommodation includes single, double, twin and family bedrooms with TV lounge and dining room. There is ample car parking and a mature garden with duck pond. Ideally located for tourists visiting Robin Hood country or for businessmen stopping overnight. Bed and Breakfast £18 nightly with reduced rates for small children. Evening Meals by arrangement. No smoking.

Nottinghamshire — Classified Advertisements

BURTON JOYCE

WILLOW HOUSE, 12 WILLOW WONG, BURTON JOYCE NG14 5FD (01602 312070). Quiet village half mile from beautiful River Trent, 5 miles Nottingham. Very comfortable accommodation. Luxury bathroom. Tea making. TV in room. Washbasins. Cot, babysitting. From £16.00 pp.

SOUTHWELL

B. KINCHIN, OLD NATIONAL SCHOOL, NOTTINGHAM ROAD, SOUTHWELL NG25 0LG (01636 814360). Former school, tastefully converted to give a high standard of comfort. Attractively furnished beamed bedrooms; four-posters, twin and family rooms, all en suite. Two Crowns.

OXFORDSHIRE

North Leigh

The Leather Bottel

EAST END, NORTH LEIGH, WITNEY, OXON OX8 6PY

Tel: 01993 882174

Joe and Nena Purcell invite you to the The Leather Bottel 16th Century Inn. Situated in a quiet hamlet near North Leigh, convenient for Blenheim Palace, Woodstock, Roman Villa, Oxford and the Cotswolds. Victorian conservatory restaurant, where you can enjoy our extensive home cooked bar snacks, vegetarian and à la carte menu, overlooking pretty gardens. Breathtaking countryside walks. 2 double en suite bedrooms, one family room (own bathroom), one single bedroom. Colour TV and coffee making facilities. B&B £18 per person per night. £26 per night for single bedroom. Children welcome. ETB 2 Crowns Commended. Open all year. *Directions: follow signs to Roman Villa off A4095*

Easington House Hotel & Restaurant

50 Oxford Road

Banbury, Oxon OX16 9AN

Enquiries & Guests

(01295) 270181 Fax: (01295) 269527

Beautifully situated in award-winning gardens just 5 minutes' walk from Banbury's famous Cross, Easington Hotel offers modern comfort in a house of exceptional charm and friendliness. There are 12 bedrooms and a beautifully appointed cottage, all decorated and equipped to the very highest standards, and a superb restaurant which is popular with visitors and locals alike. Traditional English breakfasts, including local sausages. Just one mile from the M40, 18 miles from Stratford, 20 from Oxford — ideal for touring the Cotswolds, etc.

RAC Highly Acclaimed **Johansens**

CROWN & CUSHION HOTEL & LEISURE CENTRE

Commended ♛♛♛♛
Egon Ronay and Johansens rec.

Chipping Norton, Nr Oxford OX7 5AD
Colour Brochure: Free Phone 0800 585251 Fax: 01608 642926

500-year-old Coaching Inn, tastefully modernised to provide 40 en suite bedrooms. Some four-poster suites. "Old World" bar, log fires, real ale, good food. Indoor pool, squash court, gym, solarium, snooker (subject to availability). Modern Conference Centre. Located in picturesque Cotswolds town midway between Oxford and Stratford-upon-Avon. Convenient London, Heathrow, M40. Blenheim Palace, Warwick Castle, Bourton-on-the-Water, Shakespeare Country all nearby.

Price Busters start at just £19.50 or B&B and full restaurant dinner at £34.50.

ARDEN LODGE

34 Sunderland Avenue,
(off Banbury Road), Oxford
Tel: 01865 52076

Modern detached house set in tree-lined avenue in one of Oxford's most select areas. Within easy reach of City Centre, parks, river, meadows, golf course, country inns, including world-famous Riverside Trout Inn. Excellent base for touring Cotswolds, Stratford, Warwick Castle, Blenheim Palace. All rooms have private facilities, all have colour TV and tea/coffee making. Parking. B&B from £19 per person.

MR & MRS L.S. PRICE

GORSELANDS
FARMHOUSE AUBERGE

RAC Listed

Nr Woodstock and Oxford
Convenient for Blenheim Palace, Roman Villa and Cotswold villages

Beautiful Cotswold stone farmhouse in idyllic countryside. One acre grounds. Billiards room with full-size table. Lovely dining conservatory. Log fires, exposed beams, flagstone floors. Large family/double/twin en suite rooms. Drinks licence. Tennis court.

B & B from £14.00; Evening Meal from £9.95

Brochure: Gorselands, Boddington Lane, Near Long Hanborough, Near Woodstock, Oxford OX8 6PU

Tel: (01993) 881895

Oxfordshire — Classified Advertisements

FARINGDON

FARINGDON HOTEL, 1 MARKET PLACE, FARINGDON SN7 7HL (01367 240536). Situated in historic Faringdon, with easy access to London, Bristol and the Midlands. Rooms furnished to highest standards with en suite bathroom, colour TV, telephone, hairdryer etc. 3 Crowns Commended.

FREELAND

BABS TAPHOUSE, WRESTLERS MEAD, 35 WROSLYN ROAD, FREELAND, OXFORD OX7 2HJ (Freeland [01993] 882003). Convenient for Blenheim Palace, Oxford and Cotswolds. Single, double rooms with colour television, family or twin room with colour television and en-suite shower room with washbasin and toilet. Bed and Breakfast from £15.00.

HENLEY-ON-THAMES

MRS K. BRIDEKIRK, 107 ST MARKS ROAD, HENLEY-ON-THAMES RG9 1LP (01491 572982). A large comfortable house, quiet location, near town and Thames. All rooms H&C, colour TV, tea/coffee making facilities. Full central heating. From £14.50 single, £30 double/twin. Children welcome. Regret, no dogs. Convenient for Windsor, Oxford, London. Parking. Open all year. ETB Listed.

LONG HANBOROUGH

MRS A. WARWICK, THE CLOSE GUEST HOUSE, WITNEY ROAD, LONG HANBOROUGH OX8 8HF (01993 882485). Large detached house. Set in own grounds of 1½ acres. Close to Woodstock, Oxford and the Cotswolds. Three family rooms, all en suite with tea/coffee and colour TV. ETB 2 Crowns Commended. AA Listed. Bed & Breakfast from £15.00 per person.

STANTON HARCOURT

MRS MARGARET CLIFTON, STADDLE STONES, LINCH HILL, STANTON HARCOURT OX8 1BB (01865 882256). Chalet Bungalow with four acres, including carp pond for fishing. Bedrooms en suite or private bathrooms. TV lounge with tea/coffee. Disabled persons, children welcome. Near to Oxford and Cotswolds. Dogs welcome. Bed and Breakfast from £16.

WITNEY

MRS ELIZABETH SIMPSON, FIELD VIEW, WOOD GREEN, WITNEY, OXFORD OX8 6DE (01993 705485). Attractive Cotswold stone house in 2 acres, midway between Oxford University and the Cotswolds. Peaceful setting and friendly atmosphere. Three delightful en-suite bedrooms. Bed and Breakfast from £20.00. ETB 2 Crowns Highly Commended.

SHROPSHIRE

Bucknell, Shrewsbury

THE HALL

Commended

BUCKNELL **MRS CHRISTINE PRICE** **SY7 0AA**

BUCKNELL (015474) 249

You are assured of a warm welcome at The Hall, which is a Georgian Farmhouse with spacious accommodation. The house and gardens are set in a secluded part of a small South Shropshire Village, an ideal area for touring the Welsh Borderland. Offa's Dyke is on the doorstep, and the historic towns of Shrewsbury, Hereford, Ludlow and Ironbridge within easy reach as are the Church Stretton Hills and Wenlock Edge. Three bedrooms, one twin en suite, two doubles (with washbasins), tea making facilities, TV. Guest Lounge, Bed and Breakfast from £16.00. Dinner £8. ETB Member.

SAE please for details.

SANDFORD HOUSE HOTEL

St Julian's Friars, Shrewsbury SY1 1XL

Tel: 01743 343829

Grade II Listed Town House close to the River Severn with its fine riverside walks and good fishing, yet only a few minutes' walk from the town centre. Small licensed Family Hotel run for the last nine years by Joan and Roy Jones. Warm, friendly and informal, with high standards in food and cleanliness. All rooms have coffee/tea, colour TV. En suite rooms. Easy parking.

From £19.00 per person.

Discount for Short Breaks and longer stays.

ETB Highly Commended AA QQQQ Selected

Please telephone for brochure

Shropshire — Classified Advertisements

CHURCH STRETTON

DON AND RITA ROGERS, BELVEDERE GUEST HOUSE, BURWAY ROAD, CHURCH STRETTON SY6 6DP (01694 722232). Pleasant, centrally heated family Guest House - attractive gardens. Parking. Hairdryers, shaver points, Teasmaids all rooms. Two lounges - one TV. Packed lunches available. Bed and breakfast from £21.00. Evening Meal £9.00. 10% reduction for weekly/party bookings. AA QQQQ, RAC Acclaimed. ETB 3 Crowns Commended.

MRS MARY JONES, ACTON SCOTT FARM, ACTON SCOTT, CHURCH STRETTON SY6 6QN (01694 781260). Lovely 17th century Farmhouse in beautiful village. H&C and beverage making facilities in all rooms; en suite available. Visitors' lounge. Central for touring. Bed and Breakfast from £13. ETB Two Crowns Commended.

SOMERSET

Glastonbury

NEW HOUSE FARM
Burtle Road, Westhay, Nr Glastonbury
Mrs M.A. Bell
Tel: 01458 860238

A warm welcome awaits you on this working dairy farm on Somerset Levels. 1 family room and 1 double room, both en suite with colour TV, tea/coffee facilities and central heating. BED & FULL ENGLISH BREAKFAST FROM £18, EVENING MEAL £10.

COURT LODGE
Butleigh, Glastonbury BA6 8SA
Tel: 01458 50575

A warm welcome awaits at attractive, modernised 1850 Lodge. Set in picturesque garden on edge of Butleigh, 3 miles Glastonbury. 1 Double, 1 Twin, 1 Single Bedrooms; constant hot water, central heating. Bed & Breakfast from £12.50; Evening Meal by arrangement.

Somerset — Classified Advertisements

CHEDDAR

P. A. PHILLIPS, THE FORGE, CLIFF STREET, CHEDDAR BS27 3PL (01934 742345). Comfortable old stone cottage with 'Traditional Working Forge'. Conveniently situated in the village, a few minutes' walk from gorge & caves. Tea/coffee making, television lounge; parking and cycle lock-up. Non smoking. B&B from £12.50 pp. Double and family. Lovely views of Mendip Hills. Hearty breakfast.

DUNSTER

EXMOOR HOUSE HOTEL, 12 WEST STREET, DUNSTER TA24 6SN (01643 821268). Near castle. Georgian Listed building, south-facing garden. Licensed candlelit restaurant. Non smoking throughout. B&B from £24.50. ETB Three Crowns Highly Commended, AA/RAC Two Stars.

GLASTONBURY

MRS DINAH GIFFORD, LITTLE ORCHARD, ASHWELL LANE, GLASTONBURY BA6 8BG (01458 831620). Central position for touring West Country. At the foot of the historic Glastonbury Tor and overlooking the Vale of Avalon. Colour television lounge. Washbasins. Bath and shower. Central heating. Car parking. Children welcome, cot. Pay-phone. A welcoming 'cuppa' on arrival. Bed and Breakfast from £13.50. Fire Certificate. "Which" Recommended.

MRS M. DODDS, TWELVEHIDES, QUARRY LANE, BUTLEIGH, GLASTONBURY BA6 8TE (01458 50380). 18th century cottage on the edge of picturesque village. Idyllic setting with panoramic views of Vale of Avalon. One double, two twin rooms with tea/coffee facilities. Pets welcome. Traditional breakfast. Terms from £15. Many tourist attractions within easy reach. Good pub food nearby.

HIGHBRIDGE

MRS B. M. PUDDY, LAUREL FARM, MARK CAUSEWAY, HIGHBRIDGE TA9 4PZ (0127-864 1216). Old farmhouse, Listed building. All rooms have fitted carpets, washbasins, central heating, electric blankets. Ideal for touring Glastonbury, Wells, Wookey Hole, Bath etc, or as overnight stop. Large beamed sitting room with colour TV; garages and parking. Bed and full English breakfast. Open all year.

ILMINSTER

SHEILA K. SUTTON, SHAVE FARM, DONYATT, ILMINSTER TA19 0SA (014605 2317). Close Devon and Dorset borders. An ideal overnight stop. Spacious Farmhouse Bed and Breakfast from £14.00. Tea/coffee facilities. Log fires. Easy reach of M5 Junction 25.

MARTOCK

MRS TURTON, "WYCHWOOD", 7 BEARLEY ROAD, MARTOCK TA12 6PG (01935 825601). ETB 2 Crowns Commended. AA QQQ. Grid Ref Map 2, E5. Quality, comfortable accommodation. Excellent home cooking. Just off A303, M5 25 minutes. TV, tea/coffee facilities. Double and single rooms with en suite, twin with private bathroom. Central heating. No smoking. B&B from £16, Dinner from £12. Brochure. Open all year.

OTHERY

MRS F. S. FILSELL, THE CEDARS, HIGH STREET, OTHERY, NEAR BRIDGWATER TA7 0QA (01823 698310). A small Listed Georgian country house in the centre of village situated halfway between Glastonbury and Taunton on A361. £28 double or twin room.

PAWLETT

SANDRA WEATHERHEAD, NEUYS HOUSE, OLD MAIN ROAD, PAWLETT, BRIDGWATER TA6 4RY (01278 683779). Small comfortable Guest House, good position for touring Somerset and North Devon. Rooms have tea/coffee making facilities and colour TV. Riding stables and excellent coarse fishing nearby. Warm welcome guaranteed. Children welcome. ETB One Crown.

TAUNTON

BLORENGE GUEST HOUSE, 57 STAPLEGROVE ROAD, TAUNTON TA1 1DG (01823 283005). Spacious Victorian house in quiet area near town centre, convenient for rail and bus services. Comfortable bedrooms, some en suite, with tea-making facilities and TV (4 with four-posters). Outdoor heated pool. Residential licence. Many sports and leisure facilities locally; ideal touring base.

WELLS

MRS ALCOCK, CROSS FARM, YARLEY, NEAR WELLS BA5 1PA (01749 678925). 17th century longhouse, formerly a farm. One family, one double and one twin-bedded room, all with washbasins and shaver points. Bed and Full English Breakfast from £13.50.

MRS JANE ROWE, REDHILL FARM, EMBOROUGH, NEAR BATH BA3 4SH (01761 241294). Listed Farmhouse built in Cromwellian times, situated high on the Mendips between Bath and Wells. Within easy reach of the Bath and West Showground. A working smallholding. Bedrooms have central heating, washbasins and tea/coffee facilities. Sleeps six. Bed and Breakfast from £15.00. WCTB Listed.

THE GABLES

570-572 Etruria Road
Newcastle ST5 0SU

Telephone (01782) 619748

A WARM WELCOME TO ALL GUESTS

B&B

Secluded Edwardian Town House, with extensive lawns and gardens, on the A53, with easy access to the M6. Adjacent to the New Victoria Theatre, and ideal for visitors to Stoke on Trent's pottery factories and Alton Towers. Centrally heated throughout. Colour TV lounge. Thirteen bedrooms (most with private shower). Private car park.

Bed and Breakfast

BED AND BREAKFAST FROM £17.50 SINGLE, £26.50 DOUBLE

Staffordshire — Classified Advertisements

NEWCASTLE-UNDER-LYME

DURLSTON LICENSED GUEST HOUSE, KIMERBLEY ROAD (off A34), NEWCASTLE-UNDER-LYME ST5 9EG (01782 611708). Central for the Potteries and Dales. Warm welcome assured. Discount for children. TV and hot drinks facilities in all rooms. B&B from £16. ETB One Crown, AA Listed.

READERS ARE REQUESTED TO MENTION THIS GUIDEBOOK WHEN SEEKING ACCOMMODATION (AND PLEASE ENCLOSE A STAMPED ADDRESSED ENVELOPE)

SUFFOLK

Riverview House
Ballygate, Beccles, Suffolk IP18 6SF
Tel: (01502) 713519

Nicely situated overlooking the River Waveney in the market town of Beccles. We offer a warm welcome throughout the year for mini-breaks or longer stays. Formerly an old Georgian rectory which has been completely refurbished. Central heating. All bedrooms are tastefully decorated with washbasins, colour TV and tea/coffee making facilities. Private facilities available. Ideal base for exploring the Norfolk Broads, Suffolk countryside and coast. Near Norwich with its castle and cathedral, close to Great Yarmouth and Lowestoft.

B & B £16.50. Bargain breaks – 3 nights bed and breakfast £48-£51.

SASKIAVILL

Chediston, Halesworth IP19 0AR
Tel: 01986 873067

Saskiavill is set back from the road and features its own garden. It is situated close to Norwich, coast and Minsmere Bird Sanctuary. There are two double rooms, one family and one twin with washbasins. One room has been adapted for disabled guests.

Suffolk — Classified Advertisements

FRAMLINGHAM

BRIAN AND PHYLLIS COLLETT, SHIMMENS PIGHTLE, DENNINGTON ROAD, FRAMLINGHAM IP13 9JT (01728 724036). Set in an acre of landscaped gardens on outskirts of Framlingham. Ground floor accommodation. Home-made marmalade and local cured bacon. Morning tea and evening drinks offered. No Smoking. ETB Listed "Commended". Self-Catering flats also available at SOUTHWOLD.

HITCHAM

MRS J. M. WHITE, MILL HOUSE, WATER RUN, HITCHAM, STOWMARKET IP7 7LN (01449 740315). Late Regency House, in four acres of grounds, gardens and duck ponds. Tennis court. Stables and paddock. Central heating, colour TV, washbasins, teamaking facilities. Central for Constable Country, Suffolk villages. Five miles from Lavenham. Bed and Breakfast from £12. Dinner by arrangement.

SAXMUNDHAM

C.M. STRACHAN, HALL FARM, RENDHAM, SAXMUNDHAM IP77 2AW (01728 78440). Dairy farm with traditional farmhouse. Near coast. Ideal walking/birdwatching. Large guest rooms. Washbasins. Friendly atmosphere. Children welcome. Bed and Breakfast £15. Open all year.

SUDBURY

WEANERS FARM, BEARS LANE, LAVENHAM, SUDBURY CO10 9RX (01787 247310) Comfortable modern farmhouse surrounded by cornfields but only one mile from historic village is within easy reach of Constable Country, Cambridge and National Trust Houses. On route for Felixstowe, Harwich or Stansted. One double, two twin-bedded rooms, two bathrooms. Private guests' dining-lounge area. TV.

SURREY

Gatwick, Horley

CHALET GUEST HOUSE

77 Massetts Road, Horley RH6 7EB

ONE MILE FROM GATWICK

Modern, non-smoking Guest House only 5 minutes from Airport. En-suite accommodation with GOOD showers. All rooms TV and central heating. Comfortable guests' lounge; FREE tea and coffee available all day. Easy walk Horley town centre, pubs and restaurants for Evening Meals. Holiday car parking £10 weekly. Half mile railway station; half an hour London & South Coast.

B&B from £21. AA, RAC Acclaimed. ETB 2 Crowns Commended

Tel: (01293) 821666 Fax: (01293) 821619

Chase Lodge Guest House

Kingston Upon Thames KT1 4AS
10 Park Road, Hampton Wick
Tel: 0181-943 1862 Fax: 0181-943 9363

WINNERS OF BTA TROPHY 1991

Built 1870, Chase Lodge is a fully restored small, intimate, high quality, unique Guest House ideally suited to the discerning client who requires an environment of old-world charm allied to 20th century personal service. Situated in a quiet conservation area close to Hampton Court, Bushy Park and River Thames. Train station one minute's walk-20 minutes central London and Heathrow. Chauffeuring service to/from Heathrow (free for 3 nights or more). Ideal base for tourists and business persons alike. Fast becoming recognized for a superb English Breakfast and tasty traditional home-cooked English-style Dinner.

Prices from £22.00 per person.
All major credit cards accepted.
Please book early to avoid disappointment

Oaklands is a spacious country house of considerable charm dating from the 17th century. It is set in its own grounds of one acre, about one mile from the small town of Lingfield, and three miles from East Grinstead, both with rail connections to London. Transportation and parking for Gatwick Airport can be arranged. Oaklands is ideal as a stopover or base. Dover and the Channel Ports are two hours' drive away whilst the major towns of London and Brighton are about one hour distant. One en-suite room; one double and one single bedrooms, one with washbasin; two bathrooms, two toilets; sittingroom; dining-room. Cot, high chair, babysitting and reduced rates for children. Gas central heating. Open all year. Parking. Bed and Breakfast from £16. Evening Meal by arrangement. Mrs V. Bundy **01342 834705**

Oaklands
Felcourt Road, Lingfield,
Surrey RH7 6NF

PINEHURST GRANGE GUEST HOUSE
EAST HILL (A25), OXTED RH8 9AE
Tel: OXTED (01883) 716413
Proprietors: Mr & Mrs L. Rodgers
ROOM & BREAKFAST FROM £24 per night

1 double, 1 twin, 1 single bedroom, all with hot/cold water, TV, and tea/coffee making facilities. Residents' Dining Room & Sitting Room. Close to good local amenities: 20 mins drive Gatwick Airport (M25 Jct 6 2½ miles): 7 mins walk to station: good train service to London/Croydon, close to local bus & taxi services.

Many historic & famous houses in nearby area include CHARTWELL, KNOLE, HEVER CASTLE and PENSHURST PLACE. Handy for Lingfield Park Racecourse.

Surrey — Classified Advertisements

GATWICK

LYNWOOD GUEST HOUSE, 50 LONDON ROAD, REDHILL RH1 1LN (01737 766894). Gatwick Airport 12 minutes by train or car; London 35 minutes by train. Six minutes' walk to Redhill Station and town centre. Comfortable rooms with shower, washbasin, colour TV and tea/coffee facilities. Car park. English Breakfast. AA Listed.

ROSEMEAD GUEST HOUSE, 19 CHURCH ROAD, HORLEY RH6 7EY (01293 784965; Fax: 01293 820438). Gatwick airport five minutes. Small guest house providing English Breakfast after 7.30 am, Continental before. Car parking facilities. Single £23, Double or Twin £35 (en suite £42), Famiy room £49 en suite. All rooms colour TV, tea/coffee facilities. Tourist Board Commended, AA Listed.

MRS GRETA MCLEAN, GORSE COTTAGE, 66 BALCOMBE ROAD, HORLEY RH6 9AY Tel/Fax: 01293 784402). Small, friendly, detached accommodation. Two miles Gatwick Airport, five minutes BR station for London and South Coast. English Breakfast served after 7.30am. £16 per person (double), £20 single.

GUILDFORD

MRS REILLY, CHALKLANDS, BEECH AVENUE, EFFINGHAM KT24 5PJ (01372 454936; 0378 140010 mobile). Lovely detached house overlooking golf course. 10 minutes M25 Guildford, Dorking, Leatherhead. Heathrow and Gatwick, London (Waterloo Station) 35 minutes. En suite facilities. Excellent pub food nearby. £20 B&B.

HORLEY

ERNEST AND MARCIA ATKINSON, SPRINGWOOD GUEST HOUSE, 58 MASSETTS ROAD, HORLEY RH6 7DS (01293 775998). One mile Gatwick Airport. Close to pubs, restaurants, railway station. All rooms have TV, tea/coffee facilities, washbasins. Terms from £23 single, £34 double, £40 family. Holiday parking. Courtesy transport provided. ETB One Crown. Member G.G.H.A.

LEATHERHEAD

BOOKHAM GRANGE HOTEL, LITTLE BOOKHAM COMMON, BOOKHAM, NEAR LEATHERHEAD KT23 3HS (01372 452742; Fax: 01372 450080). Country house hotel with gardens facing NT land. Excellent food and friendly service. Convenient for airports, sightseeing and business; Bookham railway station nearby. Four miles from M25, five miles from A3. 4 Crowns.

LINGFIELD

STANTONS HALL FARM, BLINDLEY HEATH, LINGFIELD RH7 6LG (01342 832401). 18th century Farmhouse set in 18 acres. Family, double and single rooms, most en suite, all with colour TV, central heating, tea/coffee making. Car parking facilities. Bed and Breakfast from £16, reductions for children sharing. Cot/high chair provided. Convenient for M25 and Gatwick.

SURBITON

JAMES L. LYNN, KINGSTON YMCA, 49 KINGSTON ROAD, SURBITON KT6 4NG (0181 390 0148). Superb budget hotel. 150 rooms: single, twin/double en suite. TV. Bed, Breakfast/Half Board. Two restaurants/bar. Health club. Beauty clinic, etc. Reasonable terms.

MRS MENZIES, VILLIERS LODGE, 1 CRANES PARK, SURBITON KT5 8AB (0181 399 6000). Excellent accommodation in small Guest House. Every comfort, tea/coffee making facilities in all rooms. Close to trains and buses for London, Hampton Court, Kew, Windsor and coast. Reasonable terms.

WALTON-ON-THAMES

MRS JOAN SPITERI, BEECHTREE LODGE, 7 RYDENS AVENUE, WALTON-ON-THAMES KT12 3JB (01932 242738). Comfortable Edwardian home in quiet avenue; station 10 minutes' walk, easy access Heathrow, Hampton Court, Thorpe Park etc. All rooms with washbasins, colour TV, tea/coffee. B&B from £14. No smoking.

EAST SUSSEX

Battle, Brighton

BRAKES COPPICE FARM – BATTLE

FARMHOUSE B&B WITH 3 EN SUITE BEDROOMS

- Farmhouse modernised and furnished to high standard
- Set in 70 acres and only five miles from coast
- Near the large towns of Hastings and Eastbourne
- Bed and breakfast £25 single, £39.50 double
- Warm welcome from Michael and Fay Ramsden.

Brakes Coppice Farm, Telham Lane, Battle,
East Sussex TN33 0SJ. Tel: 01424 830347

Children welcome - Sorry, no smoking or pets.

Avalon Guest House

7 Upper Rock Gardens, Brighton BN2 1QE
Tel: 01273 692344

Bob Sharp extends a warm welcome to his small, friendly Guest House in the centre of Brighton, close to seafront, Conference Centre, Marina and tourist attractions. Fully centrally heated. All rooms have colour TV and tea/coffee making facilities. Some rooms en suite. Good English breakfast. All from £15.00. Special rates for weekly stays. Credit cards accepted. Members of the Brighton Guest House and Hotel Association. Registered with Brighton Tourist Board. Satellite TV. In-house films.

KEMPTON HOUSE HOTEL

33/34 Marine Parade, Brighton BN2 1TR
Tel: (01273) 570248

AA/RAC Highly Acclaimed: ETB ♛♛♛ Commended
Private Seafront Hotel overlooking Beach & Pier. Rooms with full ensuite shower & toilet, central heating, tea/coffee making, telephone, radio, colour TV, hairdryer, satellite TV. Four poster available; sea views. Residents' bar; patio. Full English Breakfast or Continental. Open all year.

B&B from £22 nightly; Weekly:
7 nights for price of 6 *Please phone for details*

ETB ♛♛♛ **"BRIGHTON" MARINA HOUSE HOTEL** AA RAC *TCB, ANWB*

"Your satisfaction is our first concern"
CLEAN-COMFORTABLE-CARING
8 Charlotte Street, Marine Parade, Brighton BN2 1AG
Tel: (01273) 605349 & 679484 Fax: (01273) 605349

Double, twin, triple and family en suite and standard available. Highly recommended family Hotel. Cosy elegantly furnished, well equipped rooms. Offering a warm welcome, cleanliness, comfort and hospitality. Central for sea, Marina, Royal Pavilion, Exhibition and Conference Halls, tourist attractions. Licensed restaurant. English, Chinese and Indian cuisine. Offering all facilities. Cards accepted Best in price range.

HIGHLY RECOMMENDED

Welcome to:

GEORJAN GUEST HOUSE

27 UPPER ROCK GARDENS, BRIGHTON BN2 1QE SUSSEX
TEL AND FAX: (01273) 694951

A warm welcome and friendly atmosphere prevail at this small Guest House run by the resident proprietors. Close to the Sea, Town Centre, Conference venues, tourist attractions and Marina. All rooms have central heating, colour television, radio/alarm, tea/coffee making facilities, en-suite or private shower. Full English or Vegetarian breakfast. Children welcome (special rates). Pets welcome on request. Access at all times with your own key. Rates £16-£24 per person. Credit cards accepted. Member of the Brighton Guest House and Hotel Association. Highly recommended in "Time Out", the London Weekly Guide.

Resident proprietor: R. Palmer

Sea Breeze

Probably Brighton's friendliest Guest House
"Arrive as a guest, leave as a friend"

Sea Breeze is your home from home. All rooms are fully en suite; hospitality tray, radio alarm, colour TV with video and satellite channels. Rooms individually designed (have we your colour?). Perhaps the four-poster suite.
Brighton has much to offer: entertainments, shops, Pier, Lanes, Marina, Brighton Centre and the sea.
Sea Breeze's standards are very high; friendship and a good time at Sea Breeze guaranteed.
Own keys. Credit cards and cash accepted. Pets by request. Terms from £17.00.

12a Upper Rock Gardens, Brighton BN2 1QE
Tel: 01273 602608 Fax: 01273 607166

AMBLECLIFF HOTEL

35 UPPER ROCK GARDENS, BRIGHTON BN2 1QF
Tel: 01273 681161

This stylish hotel was recommended by the Sunday Times and on TV. Excellently located close to the sea front with the Pier, The Lanes, Royal Pavilion, Conference Centre and Marina only a short stroll away. Individually designed rooms with king-size, four-poster and non-smoking rooms available. All double, twin and family rooms are en-suite. A choice of full English breakfast in the diningroom or Continental breakfast in bed. Unrestricted access. We believe you deserve an excellent service and value for money. AA QQQQ, RAC Highly Acclaimed ♛♛♛ Bed and Breakfast from £17.50, supplements for one night stays and en-suite facilities.

Melford Hall Hotel

41 Marine Parade, Brighton, Sussex BN2 1PE

RAC ACCLAIMED **Tel: 01273 681435** AA LISTED

SEAFRONT HOTEL on a premier corner position of seafront garden square, overlooking beach and Palace Pier. Forecourt parking, allowing you to enjoy shopping, entertainment, and conference amenities in comfortable strolling distance.

All rooms en suite (shower/WC), full central heating, colour TV, tea/coffee trays, hairdryers.

Four-poster and ground floor rooms available. Bed and breakfast from £20.00 per person per night, VAT incl. Supplements for singles en suite and four-poster rooms. Reductions for 3 days or more (except Bank Holidays).

Bannings Guest House

AA QQQ Recommended

14 Upper Rock Gardens, Kemptown, Brighton BN2 1QE. Tel: 01273 681403

Comfortable, Registered and Highly Recommended small family-run Guest House centrally located for all Brighton's attractions. Close to sea and shops and not far from the famous Lanes, The Royal Pavilion and the Conference Centre. All rooms have shower, colour TV and complimentary tea/coffee facilities, and some have en-suite toilets and showers. An excellent full English Breakfast is served with alternatives available for Vegetarians, Vegans and those on gluten-free diets. The house is fully centrally heated with guests having access at all times.

BED AND BREAKFAST FROM £17

Mr and Mrs P.G. Wiggin

GRANTHAM HOUSE

Lower Dicker
Hailsham
01323 844388

Eastbourne area. Victorian ex-farmhouse. Lovely garden. Large double bedrooms. Private parking. Bed and Breakfast from £14.50

STAIRS FARMHOUSE

17th century Farmhouse, carefully modernised, offers comfortable accommodation. Each room has pleasant views, colour TV and tea/coffee. Evening meal by arrangement. Close to Hever Castle, Chartwell and "Pooh Bridge". Open all year. Tea Room and Farm Shop. SEETB Listed/Commended. B&B from £19 per person double, £25 single.

Tel: 01892 770793
High Street, Hartfield, East Sussex TN7 4AB

Mrs P. Burnaby-Davies

BANKSIDE

Rodmell, Lewes, East Sussex BN7 3EZ

Family Bed and Breakfast - en suite facilities, TV. Situated between historic Lewes and Newhaven Ferry, on the South Downs Way, close to Glyndebourne. This delightful village was once the home of Virginia Woolf.

Tel: 01273 477058

Jeake's House

Mermaid Street, Rye,
East Sussex TN31 7ET
Tel: 01797 222828 Fax: 222623

Dating from 1869, this beautiful Listed Building stands in one of England's most famous streets.

* Oak beamed and panelled bedrooms overlook the marsh to the sea.
* Honeymoon suite
* Brass, mahogany or four-poster beds with linen sheets and lace.
* Ensuite facilities, TV, radio, telephone.
* Residential licence.
* Traditional and vegetarian breakfast served.

From £19.50 per person. Access. Visa & Mastercard accepted.

AA Selected RAC Highly Acclaimed

ETB ♛♛ Highly Commended

East Sussex — Classified Advertisements

BEXHILL-ON-SEA

MRS J. GODFREY, SLEPE HOUSE, 135 DORSET ROAD, BEXHILL-ON-SEA TN40 2HU (01424 220589). Comfortable Edwardian house. Central heating, colour TV, tea/coffee facilities all rooms. En suite doubles. Parking. Full English breakfast. From £14 per person. Non Smoking.

BRIGHTON

MR & MRS P. CULPECK, FYFIELD HOUSE, 26 NEW STEINE, BRIGHTON BN2 1PD (01273 602770). Peter and Anna, English/Swiss proprietors, welcome you to their clean, centrally situated home beside the sea. En-suites, four-poster bed, hairdryer, ironing facilities. Evening Meal on request. Excellent food. Ring now for free brochure. From £16 to £27 per person, 3 Crowns, RAC Listed

EASTBOURNE

HOTEL IVERNA, 32 MARINE PARADE, EASTBOURNE BN22 7AY (01323 730768). Close to pier, shops and theatres. Magnificent sea views. Bar. All rooms with colour TV and tea-making facilities. Nothing too much trouble for your hosts, Dave and Sandra Elkin. Bed and Breakfast £16 per night. Open all year.

HASTINGS

MR AND MRS R. STEELE, AMBERLENE GUEST HOUSE, 12 CAMBRIDGE GARDENS, HASTINGS TN34 1EH (01424 439447). Town centre, 2 minutes' walk beach, shops, entertainments, rail/bus stations, adjacent car park. Very clean rooms with washbasins, central heating, colour TV. Some en-suite. All prices include tea, coffee and biscuits in your room. Bed and 4-course English Breakfast £14.00-£16.00 inclusive. Room only less £2.00. Children sharing room half price. Also holiday Flats available nearby.

HORAM

WOODGATE COTTAGE TEAROOMS B&B, MARLE GREEN ROAD, VINES CROSS, HORAM TN21 9ED (01435 812834). Peaceful rural smallholding on country lane between Eastbourne and Tunbridge Wells. Children, pets welcome. Babysitting, cot, thermos, packed lunches, maps available. We happily cater for vegetarians and disabled guests. Central to many Sussex/Kent holiday attractions. £15 per person/night.

RYE

DAVID AND ELAINE GRIFFIN, KIMBLEE, MAIN STREET, PEASMARSH, NEAR RYE TN31 6UL (01797 230514 or 0831 841004 (mobile)). Country House. Views. Rye 5 minutes' drive. Two rooms en suite; one room with adjacent private bathroom. Single possible. All rooms colour TV. radio/alarm, tea/coffee, hairdryers. CH. Pub/restaurant 250 metres. £15-£17.50 per person, discounts for longer stays. Brochure. 2 Crowns Commended.

SEAFORD

MRS ROBERTS, 'SUNNYSIDE', 23 CONNAUGHT ROAD, SEAFORD BN25 2PT (01323 895850). Comfortable family house. Washbasins in all bedrooms. 120 yards from sea. Between Eastbourne and Brighton. Three miles Newhaven Ferry and South Downs Way.

ST LEONARDS-ON-SEA

PETER & MADELEINE MANN, GRAND HOTEL, GRAND PARADE, ST LEONARDS-ON-SEA, HASTINGS TN38 0DD (01424 428510). Seafront family-run hotel, recently renovated. Spacious lounge, licensed bar, central heating. B&B from £12; EM from £8. Parking. Some rooms en suite. Open all year. Free access to clean, comfortable rooms at all times. Children welcome; half price sharing room.

WINCHELSEA

A. N. ROCHE, THE STRAND HOUSE, WINCHELSEA, NEAR RYE TN36 4JT (01797 226276). Overlooking National Trust land, Strand House (reputedly early 15th century) is quaint and charming with inglenook fireplaces, beamed ceilings, four-poster bed and residential bar. Bedrooms (most en suite) have TV and tea-making facilities. Bed and Breakfast from £28 single, £40 double. RAC Listed. ETB 3 Crowns Commended.

WEST SUSSEX

Ardingly, Arundel

Mr & Mrs M.K. Waistell

Jordans

Church Lane, Ardingly, West Sussex RH17 6UP

Tel: 01444 892681

Peaceful Victorian Listed Manor House in beautiful grounds opposite medieval church and within walking distance of Ardingly Showground. 20 minutes from Gatwick; Brighton 30 minutes

Full English Breakfast *Colour TV* *Snooker room*

RAC *** ♛♛♛Highly Commended *All major credit cards accepted*

Situated in the heart of historic Arundel the Swan Hotel has been lovingly restored to its former Victorian splendour. Many of the Hotel's original features, including English oak flooring and wall panelling are still very much in evidence, creating a wonderful ambience throughout. Both table d'hôte and à la carte menus are available in the popular award-winning restaurant, where wines can be selected from the original 200-year-old cellar. Local real ales complement the delicious hot and cold food available in the traditional bar. Close to Arundel's famous 12th century Castle, the River Arun and other local attractions.

All rooms have · En suite bathrooms · Colour TV · Tea/coffee facilities · Hairdryers · Telephone · Room Service.

Prices from £30.00 pppn including Full English Breakfast

SWAN HOTEL, 27-29 HIGH STREET, ARUNDEL, WEST SUSSEX BN18 9AG (01903) 882314

BLACK MILL HOUSE HOTEL

ALDWICK, BOGNOR REGIS, SUSSEX

Commended AA**RAC*
Ashley Courtenay Recd.

Enclosed garden, quiet situation. Sea and Marine Gardens 300 yards. 27 bedrooms (21 with private bathroom). Lift. Two lounges, one non-smoking. Attractive cocktail bar, games room. Children special offers. DOGS WELCOME. Excellent touring centre. TERMS: B&B from £23, D.B&B from £33.95. Mini Breaks: D.B&B. from £60 for 2 days and Summer Short Breaks.

Own Car park MEMBER SEETB, ETB. Accessible Award Cat. 3. Open all year

Tel: Bognor Regis (01243) 821945 for Illustrated Brochure

The Old Store Guest House

Stane Street, Halnaker,
Chichester PO18 0QL

An impressive 18th century Grade II Listed Guest House adjoining the Goodwood Estate. We offer family, double, twin and single bedrooms, all en suite, with tea/coffee making facilities and colour TV.

* Guests' lounge * * Car Park *
Bed and Breakfast from £25 per person
Situated on the Chichester - Petworth Road A285

Tel: (01243) 531977
Mr. R. S. Grocott

THE SQUIRRELS

Albourne Road, Woodmancote, Henfield BN5 9BH
Tel: 01273 492761

The Squirrels is a country house with lovely large garden set in a secluded area convenient for South Coast and Downland touring. Brighton and Gatwick 20 minutes. Good food at pub five minutes' walk. One family, one double, one twin and one single rooms, all with colour TV, washbasin, central heating and tea/coffee making facilities. Ample parking space. A warm welcome awaits you. Open all year.
Directions: from London take M25, M23, A23 towards Brighton, then B2118 to Albourne. Turn right onto B2116 Albourne/Henfield Road - Squirrels is approximately one and a half miles on left.
Bed and Breakfast £16

West Sussex — Classified Advertisements

HORSHAM

"ROSEDEAN", 10 NORTH HEATH LANE, HORSHAM RH12 5AH (01403 218812). Modern dwelling designed around part of mature arboretum, resulting in delightful natural aspect with many varieties of birds. One double bedroom, one twin, three singles, all with washbasins, TV and tea-making. Good base for touring and London visists. B&B; optional Evening Meal.

MIDHURST

DAVID AND JENNIE RANDALL, THE COACH HOUSE, BEPTON GU29 0HZ (01730 812351). 10 miles north of Chichester. Large en suite bed-sitting room for two, in peaceful rural setting with views to the South Downs. Well furnished, including small fridge, microwave and kettle. Non-smokers only. Bed and Breakfast £15 per person. Telephone for full details.

TYNE & WEAR

Newcastle-upon-Tyne

DENE HOTEL
38-42 Grosvenor Road, Jesmond,
Newcastle-on-Tyne NE2 2RP
Tel: 0191-281 1502 Fax: 0191-281 8110

Fully licensed Hotel with cocktail bar. Central heating. All rooms have washbasins. Colour TV lounge. Tea and coffee making facilities, and colour TV in all rooms. Most rooms with en suite. Car park.

Bed and Breakfast:
Single Room from £22.50
Double Room from £39.00
Dinner from £7.50

THE GEORGE HOTEL
88 OSBORNE ROAD, JESMOND
NEWCASTLE-UPON-TYNE NE2 2AP
Tel: 0191-281 4442 Fax: 0191-281 8300

Family run Hotel. Friendly service generously provided. Excellent, freshly cooked meals served all day. All rooms have en suite facilities.

AA QQ ETB ♛♛ RAC Acclaimed

WARWICKSHIRE

Nuneaton, Stratford-upon-Avon

DRACHENFELS HOTEL

25 Attleborough Road,
Nuneaton,
Warwickshire CV11 4HZ
Tel: 01203 383030

Small private Hotel, five minutes' walk from town centre. Resident Proprietor. All rooms with colour TV and tea/coffee facilities; some en suite. Licensed. Free parking. English Breakfast. Near Warwick, Coventry, Birmingham, Leicester. From £15 per person.

Telephone for Brochure ETB ♛♛ AA.

CROWN & CUSHION HOTEL & LEISURE CENTRE
♛♛♛♛ Commended
Chipping Norton, Nr Stratford-upon-Avon OX7 5AD
Colour Brochure: Free Phone 0800 585251 Fax: 01608 642926

500-year old Coaching Inn, tastefully modernised to provide 40 excellent en suite bedrooms, some four-poster suites. "Old World" bar, log fires, real ale, good food. Indoor pool, squash court, gym, solarium, snooker (subject to availability). Hotel situated in picturesque Cotswolds town midway between Oxford and Stratford-upon-Avon. Convenient London, Heathrow, M40. Blenheim Palace, Warwick Castle, Bourton-on-the-Water, Shakespeare Country all nearby. **Price Busters start at just £19.50, or DB&B from just £34.50.**

Egon Ronay and Johansens recommended

Sun Patio
Beer Garden

Tourist Board
2 Crowns

White Horse Inn

Banbury Road, Ettington, Nr. Stratford-upon-Avon CV37 7SU
Proprietors: Roy & Valerie Blower. Tel: (01789) 740641

A delightful, oak beamed English pub offering Bed and Breakfast and a warm welcome.
All our rooms are tastefully furnished and en suite, with colour TV, central heating and tea/coffee facilities.
Set in Shakespeare country close to the Cotswolds and Stratford-upon-Avon; also close to Royal Showground Stoneleigh and NEC Birmingham. Real ales and excellent food always available.
Weekend break reductions available from November to April.

HUNTERS MOON GUEST HOUSE

150 Alcester Road, Stratford-upon-Avon, Warwickshire CV37 9DR
Reservations: 01789 292888

All rooms are en suite and comfortably furnished with colour television, tea and coffee making facilities, and fitted hairdryers. Single, twin, double and family rooms are available. Hunters Moon is close to Anne Hathaway's Cottage, and is an ideal base for visiting the Cotswold villages, Warwick Castle and all other Shakespearean properties. Car parking is for guests' use and there is also a garden patio and ornamental fountain and pond to relax by. An excellent English breakfast is served by resident hosts, Stratfordians Rosemary and Dave Austin. Visa, Access, American Express accepted. Recommended by Arthur Frommer. AA Recommended QQQ. Telephone for further details and reservations.

PARK LEYS

Banbury Road, Goldicote,
Stratford-upon-Avon CV37 7ND
Tel: 01789 740691

Large late-Georgian Farmhouse in an acre of rambling grounds. Stratford 3½ miles, within easy drive of all Cotswolds attractions. We offer family, double & twin rooms, centrally heated, some with full en-suite facilities. Children welcome at reduced rates; cots, high chairs available. Open all year for Bed & Breakfast from £14 to £20.
HETB Registered

Enquiries welcomed

Commended ***AA Listed***

CHURCH FARM

A warm and friendly welcome awaits you in our Georgian farmhouse at edge of pretty village. In easy driving distance of Stratford and the Cotswolds. Family, Twin and Double Bedrooms, some en suite in converted stable block with TV. Tea/coffee facilities. Central heating. Gliding, fishing, boating and horse-riding nearby. Cot/high chair available. From £13.50 B&B.

For further details: Mrs. Marion J. Walters
Church Farm, Dorsington,Stratford on Avon CV37 8AX
Tel: Stratford on Avon (01789) 720471 and

BROOK LODGE
GUEST HOUSE

Quality accommodation that you'll be comfortable with.

Near to Anne Hathaway's cottage you will discover Brook Lodge, a guest house where quality, comfort and convenience combine to make each stay a truly memorable one. The attractively decorated, en-suite bedrooms are complete with hospitality trays, colour televisions, hair dryers and radios. Our aim is to provide you with a friendly and informative base from which you can explore the history and charm of the surrounding area.

AA QQQ

LES ROUTIERS

English Tourist Board COMMENDED

Large Car Park Major Credit Cards Accepted

192 Alcester Road, Stratford-Upon-Avon, Warwickshire CV37 9DR

Tel/Fax: (01789) 295988

PENRYN GUEST HOUSE

Situated midway between Anne Hathaway's Cottage and town centre, Penryn offers the ideal base for visitors to Shakespeare's Country.

The emphasis is on making your stay comfortable and enjoyable. All rooms are decorated to the highest of standards and have Colour Television, Tea/Coffee making facilities, fitted Hairdryers and luxury en suites with an endless supply of hot water.

After a comfortable night's sleep, a traditional English Breakfast served to your liking awaits you. These are just part of the hospitality that Debbie and Tony give to their guests.

Large car park, guests' telephone and local information are available. SAE for Colour Brochure.

126 Alcester Road, Stratford-upon-Avon CV37 9DP
Telephone (01789) 293718

AA LISTED QQ

RAC LISTED

COMMENDED

HOSTS: DEBBIE AND TONY PITT

Why try the rest when you can stay at the best

ACCESS, VISA, AMERICAN EXPRESS, DINERS, ALL WELCOME

Warwickshire — Classified Advertisements

LEAMINGTON SPA

MRS REBECCA GIBBS, HILL FARM, LEWIS ROAD, RADFORD SEMELE, LEAMINGTON SPA CV31 1UX (01926 337571). Comfortable farmhouse with friendly atmosphere on a 350-acre mixed farm. Pretty bedrooms, some en suite, all facilities. Guests' bathroom, TV lounge, dining room. Children welcome. Bed and Breakfast. AA Award winner. Tourist Board 3 Crowns. Spacious 5 caravan site available.

STRATFORD-UPON-AVON

ALLORS, 62 EVESHAM ROAD, STRATFORD-UPON-AVON CV37 9BA (01789 269982). Comfortable en suite, centrally heated accommodation. All rooms have a private sitting area, colour TV and tea/coffee making facilities. Private parking. Bed and Breakfast from £17.00 per person. 3 night breaks £47.50 per person. Sorry, no smoking. Tourist Board Listed, RAC Listed.

CHADWYNS GUEST HOUSE, 6 BROAD WALK, STRATFORD-UPON-AVON CV37 6HS (01789 269077). Bed and Breakfast in a traditionally furnished Victorian house in the Old Town. Five minutes' walk from Theatre and centre. All rooms with H&C, colour TV, tea-making facilities. Some en suite. Terms from £13-£19. Well behaved dogs. Children half price (under 5 free).

COURTLAND HOTEL, 12 GUILD STREET, STRATFORD-UPON-AVON CV37 6RE (01789 292401). Town centre situation. Comfortable Georgian house, antique furniture. 4 minutes theatre. All rooms washbasin, tea/coffee, colour TV. Homemade preserves. £14-£25 per person. En-suite available. AA Listed. ETB 2 Crowns Approved. Recommended by Arthur Frommer.

MRS J. M. EVERETT, NEWBOLD NURSERIES, NEWBOLD-ON-STOUR, STRATFORD-UPON-AVON CV37 8DP (01789 450285). Small farm and hydroponic tomato nursery close to Stratford-upon-Avon, Warwick, Cotswolds and Blenheim. Comfortable rooms with colour TV, tea/coffee. Local pub serves evening meals at budget prices. En suite available. Bed and Breakfast from £14.50. Children half price.

MRS D. M. HALL, 'ACER HOUSE', 44 ALBANY ROAD, STRATFORD-UPON-AVON CV37 6PQ (01789 204962). Double, twin, family and single rooms. Bed and breakfast £13-£16 including tea/coffee making facilities. Central heating. Television lounge. Quiet. Central. Non-smoking. ETB registered.

WARWICK

MRS D. BROMILOW, WOODSIDE, LANGLEY ROAD, CLAVERDON, WARWICK CV35 8PJ (01926 84 2446). Country House in 22 acres woodland/garden. Cottage style with antiques & period furniture. Garden views and countryside outlook. Twin/double rooms £16 - £20 B&B. TV lounge, open log fire and video. Very central Stratford-upon-Avon, Warwick NEC, M40/42. ETB 1 Crown. AA Listed.

CAROLYN HOWARD, WILLOWBROOK FARMHOUSE, LIGHTHORNE ROAD, KINETON, NEAR WARWICK CV35 0JL (01926 640475). Very comfortable house and small farm in lovely countryside, handy for Warwick, Stratford, Cotswolds. 1 double en-suite, 1 double, 1 twin. Tea trays, antiques. Friendly, attentive service. Good local eating places. B&B from £15.00. 3½ miles Junction 12 M40. A non-smoking house. ETB 2 Crowns.

WEST MIDLANDS

Birmingham, Henley-in-Arden

Wake Green Lodge Hotel

Wakegreen Road, Moseley, Birmingham B13 9EZ
(0121-449 4499) RAC★ ETB

Located on B4217 close to M6, M5 and M42. Ten minutes city, International Conference Centre, Symphony Hall, National Indoor Arena, 20 minutes NEC. 8 bedrooms, most en suite with colour TV and tea/coffee making. Licensed bar, restaurant. Car park. Terms include Bed, Breakfast & VAT. Single from £20 to £25, Double from £30 to £35. Phone or write to Peter & Sheila Smith.

Mrs Kathleen Connolly

HOLLAND PARK FARM

BUCKLEY GREEN
HENLEY IN ARDEN, SOLIHULL,
WEST MIDLANDS B95 5QF
TEL: 01564 792625

A Georgian style farmhouse set in 300 acres of peaceful farmland. Livestock includes cattle, sheep and Irish Draught Horses. Large centrally heated ensuite bedrooms with colour TV and beverage facilities. Guest dining room and comfortable lounge with log fire. Ideally situated within easy reach of Birmingham International Airport, NEC, NAC, Stratford, Warwick and the Cotswolds.

West Midlands — Classified Advertisements

BIRMINGHAM

ANGELA AND IAN KERR, THE AWENTSBURY HOTEL, 21 SERPENTINE ROAD, SELLY PARK, BIRMINGHAM B29 7HU (0121 472 1258). Victorian Country House. Large gardens. All rooms have colour TV, telephones and tea/coffee making facilities. Some rooms en suite, some rooms with showers. All rooms central heating, washbasins. Near BBC Pebble Mill, transport, University, City centre. Bed and Breakfast from £25 Single Room, from £39 Twin Room, inclusive of VAT.

WILTSHIRE

Zeals

OAK COTTAGE RESTAURANT

Zeals (on A303)
Tel: 01747 840398

Small family-run Restaurant which offers comfortable overnight accommodation in the pretty village of Zeals. Residents' Lounge with TV. Full central heating. Bed & Breakfast or Half Board. Packed lunches available.

Wiltshire — Classified Advertisements

CALNE

MRS JOAN DURSTON, BELL HOUSE, CHERHILL, NEAR CALNE SN11 8UY (01249 813938). Converted coaching inn where Dickens' 'Pickwick Papers' is reputed to have been written. Overlooks Cherhill Downs and White Horse. Bedrooms blend antiques and modern furniture. Beverage facilities, colour TV. Cots, highchairs, babysitting. Licensed restaurant, evening meals, including Vegetarian, by arrangement. Bed and Breakfast from £16.

MAIDEN BRADLEY

PAULINE MARTIN, SOMERSET ARMS, CHURCH STREET, MAIDEN BRADLEY, WILTSHIRE BA12 7HW (01985 844207). Friendly village inn serving Wadworth real ales and home cooked country food. Open fires. Three large bedrooms. Two bars - one with pub games - barbecue and small dining room. Close to fine walking, Stourhead Gardens and Longleat.

SALISBURY

ALAN AND DAWN CURNOW, HAYBURN WYKE GUEST HOUSE, 72 CASTLE ROAD, SALISBURY SP1 3RL (01722 412627). Situated half-mile from the city centre, the Cathedral and Old Sarum and nine miles from Stonehenge. Some rooms en-suite, all with washbasin, TV and tea/coffee making facilities. Bed and Breakfast from £15.00. ETB One Crown. AA QQ, RAC listed.

WORCESTERSHIRE

Evesham, Malvern

EVESHAM
WATERSIDE HOTEL

Luxury Lodge rooms with bath ensuite.

£23 per person.

Only with this ad. Quote BBB23

Tel 01386-442420

LINDEN MANOR

& Victorian Restaurant

Colwall, Malvern, Worcestershire WR13 6PP

Tel and Fax: 01684 540231

A delightful Country Manor House situated on the western slopes of the MALVERN HILLS provides peace and tranquillity in 12 acres of park and woodland - tennis and croquet lawns. En suite accommodation with tea/coffee facilities and full central heating. Enjoy a candlelit meal in the Victorian Restaurant with excellent cuisine served by staff dressed in clothes of that era.

Single Room £30; Double/Twin from £27.50 per person;
Family from £80 per room for Bed and Full English Breakfast.

ROCK HOUSE

**144 West Malvern Road,
Malvern WR14 4NJ
Tel: 01684 574536**

COMMENDED

Attractive Victorian Guest House on Malvern Hills in quiet atmosphere with superb views. 10 comfortable bedrooms with H & C, Showers/Bathroom, most with view. TV lounge. Licensed. Delicious home cooking carefully prepared by Proprietress with Diplomas. Groups, Families & Pets welcome. Parking on Premises. From £17. Mid-week breaks available. Also pretty Self Catering Cottage.

SAE or phone Jean & John Mobbs

BURGAGE HOUSE

**4 College Precincts
Worcester WR1 2LG**

Comfortable Georgian house in cobbled street next to the Cathedral. Large relaxing rooms, all with TV. A hearty English or vegetarian Breakfast served in large dining room. Close by are the Royal Worcester Porcelain Works, the Commandery, cricket ground and river.

Bed and Breakfast from £17.00.

Tel: 01905 25396

**Mrs M Peters
Tytchney, Boreley,
Ombersley WR9 0HZ
Tel: 01905 620185**

16th century medieval Hall House cottage in peaceful country lane. 2 1/2 miles from Ombersley, ideal walking, touring Heart of England, fishing River Severn, 1/2 mile Ombersley Golf Course. Double, family and single rooms; cot available.

Bed and Breakfast from £13.50

Worcestershire — Classified Advertisements

BROADWAY

DES AND IRIS PORTER, PATHLOW HOUSE, 82 HIGH STREET, BROADWAY WR12 7AJ (01386 853444). A small comfortable and friendly family-run Guest House. All rooms en-suite with washbasins, tea/coffee making facilities and TV. Terms on request.

BROMSGROVE

"THE GRAHAMS", 95 OLD STATION ROAD, BROMSGROVE B60 2AF (01527 874463). ETB "Listed". Modern house in quiet pleasant location close to A38; 3 miles from M5, 1½ miles M42, within easy reach NEC/ICC, Worcester and Stratford. Tea/coffee facilities. TV lounge, car parking. Non smokers welcomed. £15 pppn. One twin, two single rooms.

WORCESTER

"ST. HELEN'S", GREEN HILL, LONDON ROAD, WORCESTER WR5 2AA (01905 354035). Good quality accommodation in beautiful Georgian rectory. Close to town centre. Car parking. TV lounge. Tea facilities. Airport collection/return. Single £20, double £30, family room £40.

EAST YORKSHIRE

East Yorkshire — Classified Advertisements

BEVERLEY

(01482 862752). Interesting Victorian house in quiet conservation area, yet only two minutes' walk from centre of charming historic market town. Home cooking. Wine cellar. Library. Children welcome. No smoking in bedrooms. Hull 7 miles, Humber Bridge 9 miles, easy run York 30 miles.

NORTH YORKSHIRE

Bedale, Filey

TOWN HEAD GUEST HOUSE

1 Low Lane, Grassington,
North Yorkshire BD23 5AU

COMMENDED

Our friendly, family-run Guest House stands at the head of this beautiful village, between the cobbled streets and the Moors. The ideal location for unspoilt walks and for touring the Dales. We offer comfortable accommodation: all rooms with colour TV and tea/coffee making, some with en suite facilities. Fire Certificate.

R&M Lister ***Tel: 01756 752811***

AA THE RICHMOND

56 Dragon View, Skipton Road
Harrogate Tel: 01423 530612

The Richmond Guest House is conveniently situated towards the end of the Stray. Close to the town centre and all amenities. All rooms have en suite facilities, colour television, tea/coffee making, clock/radio alarm and baby listening. Full Fire Certificate. Easy parking. Under the personal supervision of the resident proprietors, Chris and Kathryn Dale. Yorkshire & Humberside Tourist Board member. Access, Visa & American Express welcome.

VIVERS MILL

Mill Lane, Pickering
YO18 8DJ
Tel: 01751 473640
Stan & Hilary Langton

Ancient watermill in peaceful surroundings, excellent centre for exploring North Yorks Moors and Heritage Coast; historic York only 26 miles. Visitors are assured of a friendly welcome and nourishing, traditional food. Large lounge and six comfortable ensuite bedrooms. Tea/coffee making facilities. Bed and Breakfast from £22 per day, £135 per week. Reductions for family rooms. Pets welcome.

THE BRIDGE INN

GRINTON

Richmond, North Yorkshire DL11 6HH

In the National Park in glorious Swaledale, the Hotel is on the River Swale and has its own 1½ miles of private trout fishing. Spectacular views of the hills and moors. Some rooms en suite. Central heating throughout. Large car park. Pets welcome. Open all year. 2 crowns.

Tel: 01748 884224.

Good food and drink offered with traditional Yorkshire hospitality.
Proprietors: Trevor and Margaret Hird.

FLASK INN

Fylingdales, Robin Hood's Bay,
Whitby YO22 4QH
Tel: 01947 880305

A traditional 16th Century country Inn originally a monks' hostelry situated in the glorious North Yorkshire Moors National Park with panoramic views, overlooking Robin Hood's Bay. En suite bedrooms recently refurbished include TV and tea making facilities. Large car park.

WHEATCROFT MOTEL

156 Filey Road
Scarborough
YO11 3AA Tel: 01723 374613

Privately run, purpose built, modern motel which has a high reputation for cleanliness and standard of facilities. All rooms en suite with colour TV and tea/coffee facilities. Central heating. A substantial Continental breakfast is served directly into the rooms. Large private car park. Room and breakfast from £16.00. RAC Listed. Open most of the year.

THE TERRACE

69 Westborough, Scarborough
North Yorkshire YO11 1TS

THE TERRACE is a small family-run hotel situated between North and South Bays. Close to all Scarborough's many attractions, only a short walk from town centre, rail and bus stations.

We serve good home cooking in our pleasant dining room. Bedrooms are on 2 floors with bath/shower, toilet on each floor. Private Car Park; Licensed Bar; colour TV in all rooms. B&B £14.00 per day, B&B and EM £19.00. En suite £2.50pppn supplement.

Tel: 01723 374937

Wellgarth House

Wetherby Road, Rufforth,
York YO2 3QB
Tel: 01904 738592 or 738595

Most attractive detached house in delightful village, 5 minutes' drive from historic York. Ideal for touring moors, Dales and East Coast. All rooms have colour television, tea/coffee making, and ensuite facilities. Residents' lounge and dining room. Private parking.

Mrs Jackie Cundall

AA Listed

JUBILEE GUESTHOUSE

120 Haxby Road, York YO3 7JP
ETB AA QQQ

The Jubilee is situated 12 minutes' walk from York Minster and city centre. Our beautifully refurbished rooms offer CTV, tea and coffee tray, clock radio etc. Most rooms en suite. We have central heating, tourist information and a guests' car park. A bank, shops and launderette are close by.

B&B £14 to £19pp depending on room and season.

Tel: 01904 620566

Hobbits Hotel

9 ST. PETER'S GROVE, CLIFTON, YORK YO3 6AQ
TEL: 01904 624538
ETB Commended

Hobbits is a small, quiet and friendly hotel and only ten minutes' walk from York Minster. All bedrooms beautifully decorated and en suite, with TV, mini bars and tea/coffee making. Off street parking. Children welcomed. Great breakfasts - vegetarian or otherwise! Non smoking bedrooms.

£27 per person for B&B.

Pauleda House Hotel

123 Clifton, York YO3 6BL
Tel & Fax: 01904 621327

Enjoy superb accommodation centrally situated only minutes away from all the historic attractions. A warm and friendly welcome awaits you at Pauleda, a small family run hotel offering excellent value for money. All rooms are en suite and tastefully equipped, some with four-poster, colour television with satellite, tea/coffee tray, etc. Car park. Reduced rates for weekly bookings. Free bottle of house wine per couple with your first evening meal. Bed and Breakfast from £16.00 to £25.00. Dinner, Bed and Breakfast from £27.00 to £36.00.

Clifton Green Hotel

8 Clifton Green, York YO3 6LH
Tel: 01904 623597

Small elegant hotel privately owned and managed. Attractive location overlooking Clifton Green, just ten minutes' walk city centre and York Minster. Spacious bedrooms, some with en-suite bathrooms and all with colour TV and heating.

Private car parking

Proprietor: D. G. Tree

Off the beaten track . . . yet only 4½ miles from the City . . . alongside the River Ouse . . . right at the heart of Yorkshire.

The Manor

Country Guest House

Acaster Malbis York YO2 1UL
Tel: York (01904) 706723
Fax: York (01904) 706723

Atmospheric Manor in rural tranquillity with own private lake set in 5½ acres of beautiful mature grounds. Preservation orders on all trees with abundant bird life. Fish in the Lake, cycle or walk, bring your own boat for river cruising. Close to Racecourse and only 10 minutes' car journey from the city or take the leisurely river bus (Easter to October). Conveniently situated to take advantage of the Dales, Moors, Wolds, and splendid coastline.

Find us via A64 exiting for Copmanthorpe-York, Thirsk- Harrogate or Bishopthorpe (Sim Balk Lane).

Centrally heated. 10 ensuite bedrooms with direct dial telephone, hairdryer, TV and courtesy tray. Dining room with open coal fire. Licensed - optional evening meal. B&B from £19 to £26 per person per night.

For details,
SAE or telephone
Susan Viscovich

AWARDED ETB

Easton's

Fine Period Bed & Breakfast

90 BISHOPTHORPE ROAD,
YORK, YO2 1JS

Telephone 01904 626646

RAC ACCLAIMED

Bed & Breakfast of the Year Runner-up 1994

Centrally situated just 250 yards from the City Walls, you can leave the car here and explore York at leisure. The period furniture, William Morris decor and open fires are in accord with the gracious Victorian character of the building and with the standard of excellence the owners strive for. Individually designed en-suite and standard bedrooms benefit from colour TV, clock radios and tea/coffee making facilities alongside personal touches such as toiletries. Breakfast, chosen from the 'Victorian Sideboard' menu, only adds to the atmosphere and includes traditional and vegetarian dishes. Easton's is non-smoking and has a private car park. Bed & Breakfast from £15.00 to £21.50 per person per night, with reduced rates for children and 'Winter Warmer' Breaks. Brochure available on request.

BLOOMSBURY HOTEL

ETB
AA QQQ
RAC Listed

127 Clifton, York YO3 6BL

Situated in the ideal central location for your visit to York. This fine Victorian Town House offers warm comfortable hospitality with adequate car parking. All rooms have en suite facilities, TV and hospitality trays in a no-smoking environment.

Tel: 01904 634031

AVIEMORE HOUSE HOTEL

Mr and Mrs Steele

78 Stockton Lane, York YO3 0BS

Tel: 01904 425556

An Edwardian house situated on the East side of the city, now a small comfortable, friendly family-run hotel. All rooms have colour TV, tea/coffee making facilities, hairdryers, clock radios. All are en suite. Residents' lounge * Private Parking * Fire Certificate * RAC Acclaimed * Bed and full English Breakfast £18-£24, single, £18-£25 double/twin per person per night. Reduced rates for children. Special Autumn and Spring Breaks available from £32 for Bed and Breakfast; Minimum of two nights.

Mont-Clare Guest House

32 CLAREMONT TERRACE, GILLYGATE, YORK YO3 7EJ

RESERVATIONS TEL: 01904 627054 AND FAX: 01904 651011

Take advantage and enjoy the convenience of City Centre accommodation in a quiet location close to the magnificent York Minster. A warm and friendly welcome awaits you at the Mont-Clare. All rooms are tastefully decorated, en-suite and have colour TV with Satellite, Radio Alarm, Telephone, Hairdryer, Tea/Coffee Tray, Shoe Cleaning etc. All of York's attractions are within walking distance and we are ideally situated for the Dales, Yorkshire Moors and numerous Stately Homes. Fire and Hygiene Certificates. Cleanliness, good food, pleasant surroundings and friendliness are our priorities. Open all year. Private Car Park. B/B from £16.00 per person per night. **Reduced** rates for weekly stay.

Valley View Farm

Old Byland, Helmsley, York YO6 5LG

Tel: 01439 798221

A working farm on the edge of a small village within the North York Moors National Park, with outstanding views across beautiful countryside. Four en suite rooms with tea/coffee facilities, colour TV and central heating. Residents' lounge furnished traditionally with open fires and your comfort always in mind. Excellent walking country. Open all year.

Highly Commended **B&B from £25; D,B&B from £37**

ETB ♛♛♛

INGLEWOOD GUEST HOUSE

7 Clifton Green, York YO3 6LH
Tel: 01904 653523

Relax and make yourself at home in this delightful Guest House, renowned for its warm and friendly atmosphere. All the comfortable bedrooms have TV and some have en-suite facilities. Central heating. Pleasant dining room. Parking. Reduced rates for children. Open all year for Bed and Breakfast - details on request.

"Chimneys"

18 Bootham Crescent, York YO3 7AH
Tel: (01904) 644334

Bed & Breakfast is offered in this beautifully decorated house less than 5 minutes' walk from the historic City Walls. All bedrooms have colour TV, tea/coffee facilities etc, and ground floor accommodation is available. Relax and enjoy Breakfast in our olde-worlde dining room before embarking on your day's sightseeing in historic York. We guarantee you a wonderful Yorkshire welcome! **MRS SANDRA HARE**

ORILLIA HOUSE

89 The Village, Stockton-on-Forest, York YO3 9UP
Tel: 01904 400600 Or 01904 738595

A warm welcome awaits you at Orillia House, conveniently situated in the centre of the village 3 miles north-east of York, one mile from the A64. The house dates back to the 17th century and has been restored to offer a high standard of comfort with modern facilities, yet retaining its original charm and character. All rooms have private facilities, colour TV and tea/coffee making. Our local pub provides excellent evening meals. We have our own private car park. ETB ♛♛

Bed and Breakfast from £16. Telephone for brochure or write.

♛ ETB

MRS D. TINDALL

NEWTON GUEST HOUSE

Neville Street, Haxby Road, York YO3 7NP
Tel: (01904) 635627

John and Diana offer a warm, friendly welcome to their home, 10 minutes' walk from city centre. Central heating, tea and coffee making facilities, colour TV, private showers. All rooms private facilities.
* Choice of Breakfast * Private Parking * Fire Certificate
* Personal attention * **Non-smokers only please**
Ideal base for touring Dales and Moors

IVY HOUSE FARM

Kexby, York YO4 5LQ
Tel: 01904 489368
Mrs K.R. Daniel

Bed and breakfast on a mixed dairy farm six miles from the ancient city of York on the A1079. Central for the east coast, Herriot country and Dales. We offer a friendly service with comfortable accommodation consisting of double or family rooms all with colour TV and tea/coffee making facilities. We provide a full farmhouse English Breakfast served in separate dining room; colour TV lounge. Ample car parking with play area for children, who are most welcome. We are within easy reach of local restaurants and public houses serving excellent evening meals. AA and RAC Listed. B&B from £14.00 per night.

The Green ♛ Guest House

31 Bewlay Street, Bishopthorpe Road, York YO2 1JT
Tel: 01904 652509

Norma and Ted welcome you to their small non-smoking Guest House and offer you a Full English or Vegetarian Breakfast. Open all year with en suite rooms available. Colour TV and hospitality trays in all rooms. Only 10 minutes' walk to city centre. Evening Meal on request. Children welcome at reduced. rate. Bargain Breaks from October to March. A warm welcome awaits you with tea and biscuits on arrival. Bed and Breakfast from £15.

Proprietors: Norma and Ted Long

North Yorkshire — Classified Advertisements

BEDALE

BOBBIES XVII CENTURY COTTAGE B&B, AISKEW, BEDALE DL8 1DD (01677 423385). Charming beamed Cottage with pretty cottage gardens and car park. All rooms have washbasins, tea/coffee making, razor points, TV, central heating. Friendly atmosphere. From £15 per person. Personal attention.

GREWELTHORPE

MRS DOROTHY BARKER, HIGH BRAMLEY GRANGE, GREWELTHORPE, RIPON HG4 3DH (01765 658349). 18th century farmhouse on 100-acre dairy farm, 9 miles from Ripon. One double, one family room; sitting room, dining room; bathroom, two toilets; colour television; central heating. No pets. Parking space. Bed and Breakfast from £12.

HARROGATE

MRS A. WOOD, FIELD HOUSE, CLINT, HEAR HARROGATE HG3 3DS (01423 770638). Peaceful position, overlooking Nidd Valley. Ideal for Moors, Dales, market towns, historic buildings. One twin, one double bedrooms with washbasins. Private bathroom. Sitting room with TV and tea-making facilities. Bed and Breakfast from £12.50. Evening Meal readily available.

MRS JOYNER, 90 KINGS ROAD, HARROGATE HG1 5JX (01423 503087). Near all amenities. Valley Gardens, Conference Centre, Dales. Comfortable. Home cooking. Separate lounge, dining room. Colour TV in all rooms. Bed and Breakfast. Dinner if required. Centrally heated. Washbasins. Tea and coffee in all rooms. En suite rooms. AA QQQ, RAC Listed. Two Crowns Commended. Well recommended. FHG Diploma Winners.

PETER AND PENNY BELL, DENE COURT GUEST HOUSE, 22 FRANKLIN ROAD, HARROGATE HG1 5EE (01423 509498). Friendly family-run Guest House, close to Town Centre, Valley Gardens, Conference Centre and Exhibition Halls. Six bedrooms, tea/coffee making facilities. TV lounge, dining room. Bed and good Breakfast from £15. Evening Meals by arrangement. Reductions for children. ETB registered.

INGLETON

MRS MOLLIE BELL, 'LANGBER COUNTRY GUEST HOUSE'. INGLETON (VIA CARNFORTH) LA6 3DT (015242 41587). Good centre for Dales, Lakes and coast. Comfortable accommodation; home cooking, friendly personal service. Value for money. Ideal for families. Bed and Breakfast; Evening Meal optional. AA, RAC Listed.

KNARESBOROUGH

MR O'DOWD, MITRE HOTEL, STATION ROAD, KNARESBOROUGH HG5 9AA (01423 863589). Two minutes' walk to pretty market square, castle and beautiful river gorge. We offer facilities for families and business people. All bedrooms en suite and a menu to suit all. Harrogate 2 miles, York 15 miles. On edge of Yorkshire Dales.

LEEMING BAR

THE WHITE ROSE HOTEL, LEEMING BAR, NORTHALLERTON DL7 9AY (01677 422707/424941; Fax: 01677 425123). Eighteen bedrooms, 2 star private hotel situated in village on A684 half mile from A1 Motorway. Ideal base for touring North Yorks Moors, Dales and Coastal resorts. Three Crowns Commended.

MALTON

MRS ANN HOPKINSON, THE BROW, 25 YORK ROAD, MALTON YO17 0AX (01653 693402). Large Georgian house with spectacular view over the River Derwent and the Wolds. Convenient for York, Castle Howard, North Yorks Moors, Pickering steam railway and Flamingoland. Guests often return here so they must be very satisfied! Ample car parking space. ETB and YHTB Registered.

NORTHALLERTON

MRS D HODGSON, LITTLE HOLTBY, LEEMING BAR, NORTHALLERTON DL7 9LH (01609 748762). Period farmhouse at gateway to Yorkshire Dales, just 100 yards off A1 Retains original character with open fires and original beams in many rooms. All bedrooms with colour TV, tea/coffee; some en suite. Bed and Breakfast from £17.50; Evening Meal available. 2 Crowns Highly Commended.

PATELEY BRIDGE

MRS J. LUBECK, WINDY NOOK, WATH, PATELEY BRIDGE HG3 5PL (01423 711088). Oak-beamed cottage in peaceful village; panoramic views. Excellent touring and walking country (by Nidderdale Way). Lounge, double/single bedrooms. Bed and Breakfast from £12.

RICHMOND

MRS D. WARDLE, GREENBANK FARM, RAVENSWORTH, RICHMOND DL11 7HB (01325 718334). 4 miles west of Scotch Corner, within easy reach of Dales, Lake District. One double room en suite, one twin and one single, all with washbasins, tea/coffee facilities. Children welcome, play area. Sorry, no pets. B&B from £11.50, Evening Meal available.

HOLMEDALE, DALTON, RICHMOND DL11 7HX (01833 621236). A Georgian house in a quiet village midway between Richmond and Barnard Castle. Personal attention with good home cooking. Central heating, open fires. Washbasins in both rooms. Bed and breakfast from £12.50; Bed, Breakfast and Evening Meal from £20. Single room from £15. ETB 1 Crown Commended.

ROBIN HOOD'S BAY

MRS M. NOBLE, MINGO COTTAGE, FYLINGTHORPE, ROBIN HOOD'S BAY, WHITBY YO22 4TZ (01947 880219). Bed and Breakfast in charming 17th Century cottage in picturesque village. Central heating. TV lounge.

THORNTON-LE-DALE

MRS S WARDELL, TANGALWOOD, ROXBY ROAD, THORNTON-LE-DALE, PICKERING YO18 7SX (01751 474688). A warm welcome awaits all guests and clean, comfortable accommodation, with good food provided. Two double rooms, (one en-suite available, all with TV and tea-making facilities. Private Parking. Easy access coast, moors, NYM railway, Heartbeat country. From £12.50. ETB registered.

YORK

BRIAN & CAROL DAVIES, BIRCHFIELD GUEST HOUSE, 2 NUNTHORPE AVENUE, YORK YO2 1PF (01904 636395). Delightful, family-run, unspoiled Victorian house. Just 10 minutes' walk from city centre, railway station, racecourse and Minster. TV, tea and coffee all rooms. Super English Breakfast, alternative diets catered for on request. Bed and Breakfast from £12. See you!

MRS R FOSTER, BROOKLAND HOUSE, HULL ROAD, DUNNINGTON, YORK YO1 5LW (01904 489548). York - east on A1079 four miles (after turn-off to Dunnington village). A warm welcome, good facilities. Superb Yorkshire breakfast. Private parking. From £13, reductions children. Local Pub (5 minutes' walk) serves Evening Meals.

MR ROY DODD, CHARLTON HOUSE, 1 CHARLTON STREET, BISHOPTHORPE ROAD, YORK YO2 1JN (01904 626961). Double/family en-suite rooms with TV, tea/coffee facilities. Easy walking distance from city centre, racecourse, museums etc. Ground floor accommodation. Parking facilities. Bed and Breakfast from £15 per person.

MRS S. STURDY, GLENVILLE GUEST HOUSE, 132 EAST PARADE, HEWORTH, YORK YO3 7YG (01904 425370). Warm, friendly accommodation. Quietly situated. University nearby. Minster and City Centre 12 minutes' walk. Good English Breakfast. From £14. Y&HTB 2 Crowns.

MRS PEARL COOK, BEECH CROFT, WHITWELL-ON-THE-HILL, YORK YO6 7JJ (01653 618207). Old stone Cottage in quiet Country Village. Ideally situated for Castle Howard, York, Moors and coast. Twin and double rooms. Non-smokers only please. Bed and Breakfast from £13.

BOOTHAM PARK HOTEL, 9 GROSVENOR TERRACE, YORK YO3 7AG (01904 644262). Brian & Viv Baker extend a warm welcome to their Victorian town house just five minutes from the city centre. All rooms en suite with CTV, hairdryers, welcome trays, telephones, etc. Generous choice of breakfasts, also freshly cooked evening meals by request. Three Crowns.

SOUTH YORKSHIRE

South Yorkshire — Classified Advertisements

SHEFFIELD

MILLINGTONS PRIVATE GUEST HOUSE, 70 BROOMGROVE ROAD, SHEFFIELD S10 2NA (01742 669549). Small, friendly guest house, approximately one mile city centre. All rooms H&C (some with shower or toilet en-suite), central heating, tea/coffee making, colour TV. Full English breakfast. Easy reach Peak District National Park. Near Universities, Hallamshire Hospital. B&B single from £23, double from £39. AA QQQ, RAC.

WEST YORKSHIRE

West Yorkshire — Classified Advertisements

HAWORTH

BRIDGE HOUSE PRIVATE HOTEL, BRIDGEHOUSE LANE, HAWORTH BD22 8PA (HAWORTH (01535) 642372). Small family-run Licensed Hotel. Formerly mill owner's Georgian residence situated in the famous tourist village of Haworth, home of the Brontës. Close to Keighley and Worth Valley railway. Parking available.

ILKLEY

MRS S. READ, 126 SKIPTON ROAD, ILKLEY LS29 9BQ (01943 600635). House overlooks beautiful Wharfe Valley. Ideal centre for touring Yorkshire Dales. One twin-bedded room with en suite bathroom. Parking. TV. Non-smoking. Bed and Breakfast from £16.50.

PONTEFRACT

MRS I. GOODWORTH, THE CORNER CAFE, WENTBRIDGE, PONTEFRACT WF8 3JJ (01977 620316). A 16th century Cottage, with car park, in lovely village where Evening Meals are available from Inn and restaurant. Guests are accommodated in 2 single rooms, 2 family rooms en suite, one double and one twin (with bathroom). All with washbasins, TV, teamaking. Terms from £16. Listed.

WETHERBY

SHEILA SMITH, MUDDY LANE, GLENDALES, LINTON, NEAR WETHERBY LS22 4HW (01937 585915). Glendales is a lovely detached house overlooking village green. In a country setting yet you are still only 10 minutes from A1. Halfway between London and Edinburgh. 20 minutes Leeds, York and Harrogate. NO SMOKING. Two Crowns.

FHG DIPLOMA WINNERS 1994

Each year we award a small number of diplomas to holiday proprietors whose services have been specially commended by our readers and the following advertisers were our FHG Diploma winners for 1994.

ENGLAND

Mrs Judith Goddard, Cherry Tree Villa, 7 Newbridge Hill, Bath, Avon
Mrs S. Briggs, High Wray Farm, High Wray, Ambleside, Cumbria
Mr & Mrs F. Cervetti, Lightwood Farmhouse, Bowland Bridge, Cumbria
Mrs Jenny Fox, Highstead Farm, Bucks Cross, Near Bideford, Devon
Mrs B. Williams, Abbots Court, Church End, Twyning, Gloucestershire
Mr & Mrs Hayward, Castlemere Hotel, 13 Shaftesbury Avenue, Blackpool
Mrs Wainwright, Homestead House, 5 Ashley Road, Medbourne, Leics
Mrs Sheila Potts, Aydon, 1 Osborne Avenue, Hexham, Northumberland
Mr & Mrs B. Joyner, Anro, 90 Kings Road, Harrogate, N. Yorks

SCOTLAND

Mr & Mrs I. Weir, Appin Holiday Homes, Appin, Argyll

WALES

Mrs J.E. Thorn, The Grange, Penrose, Raglan, Gwent

WALES

ANGLESEY

Anglesey — Classified Advertisements

BRYNSIENCYN

MRS M. E. WILLIAMS, TYDDYN GOBLET, BRYNSIENCYN (01248 430296). Character farmhouse set back 200 yards from A4080 Newborough Road. Ground floor en-suite bedrooms, colour TV, tea-making facilities. Full central heating. B&B £14-16 per night. Evening dinner optional. Brochure. Two Crowns Highly Commended.

CLWYD

Rhos-on-Sea

SUNNYDOWNS HOTEL

66 ABBEY ROAD, RHOS-ON-SEA, NEAR LLANDUDNO LL28 4NU
TEL: 01492 544256 FAX: 01492 543223
Proprietors: Mr & Mrs Mike Willington

A 4 crown family-run hotel just 2 minutes' walk to beach & shops. All rooms en suite with colour TV, video & satellite channels, tea/coffee facilities, mini bar and central heating. The hotel has a bar, pool room, restaurant and sauna. Only five minute's drive to Llandudno & Colwyn Bay, and ten minutes' to the mountains and castles of Snowdonia.

Open all year **Telephone for brochure**

DYFED

Llanelli

Jackie & John Rawlings

DAN-Y-CWARRE FARM
FIVE ROADS, LLANELLI SA15 5JA
TEL: 01269 860187

Enjoy a genuine WELSH Farm Holiday in a 200-year-old Farmhouse with superb views across CARMARTHEN BAY. Ideal centre for touring: Gower, Brecon Beacons & Pembrokeshire easily accessible; fine beaches; SWANSEA with its many attractions, Marina, leisure centres etc. All guest bedrooms have private bathrooms and tea making facilities. Lounge with TV. Children welcome; highchair, babysitting; family horse for children to ride. Open all year for Bed and Breakfast.

£15 PER PERSON PER NIGHT

Write or phone for further information.

Dyfed — Classified Advertisements

GLYNARTHEN

MRS KATHLEEN DRAPER, RAINBOW FOUNTAIN RESTAURANT, HENDRAWS FARM, RHYDLEWIS, LLANDYSUL SA44 5QR (01239 851 345). Homely Guest House. Licensed restaurant, home-cooked food. All rooms en suite, colour TV, tea/coffee facilities. Near beaches. Open all year. Bed and Breakfast £16 per person per night.

HAVERFORDWEST

MRS C. DI SANDOLO, VILLA HOUSE, ST THOMAS GREEN, HAVERFORDWEST SA61 1QN (01437 762977). A warm welcome given to all our visitors at this Tourist Board Listed Guest House. English and Italian meals catered for. Beaches and coastal paths nearby; five minutes' walk to town centre. B&B from £14.

NARBERTH

MRS N. JONES, HIGHLAND GRANGE FARM, ROBESTON WATHEN, NARBERTH SA67 8EP. (Tel and Fax: 01834 860952). Lovely family home centrally situated on A40 amidst beautiful countryside. Ground floor accommodation. Guest lounge. Ideal for touring; extensive information and helpful host. Country Inn 200 yards; beach 7 miles. Two Crowns.

PONTRHYDFENDIGAID

MRS W. HARRIS, "HEDDLE", PONTRHYDFENDIGAID, YSTRAD MEURIG SY25 6EF (01974 831686). A warm welcome awaits you in Red Kite country between Devil's Bridge and Tregaron. Three double/twin rooms with washbasins, tea/coffee making facilities. Non-smoking. Good home cooking; vegetarians catered for. Dogs welcome. B&B £15, Evening Meal (by arrangement) £8.

PUNCHESTON

MRS B. DEVONALD, PENYGRAIG, PUNCHESTON, HAVERFORDWEST SA62 5RJ (Tel/Fax: 01348 881277). Working farm at foot of Preseli Hills. Ideal base for North Pembrokeshire; coast 8 miles. Spacious rooms: one double en suite, one family room. Tea trays. Two Crowns Highly Commended.

ST DAVID'S

Y-GORLAN GUEST HOUSE, 77 NUN STREET, ST DAVID'S, HAVERFORDWEST SA62 6NU (Tel and Fax: 01437 720837). Relax in a warm and friendly atmosphere in a family-run guest house. Comfortable lounge with colour TV. All rooms with tea/coffee facilities, hairdryer, radio, and colour TV. Two miles from sandy beaches and golf course; ideal base for walkers. Licensed. Open all year. Tourist Board Listed "Commended".

SOUTH GLAMORGAN

South Glamorgan — Classified Advertisements

CARDIFF

AUSTINS HOTEL, 11 COLDSTREAM TERRACE, CARDIFF CF1 8LJ (01222 377148). In the centre of Cardiff, 300 yards from the castle, 5 single and 6 twin bedrooms, 5 with full en suite facilities. All have washbasins, tea and coffee, colour TV. Full English Breakfast. Bus and train station 10 minutes' walk. Fire certificate. Warm welcome offered to all nationalities. WTB 2 Crowns.

GWENT

Monmouth, Newport

Tresco Guest House
Redbrook, Nr. Monmouth, Gwent
Situated in the Wye Valley in Wales. Near the River Wye. Drying facilities. Wye salmon and other evening meals available. Packed lunches. Special rates for children. Ground floor bedrooms have views of flower gardens. Ample parking.
Bed & Breakfast from £13.50
Tel: 01600 712325

Church Farm Guest House
Mitchel Troy, Monmouth, Gwent NP5 4HZ
A 16th century former farmhouse with oak beams and inglenook fireplaces. Large attractive garden with stream. Easy access to A40; Monmouth 2 miles.
**Open all year * Central Heating **
**Large Car Park * Some en suite bedrooms **
Bed and Breakfast from £16.50 to £19.00
WTB Commended
Rosemary and Derek Ringer Tel: 01600 712176

BRICK HOUSE COUNTRY GUEST HOUSE
Situated 3 miles off M4 motorway Exit 23
Large Georgian Country Guest House. Ideal centre for touring the Wye Valley and South Wales. Every comfort. All rooms with central heating and en suite bathrooms. Open all year. Bed and Breakfast from £19.50 per person. Evening Meal (optional) from £9.50.
Mr C.T. Park, Brick House Country Guest House, Redwick, Near Newport, Gwent NP6 3DX
Tel: (01633) 880230

Good Hotel Guide
WEST USK LIGHTHOUSE
St Brides, Near Newport, Gwent NP1 9SF
Tel: (01633) 810126/815860
Unique opportunity to stay in a 170-year-old Lighthouse converted to a superb Guest House. Facilities include waterbed, four-poster bed in wedge-shaped en suite rooms; colour TV, tea/coffee making. Relaxation floating, aromatherapy and champagne breakfast available to make up an unforgettable short break. 3 miles Newport and 10 miles Cardiff. Exit Junct. 28 M4. From £22 nightly. Full tariff on request.

GWYNEDD

Aberdaron, Betws Garmon

BRYN MOR
Aberdaron, Gwynedd LL53 8BS
Tel: 0175-886 344
BRYN MOR GUEST HOUSE stands in its own grounds in the village of Aberdaron at the tip of the Lleyn Peninsula, with panoramic views of the Bay. Beautiful walks, fishing, golf, sailing and riding in the area. Comfortable rooms, access at all times. Lounge and separate dining room. Bathroom and shower facilities. Bed and full English Breakfast £14.50; Bed, Breakfast and Evening Meal £21.00. Reduced rates for children, but sorry, no pets.
Contact **Mrs V. Bate** for details.

Beautiful Snowdonia
PLAS-Y-COED HOTEL
Betws Garmon, Gwynedd LL54 7YR
Telephone for brochure (01286) 650284
Mountain-side fully licensed hotel, standing in 11 acres of wooded grounds, and with superb views over the valley. Spacious family and en-suite rooms, all with tea/coffee facilities. Bar meals are served all day, and you can be sure of a friendly atmosphere.
B & B from £15.00. Also self-catering garden flat available. Sleeps 5. Pets welcome.

Sunray
(GUEST HOUSE)
THE QUAY, BARMOUTH
GWYNEDD . LL42 1ET
Telephone: 01341 280985

All rooms high standard

• En suite • Ground floor • Central Heating •
Self contained • Private parking •

Fabulous harbour and sea views; short level walk to all amenities

Superb Accommodation at B&B Rates

Danny & Roe Brooks

BRON CELYN GUEST HOUSE

Llanrwst Road, Betws-y-Coed,
Gwynedd, North Wales LL24 0HD
Phone (01690) 710333

HIGHLY COMMENDED

A warm welcome awaits at this delightful Guest House overlooking the Gwydyr Forest, Llugwy/Conwy Valleys and village of Betws-y-Coed in Snowdonia National Park. Ideal for touring, walking, climbing, fishing, golf. Excellent overnight stop en route to Holyhead ferries. Easy walk to village and close to Conwy/Swallow Falls and Fairy Glen.
Lovely house, most rooms en-suite, all with colour TV and beverage makers. Central heating. Lounge. Garden. Car Park. Full hearty breakfast, Packed Meals, Snacks, Evening Meals. Special Diets catered for. Open all year.

Terms from £16-£19, reduced rates for children under 12 years.

White Lodge Hotel

Central Promenade, Llandudno LL30 1AT
Tel: 01492 877713

AA★★ WTB Highly Commended RAC ★★
Have a holiday to remember at the family-run WHITE LODGE HOTEL, set on the Promenade in beautiful Llandudno. Comfortable Lounge with Bay views, dining room with separate tables and superb food from our Chef. All rooms en-suite with colour TV and tea-making facilities. Central heating. Parking for all guests' cars.
THE PERFECT BASE FOR TOURING SCENIC SNOWDONIA!

OLD SCHOOL

Hen Ysgol, Bwich Derwin, Pant Glas, Garndolbenmaen Gwynedd LL51 9EQ

Peaceful, rural school between Porthmadog and Caemarvon. Central for outdoor activities, Snowdonia and Lleyn Peninsula with railways, castles and beaches. Golf and fishing within easy reach. Open all year with access at all times. Most rooms on ground floor, providing easy access for disabled visitors, and centrally heated, with drinks facilities. Family room en suite. Babies and pets welcome. Good home cooking; full hearty breakfast; evening meal optional. Vegetarians catered for. Local information available, plus babysitting and laundry services. Bed & Breakfast from £13.
Also: self catering bunkhouse.

Terry and Joan Gibbins 01286 660701 WTB

Highly Commended

Hên - Dy Hotel

10 North Parade, Llandudno, Gwynedd LL30 2LP
Telephone: (01492) 876184

CHARLES & IRENE WATTS welcome you to Hên-Dy Hotel, on the promenade, opposite the Pier, with panoramic views over the Bay. Bedrooms have radio, TV, teamakers, central heating; some ensuite. Shops, Happy Valley, Dry Ski Slope, Haulfre Gardens, Tram & Cable Car to Great Orme Summit are close by. Enjoy the Chef/Proprietor's menu and the cosy residential Bar.
Your comfort and enjoyment is our priority. Pets by arrangement.

TARIFF FROM £17.50-£27.00 PER NIGHT

Gwynedd — Classified Advertisements

BETWS-Y-COED

ROY AND BETTY LAMPARD, GLAN LLUGWY, HOLYHEAD ROAD, BETWS-Y-COED LL24 0BN (01690 710592). On A5, central for Snowdonia and coast. Central heating, showers. Fire Certificate. All rooms washbasins, colour TV, tea-making facilities. WTB One Crown.

CRICCIETH

MRS A. REYNOLDS, GLYN Y COED HOTEL, PORTMADOC ROAD, CRICCIETH LL52 0HL (01766 522870; Fax: 01766 523341). Lovely Victorian house, centrally situated. En suite bedrooms, colour TV, full central heating, tea-making facilities. Parking. Licensed. Recommended home cooking. Children welcome. Moderate rates. Brochure. 3 Crowns Highly Commended. Also self-catering house, sleeps 8, with ground floor bedroom.

FFESTINIOG

MORANNEDD GUEST HOUSE, FFESTINGIOG LL41 4LG (01766 762734). Snowdonia Guest House with mountain views, log fires, home-cooked food including vegetarian and breakfast choices. Most of our five bedrooms are en suite; all have tea-making facilities. Ideal for walking, beaches, tourist attractions, including slate caverns, Portmeirion, Ffestiniog Railway.

LLANDUDNO

MRS T. WILLIAMS, ROSELEA, DEGANWY AVENUE, LLANDUDNO (01492 876279). Comfortable Bed and Breakfast. Few minutes sea-front and near ski slopes. TV lounge. Car park. All amenities. Well situated for touring and sightseeing. B&B from £13.

MRS R. HODKINSON, CRANLEIGH, GREAT ORME'S ROAD, WEST SHORE, LLANDUDNO LL30 2AR (01492 877688). A comfortable, late Victorian private residence and family home situated on the quiet West Shore of Llandudno. Only yards from the Beach and magnificant Great Orme mountain. Parking no problem. Two en-suite rooms available. Conforms to S.I. 1991/474. Highly Recommended.

LLANWNDA

MRS E. L. THOMAS, 'MOROGORO', DINAS, LLANWNDA, NEAR CAERNARFON LL54 5UB (01286 830 498). Two large double bedrooms, + extra camp bed; washbasins, shaving points; guests' bathroom; ample parking. Close to lovely beaches, Snowdonia; Caernarfon two miles. B&B £16 per night, reductions weekly bookings.

PWLLHELI

PENARWEL HOUSE, LLANDEDROG, PWLLHELI LL53 7NN (Tel/Fax; 01758 740719). Beautiful large castellated country mansion privately set in five acres of lovely woodland gardens. Relax in comfort. Oak-panelled public rooms; all bedrooms en suite, with colour TV, tea/coffee making facilities. Licensed. Near sea; outdoor swimming pool. Also cottage and caravan.

POWYS

Brecon, Crickhowell, Builth Wells

Lower Rhydness Bungalow

Llyswen, Brecon LD3 0AZ
Tel: 01874 754264

Set on a 150 acre farm carrying beef cows and sheep, Lower Rhydness Bungalow is very comfortable, fully centrally heated, with views across open fields to Wye Valley. Accommodation in two bedrooms, one with a single bed and the other with a double and a single beds; both rooms have washbasins and are close to bathroom with shower. Colour TV in lounge. Home produce served in season. Bed, Breakfast and Evening Meal or Bed and Breakfast only. SAE for Brochure from MRS M.E. WILLIAMS

WHITE HALL

Glangrwyney, Crickhowell NP8 1EW
Tel: 01873 811155 or 840267

Comfortably furnished and well placed for Brecon Beacons National Park and Big Pit Mine. Bed and Breakfast with TV and tea making from £15 per person, some en suite. Small single room £13. Reduced rates for three nights. Evening Meals available locally.

WTB

HALCYON HOUSE

Cilmery, Builth Wells LD2 3NU
Tel: (01982) 552838 or (0831) 101052

Enjoy the relaxed ambience of Halcyon House, ideally situated for touring the 'secret' heart of Wales. Panoramic southerly views. All bedrooms have colour TV, tea/coffee making and central heating. Billiard room. Shower and jacuzzi bathrooms. Conference facility for 30. Dormitory accommodation available. Adjacent inn/restaurant. Nearby golf, fishing, riding, bowls, tennis, swimming, theatre and sports centre. Visit the Brecon Beacons, Cardiff, Hereford, Hay-on-Wye and Worcester. Close to railway and bus stations. Bed and Breakfast from £16.

Powys — Classified Advertisements

NEWTOWN

MRS V. J. MADELEY, GREENFIELDS, KERRY, NEWTOWN SY16 4LH (01686 670596; Fax: 01686 670354). Comfortable Guest House situated east of the village of Kerry on A489. Washbasins, shaving points, tea/coffee making facilities, heating all rooms. TV lounge with open fire. Good base for exploring mid-Wales and the Borderlands. Ample off-road parking. One Crown.

NOTE: All the information in this book is given in good faith in the belief that it is correct. However, the publishers cannot guarantee the facts given in these pages, neither can they accept responsibility for errors or omissions or matters arising therefrom. Readers should always satisfy themselves that the facilities are available and that the terms, if quoted, still apply.

SCOTLAND

BORDERS

Borders — Classified Advertisements

GALASHIELS (SELKIRKSHIRE)

DIANA FINDLAY, WHEATLANDS HOUSE, LEE BRAE, GALASHIELS TD1 1QR (01896 753068; Fax: 01896 755536). Victorian mill owner's residence with many original features. Central for exploring beautiful Border region - only 33 miles from Edinburgh. Car parking. TV lounge. Coffee/tea facilities. Listed 'Commended'.

MRS I. BROWN, ISLAND HOUSE, ISLAND STREET, GALASHIELS TD1 1PA (01896 752649). Small friendly guest house. Comfortable accommodation in centre of town. Ideal for exploring Borders. One en suite room and two twin rooms. Colour TV in rooms. Tea/coffee facilities.

HAWICK (ROXBURGHSHIRE)

MRS JEAN DANNAH, BRANXHOLME CASTLE, HAWICK TD9 0JT (01450 377253). Fully modernised wing of 11th century historic building set in its own grounds and parkland. Two double and one twin bedrooms. Evening Meals available. Situated three miles south of Hawick on A7 Carlisle Road. Tourist Board Approved.

KELSO (ROXBURGHSHIRE)

MR AND MRS ARCHIE STEWART, CLIFTONHILL, EDNAM, KELSO TD5 7QE (01573 225028). Beautiful countryside with River Eden running through farm. Good walks, wildlife, fishing, swimming. Tennis Court. Double room with private bathroom, two twin rooms. Bed and Breakfast from £17. Special Winter offers for cottages. 2 Crowns.

CENTRAL

Callander

Central — Classified Advertisements

STIRLING (STIRLINGSHIRE)

WALMER HOTEL, HENDERSON STREET, BRIDGE OF ALLAN, STIRLING FK9 4HD (01786 832967). Family-run Hotel with eleven bedrooms, most en suite. Excellent food, modest prices, friendly atmosphere. Public Bar, Restaurant, Beer Garden and large car park.

DUMFRIES & GALLOWAY

Moffat

Dumfries & Galloway — Classified Advertisements

CASTLE DOUGLAS (KIRKCUDBRIGHTSHIRE)

MRS PAULINE SMITH, BREAD AND BEER COTTAGE, CORSOCK, CASTLE DOUGLAS DG7 3QL (016444 652). 18th century Drovers' Inn off A712. New Galloway 6 miles. Plenty to do and see in area. Ample parking. Double/twin rooms; bathroom and toilet; own sitting room with colour TV. Central heating, electric blankets. Evening cuppa. Children welcome. B&B £12; Evening Meal £5.

MOFFAT (DUMFRIESSHIRE)

MR G. HALL, THE LODGE, SIDMOUNT AVENUE, MOFFAT DG10 9BS (01683 20440). Bed and Breakfast in quiet cul-de-sac off Well Road. Large garden; ample parking. Lounge; single, twin, double and family rooms with tea-making facilities and TV. Shower. Central heating. B&B from £14, children half price.

FIFE

St. Andrews

Brownlees
Bed & Breakfast Guest House
7 Murray Place, St. Andrews
Fife KY16 9AP
Tel: 01334 473868
RAC Listed.
Situated only a few minutes' walk from golf courses, beaches and the town centre. All bedrooms have hot/cold water. TV Lounge.
Contact Mrs J. Smith

Escape to Tranquillity

Value for money holidays at Scotland's oldest University
Enjoy a warm welcome and a high standard of service in beautiful St. Andrews. We have attractive and comfortable residences in delightful locations offering holiday accommodation from June to August. STB Listed to 3 Crowns.
FOR FULL DETAILS ASK FOR BROCHURE
Holiday Accommodation
University of St Andrews,
79 North Street, St Andrews, Fife KY16 9AJ
Telephone: 01334 462000 (24 hours)

Fife — Classified Advertisements

ST ANDREWS

MRS ANNE DUNCAN, SPINKSTOWN FARMHOUSE, ST ANDREWS KY16 8PN (01334 473475). Bright, spacious farmhouse with double and twin rooms, all with washbasins or en suite facilities. Substantial breakfast; evening meals by arrangement. Ideal for golf, historic houses, beaches etc.

FREE and REDUCED RATE Holiday Visits! Don't miss our Reader's Offer Vouchers on pages 5 to 22.

HIGHLAND

Dulnain Bridge, Fort William, Invergarry, Inverness, Tain

Mrs F. Watson

ROSEGROVE GUEST HOUSE

Skye of Curr, Dulnain Bridge
Grantown on Spey PH26 3PA Tel: 01479 851335
Commended

Situated in the beautiful Spey Valley, 10 miles from Aviemore. Ideal for walking, fishing and exploring the Scottish Highlands. After a special dinner relax by the log fire enjoying the views over the valley to the Cairngorms. Accommodation in double, twin, single and family rooms, some en suite. Rosegrove is a holiday for all the family, children and pets are welcome. Open Christmas and New Year. B&B from £15, D,B&B from £22.50. Weekly terms available.

Mrs M.B. Howie
Glenfalloch, Argyll Road
Fort William, Inverness-shire PH33 6LD
Tel: 01397 702592

A warm welcome awaits you at Glenfalloch, which is a family-run guest house. Facilities include a TV lounge and full central heating. Access at all times. Private car parking. Open all year. Physically handicapped persons especially welcome.
A relaxing, quiet break away from it all in a friendly and comfortable atmosphere. There are three bedrooms, all with washbasins.
Bed and Breakfast from £12. Details on request.

"BEINN ARD"
Argyll Road, Fort William PH33 6LF
01397 704760

Situated in a quiet street in an elevated position just above the town with panoramic views of Loch Linnhe and surrounding hills. Only five minutes' walk from town centre, pier and station. This is a most attractive wooden house which has recently been extended and renovated to a high standard. We offer our guests a pleasant informal and comfortable base from which to view the magnificent local scenery and experience the many attractions Fort William has to offer. One family room en-suite, one double room en-suite, one twin room and two single rooms; all have colour TV and tea/coffee making facilities. Open January to Mid-October. Skiers welcome. Bed and Breakfast from £13.50 to £17.50.

ARDFRISEAL
MANDALLY, INVERGARRY PH35 4HR
Commended

Small working farm in secluded position overlooking River Garry, one and a half miles south west of Invergarry village. Central for touring, hill walking, fishing and bird watching. Fort William 24 miles, Inverness 42 miles, Skye ferry one hour's drive. Tea/coffee facilities. Log fires.
Bed and Breakfast from £13.50
Evening Meals on request
Mrs H. Fraser **Tel: 01809 501281**

Ivanhoe
GUEST HOUSE
68 Lochalsh Road
Inverness IV3 6HW
Tel. & Fax: 01463 223020

Comfortable family-run Guest House, 10 minutes' walk from town centre. All rooms with washbasins, tea/coffee making facilities and TV. One family room en suite; one double en suite; one twin; two singles.

LYNDALE GUEST HOUSE
2 Ballifeary Road, Inverness IV3 5PJ

Delightfully situated close to River Ness and within 8 minutes' walk from town centre. Eden Court Theatre, golf course and loch cruise departure point nearby. Attractive dining room; all bedrooms with washbasins, central heating, colour TV and tea/coffee facilities. Private parking in grounds.
Bed and Breakfast from £14
Mrs F. McKendrick Tel: 01463 231529

"CARRINGTONS"
Morangie Road, Tain IV19 1PY

Overlooking Dornoch Firth, two minutes from town centre. Single, double, twin and family rooms. Full en suite in family room. En suite shower in other rooms. All rooms colour TV/tea & coffee facilities/washbasins. Guest lounge with colour TV.
CHILDREN UNDER 2 FREE!
Reduced rates for children
PETS ALSO WELCOME
Bed and Breakfast from £13
Phone Mrs Roberts for details
01862 892635 STB Commended

Highland — Classified Advertisements

BROADFORD (ISLE OF SKYE)

MRS MORAG ROBERTSON, EARSARY, HARRAPOOL, ISLE OF SKYE IV49 9AQ (01471 822697). Situated on a working croft you will find all the comforts of home. Panoramic sea view, private facilities, central heating, guests' lounge. Open all year. B&B from £17. STB 2 Crowns Highly Commended.

BRORA (SUTHERLAND)

MR AND MRS D. ROBERTSON, BRAES HOTEL, FOUNTAIN SQUARE, BRORA KW9 6NX (01408 621217). Licensed. Tea/coffee and washbasins all rooms; some with TV. Golf; sea, river, loch fishing; hill-walking. Some rooms en suite. B&B from £16-£21.

INVERNESS (INVERNESS-SHIRE)

WINDSOR HOUSE HOTEL, 22 NESS BANK, INVERNESS (01463 715535/233715). Traditional Scottish hotel with lovely conservatory on banks of River Ness opposite the cathedral. Easy walking distance to town centre and short drive to Loch Ness. Attractive en suite bedrooms, all with colour TV, telephone and coffee making facilities. From £28 per person sharing double/twin room. STB 3 Crowns.

MRS A. MACLEAN, WATERNISH, 15 CLACHNAHARRY ROAD, INVERNESS IV3 6QH (01463 230520). On main A862 to Beauly, five minutes from Inverness town centre. Ideal for touring. Three double/twin rooms, one en suite, all with tea/coffee making. TV lounge. Full Scottish Breakfast. Open March to October. B&B from £12.50

ELIZABETH MACKAY, 12 GLENBURN DRIVE, INVERNESS IV2 4ND (01463 223809). Comfortable accommodation in quiet area within walking distance of town centre.One double and one twin bedroom; bathroom with shower. No pets. B&B £11 per person.

MRS E. MACKENZIE, THE WHINS, 114 KENNETH STREET, INVERNESS IV3 5QG (01463 236215). A warm welcome awaits you. Accommodation has TV, tea making and washbasins in rooms. 10 minutes bus/railway and town centre. Two double/twin rooms. £12.50 per person.

MRS JOAN HENDRY, 'TAMARUE', 70A BALLIFEARY ROAD, INVERNESS IV3 5PF (01463 239724). Well recommended Bed and Breakfast accommodation; one double with private facilities and one double and one twin; washbasins, tea/coffee making facilities, central heating. TV lounge. Separate shower for visitors' use. Parking. Long-established reputation. Completely non-smoking house. STB One Crown Commended.

HIGHLAND/KINGUSSIE (INVERNESS-SHIRE)

MRS J. STEWART, INVERTON HOUSE, KINGUSSIE PH2 1NR (01540 661866). "Inverton" is 2½ miles past the Newtonmore junction, on the main A9, heading North, on the left. Leisure facilities and Aviemore nearby. Family, double and single bedrooms; TV lounge, dining room. Heating throughout. Bed and Breakfast from £12.00; Evening Dinner optional. Half-price for children.

KYLESKU (SUTHERLAND)

MRS JOAN MOFFAT, "ARDALOCH", KYLESKU IV27 2HN (0197150 2239). Comfortable accommodation overlooking Loch Glen Coul. One double and one twin room with washbasins and central heating. B&B £14; DB&B £20.

STRUAN (ISLE OF SKYE)

MRS MORAG MACCUSBIC, 4 TOTARDER, STRUAN, ISLE OF SKYE IV56 8FW (01470 572253). Situated on a 40-acre croft at the head of a sea loch. Approximately 10 miles from Dunvegan and Portree. One twin room en suite, one double room with private bathroom.

MRS M. MACKINNON, "SEAFORTH", COILLORE, STRUAN, ISLE OF SKYE IV56 8FX (01470 572230). Comfortable accommodation: one double, one twin, one family room with electric blankets. Good home cooking. Centrally situated for touring. Take A863 from Sligachan for approximately 10 miles. B&B from £14; DB&B from £23 by arrangement.

UIG (ISLE OF SKYE)

MRS G. J. WILSON, GARYBUIE GUEST HOUSE, GLENHINNISDAL, SNIZORT IV51 9UX (0147-042 310). Situated in glen by side of river off A856. Warm family house; family, double, twin and single rooms, all with TV. Home cooking, dinner on request. 10 minutes from Uig Ferry. Tourist Board Listed. Bed and Breakfast from £14 to £15.

LOTHIAN

Dunbar, Edinburgh

Redheugh Hotel

Bayswell Park, Dunbar EH42 1AE

Tel: 01368 862793

Cliff top location. Small family-run licensed hotel with the emphasis on personal attention. All rooms en-suite with colour TV, tea/coffee making facilities, telephones, etc. Good home cooking and menu changed daily. Only 28 miles from Edinburgh yet set in the heart of golfing country — 14 courses within a half-hour drive, with two in Dunbar itself. Also ideal for touring the Borders. STB 4 Crowns Commended. AA/RAC two star. Les Routiers, Logis (GB). Bed and Breakfast £55 for two people sharing double/twin room. Please telephone for more details.

BEVERLEY HOTEL

40 Murrayfield Avenue

Edinburgh EH12 6AY

Tel: 0131 337 1128

Commended

The Beverley Hotel is situated in a quiet tree-lined avenue (5 minutes from Princes St.) and offers a high standard of comfort at reasonable cost. Situated just off the main trunk road to the airport, the west and the north. Free car parking. Some rooms en suite. Restricted licence. Full central heating. B&B from £18.

THE IVY GUEST HOUSE

Tel: 0131 667 3411

7 Mayfield Gardens

Edinburgh EH9 2AX

STB Commended

RAC Acclaimed; AA "QQQ Recommended"

B&B; Victorian villa. Open all year. Private car park. Close to city centre. All rooms have central heating, H&C, colour TV, tea/coffee making facilities. En suite or standard rooms. Public phone.

Lugton's B & B,
29 Leamington Terrace, Edinburgh EH10 4JS
Tel: 0131-229 7033

Small guesthouse with a worldwide reputation for friendliness and value for money. Each room is well decorated, with central heating, washbasin, tea/coffee facilities, radio/alarm, colour TV and hairdryer. Full cooked breakfast. Central situation, on main bus routes.

PRICE £14.00 to £17.00

CHALUMNA GUEST HOUSE

5 Granville Terrace, Edinburgh EH10 4PQ

Friendly, family-run Guest House with private car parking. Situated close to the City Centre, tourist attractions and all amenities. An ideal base from which to explore Scotland and its historic capital. STB ♛ Approved

TEL: 0131-229 2086

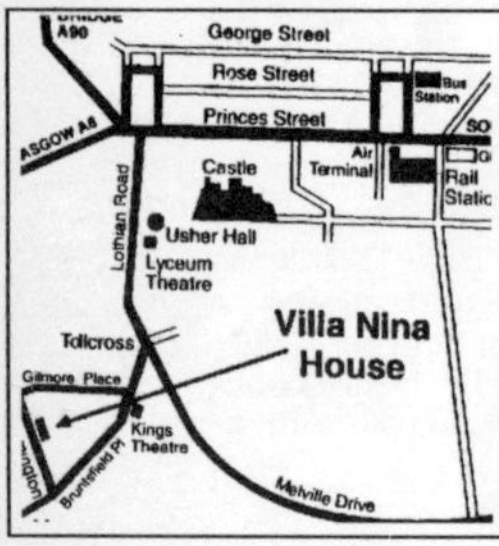

VILLA NINA HOUSE
39 Leamington Terrace, Edinburgh EH10 4JS
Tel and Fax: 0131-229 2644

Situated in a residential part of the City, yet only 10 minutes' walk to Princes Street, the Castle, theatres, shops and other major attractions.

TV in all rooms. Some rooms with private showers
Full cooked Breakfast. Member STB, AA.
Bed and Breakfast from £15.00 pp.

Mr. and Mrs. J. F. Kidd

BRIG O'DOON GUEST HOUSE

262 Ferry Road, Edinburgh EH5 3AN
Tel: 0131-552 3953

* Close to city centre
* Parking available
* Washbasins, TV and tea/coffee facilities in all bedrooms
* Central heating
* View of the Castle

Bed and Breakfast from £15.00 per person and reduction for children under 12 sharing with adults.

Sorry no dogs *Non-smokers preferred*

♛♛♛ ROTHESAY HOTEL (Central)

Commended

Within Edinburgh's Georgian New Town, situated 5 minutes, walk from Princes Street - Edinburgh's shopping and commercial centre. 36 rooms with private bathroom and colour TV, tea/coffee facilities. Elevator. Bar and restaurant offering traditional Scottish Fayre. Children welcome. Reasonable terms, open all year. Contact Mr. Fariday.

Tel: 0131-225 4125/6

8 Rothesay Place, Edinburgh EH3 7SL Fax: 0131-220 4350

EDINBURGH
Mrs Eileen Dickie
STB ♛♛ *Commended*

"No. 22", East Claremont Street, Edinburgh EH7 4JP
Tel: 0131-556 4032 Fax: 0131-556 9739

Comfortable, centrally heated Victorian Guest House 15 minutes' walk from Princes Street, railway and bus stations. Unrestricted street parking. Four bedrooms, two en-suite (shower, toilet and washbasin), all with colour TV, radio. Superb breakfasts, choice of cooked, Continental, vegetarian and a 'Taste of Scotland'. Tea/coffee, biscuits at any time. Children welcome (reduced rates). Bed and Breakfast from £20-£26. All inclusive - no extra or hidden charges. "No. 22" is an ideal friendly and relaxing base for exploring Edinburgh and surrounding countryside - just read the comments in our Visitors' book!

Averon Guest House
44 Gilmore Place,
Central Edinburgh EH3 9NQ
Tel: 0131-229 9932

- City Centre
- Private Car Park
- Near Castle and Princes Street
- Full Scottish Breakfast
- Colour TV/Satellite TV all rooms
- Bed and Breakfast from £12pp
- All credit cards welcome

MARDALE GUEST HOUSE
11 HARTINGTON PLACE,
EDINBURGH EH10 4LF
TEL: 0131 229 2693

Props. Robert & Frances Martin

Centrally located Victorian Villa offering excellent B&B at very reasonable prices. Extremely comfortable and stylish bedrooms. En suite available. Overseas visitors' comments: "Very comfortable", "Excellent! Want to come back"; "Best B&B on our trip!"

AA Listed STB ♛♛ Commended

WEST LOTHIAN

Livingston New Town is 15 miles from Edinburgh, with easy access to motorway for touring north or south: Fife, Borders, Trossachs, Loch Lomond. Accommodation in one twin room, one single, one with double and single beds and one triple-bedded room (all upstairs, 1st and 2nd floors); bathroom with shower, two toilets; sitting/dining room. TV in all rooms. Tea/coffee making facilities. Children welcome, but sorry, no pets. Parking nearby. Bed and Breakfast from £12.50; reductions for children under 10.

Open all year except Christmas and New Year

Mrs M. Easdale, 3 Cedric Rise, Dedridge, Livingston EH54 6JR. Tel: 01506 413095

Lothian — Classified Advertisements

EDINBURGH (LOTHIAN)

SOUTHDOWN GUEST HOUSE, 20 CRAIGMILLAR PARK, EDINBURGH EH16 5PS (0131-667 2410). On main bus route, 10 minutes from Princes Street. All rooms with showers, tea/coffee making; fully en-suite rooms available. Colour satellite TV lounge. Central heating. Cot, high chair, babysitting. Open February to November. B&B from £17.50; reduced rates families and groups. STB registered.

MR VEITCH, DUNSTANE HOUSE HOTEL, 4 WEST COATES, EDINBURGH EH12 5JQ (0131-337 6169). Private Hotel, Licensed, ideally situated 15 minutes from town. Bed and Breakfast from £25.00. Very comfortable Victorian detached property. Private car park. Send for brochure. AA Listed.

ANGUS BEAG GUEST HOUSE, 5 WINDSOR STREET, EDINBURGH EH7 5LA (0131-556 1905). Georgian Guest House, close to all amenities. Ten minutes Princes Street, adjacent Playhouse Theatre, bus and railway stations. All rooms have washbasins, TV, tea/coffee facilities. STB Listed.

MRS E. A. DALE, 29 DRUMMOND PLACE, EDINBURGH EH3 6PN (0131-556 6734). Bed and Breakfast, very central, close to bus and train. Large rooms with TV and tea/coffee making. Twin/double from £15, single from £18. Open July to September.

RAEBURN HOUSE HOTEL, 112 RAEBURN PLACE, STOCKBRIDGE, EDINBURGH EH4 1HG (0131 332 8000; FAX: 0131 315 2381). Tourist Board Approved hotel half-mile from city centre. Conservatory, ale and chop house restaurant, two lounge bars. Luxury apartments. Security car parking. B&B from £19 per person.

GILMORE GUEST HOUSE, 51 GILMORE PLACE, EDINBURGH EH3 9NT (0131-229 5008). Ideally situated, short walk from Princes Street, shops, entertainments, restaurants etc. Rooms with washbasins, colour TV, central heating etc; most rooms en suite. Prices from £12. Prices seasonally adjusted. Bus tours can be booked. Parking. STB Approved. 1 Crown.

SOUTH QUEENSFERRY (West Lothian)

MRS VIVIENNE DUNCAN, NEWTON HOUSE, NEWTON VILLAGE, BY SOUTH QUEENSFERRY, EDINBURGH EH52 6QE (0131-331 3298). Small friendly guest house in rural setting, offering Bed and Breakfast. Five minutes Forth Road Bridge, 20 minutes Edinburgh city centre. Central heating, colour TV, clock/radios and kettles all bedrooms. Bed and Breakfast from £14.50.

STRATHCLYDE

Ayr

STB ♛ Commended

TEL: 01292 264947

Well-appointed house, sleeps 4, close to pitch and putt and lovely river walk. Choice of golf courses nearby. Town Centre, railway station and sea front only 10/15 minutes' walk. Parks, Ayr Racecourse easily accessible. Private parking. Central heating. All bedrooms with washbasins, and are 'no smoking' areas.

Mrs J. Mair *Terms from £14.00*

Laggan, 42 Craigie Road, Ayr KA8 0EZ

Busbiehill Guest House

KNOCKENTIBER, BY KILMARNOCK, AYRSHIRE KA2 0DJ
TEL: 01563 532985

Situated in rural setting almost in the centre of Ayrshire, looking westwards towards the Arran hills on the Firth of Clyde. Within easy reach of all the popular seaside towns, Burns' Country, Culzean Castle. Day trips available to Loch Lomond, Edinburgh and Isle of Arran; sailings on Firth of Clyde. Also many golf courses. Kilmarnock 4 miles, Ayr 13, Troon 10, Irvine 5, Ardrossan 13. 8 rooms, 5 bathrooms; 2 double rooms with own bathrooms. Tea making facilities, electric blankets. Terms from £11.00 Bed & Breakfast. No dogs.

Mr & Mrs Gibson - 35 years' service to tourists

Tel. and Fax:
0141 248 3458
Mobile no: 0836 312520

Carole Divers
KIRKLAND HOUSE
42 St Vincent Cres., Glasgow G3 8NG

City centre guest house located in Glasgow's little Chelsea, a beautiful Victorian Crescent in the area known as Finnieston, offers excellent rooms, most with en suite facilities, full central heating, colour TV and tea/coffee makers.

The house is located within walking distance of the Scottish Exhibition Centre, Museum/Art Gallery and Kelvingrove Park. We are very convenient to all City Centre and West End facilities and only ten minutes from Glasgow's International Airport. STB Listed and Commended. Member of Harry James Appreciation Society, details on request.

Rooms; Singles from £25 to £35, Twins/Doubles from £46 to £55.

HOLLY HOUSE

Holly House offers spacious rooms, most with en suite facilities. Situated in an early Victorian tree-lined terrace in the city centre South area. Convenient for all city centre amenities. 10 minutes from S.E.C.C. Prices include Bed and Breakfast.

Member of Harry James Appreciation Society: details on request. STB Listed "Commended".

Singles £20 to £25; Twins £36 to £50; Doubles £36 to £50
Holly House, 54 Ibrox Terrace, Glasgow G51 2TB
Telephone Peter Divers: 0141 427 5609
Portable No. 0585 562382

Brown's Guest House

2 Onslow Drive, Dennistoun, Glasgow G31

Family-owned Guest House near City Centre and convenient for M8. Ideal for visiting Stirling and Edinburgh and as a base for touring.

Comfortable bedrooms have tea-making facilities, TV and washbasins.

BED & BREAKFAST FROM £13. FAMILY, TWIN OR DOUBLE ROOMS. £15 FOR SINGLE

0141-554 6797

Mrs Mary Howie
Hill House Farm,
Grassyards Road,
KILMARNOCK
KA3 6HG

Working dairy farm 2 miles east of Kilmarnock (25 minutes from Glasgow), with three large bedrooms, one en suite, washbasins; lounge, dining room. Central heating and home baking. Bed and Breakfast from £13 including supper. Self catering cottages available.

Tel: 01563 23370 Commended

Strathclyde — Classified Advertisements

HARTHILL (LANARKSHIRE)

MRS M. IRELAND, BLAIR MAINS FARM, HARTHILL (01501 751278). Attractive farmhouse on small working farm. Fishing, golf, clay pigeon shooting nearby. Family, double/twin and single bedrooms. Children welcome - babysitting available. Car essential. Ideal for touring Edinburgh, Glasgow, Stirling. Tourist Board Award pending.

SANDILANDS (LANARKSHIRE)

MARY AND RAY THOMSON, EASTERTOWN GUEST HOUSE, SANDILANDS LANARK ML11 9TX. (01555 880236). Ideally situated for Southern and Central Scotland, M74 three miles. 18th century farmhouse, ground floor rooms available. No smoking in bedrooms. B&B from £14; Evening Meal by arrangement.

TAYSIDE

Kinloch Rannoch, Perth

CRAIGHALL FARMHOUSE
Forgandenny, Near Bridge of Earn
Perth PH2 9DF Tel: 01738 812415

Come and stay in a modern and warm farmhouse with a cheerful, friendly atmosphere situated in lovely Earn Valley. True Highland hospitality and large choice of breakfast served. Open all year. Fishing, golf, tennis, swimming locally. Hill walking amid lovely scenery. Two rooms with private en suite facilities, others with washbasins. Double, twin and family rooms, tea making facilities. Bathroom, sittingroom. Reduced rates for children. B&B from £15.00. AA/RAC Acclaimed, ♛♛ Commended.

THE MOULIN HOTEL
Pitlochry, Perthshire
PH16 5EW

17th Century Inn extended to the present 16 en-suite bedroomed hotel. We are situated in the historic village of Moulin on the Old North Road. Overlooking the village square to the front and the Moulin Burn and gardens to the rear, this hotel offers real hospitality in its restaurant and two bars. Moulin is the starting point for a number of easy walks in the area, maps and brief guides are available.

Tel: 01796 472196 or Fax: 01796 474098

ADDERLEY PRIVATE HOTEL
213 Toberargan Road, Pitlochry,
Perthshire PH16 5HG Tel: 01796 472433

A warm and friendly welcome awaits you at our family run hotel. All rooms en suite with tea/coffee, colour TV. 4 course dinner with free glass of wine. Home cooking, ample parking in own grounds. STB ♛♛♛ Approved. Les Routiers Commended.

Tayside — Classified Advertisements

CAPUTH (PERTHSHIRE)

MRS RACHEL SMITH, STRALOCHY FARM, CAPUTH, MURTHLY PH1 4LQ (0173 871 250). Modern farmhouse in a lovely spot four miles from Dunkeld. One double, one twin bedroom. Open May to October. Central for touring Perthshire. Car essential, parking.

KIRRIEMUIR (ANGUS)

MRS J. LINDSAY, 'CREPTO', 1 KINNORDY PLACE, KIRRIEMUIR, ANGUS DD8 4JW (01575 572746). Situated in quiet cul-de-sac 10 minutes' walk from town centre. Ideal for exploring surrounding hills and glens. Warm welcome. Comfortable twin, single, and double rooms. STB Commended.

AIRPORTS AND FERRIES

Accommodation Convenient For
AIRPORTS AND FERRIES

The entries which follow provide contact details for overnight accommodation which is convenient for a particular airport or ferry. For AIRPORTS, entries are listed alphabetically by airport. For FERRIES, there are sub-sections for the Continent, Isle of Wight, the Channel Islands and the Scillies; Ireland and the Isle of Man; the Scottish Islands; and ports are listed alphabetically.

Breaking an inward or outward journey has become one of the commonest overnight stops and finding a suitable 'B&B' is often a frustrating experience. Only a brief description is given here but you will find fuller information for each entry in the appropriate county section preceding this Supplement.

The usual procedures for direct booking apply but with Airports and Ferries it is even more important to make sure that advance bookings are confirmed, that you arrive in good time and that your host knows when you want to leave. Early notice of any cancellation or change in plan is also essential.

In your own interests, you should double-check with the establishment before booking what the distance or average travelling time is from the airport or ferry you are using.

CHANNEL TUNNEL

ANNE AND NICK HUNT, BOWER FARMHOUSE, STELLING MINNIS, NEAR CANTERBURY CT4 6BB (01227 709430). Traditional farmhouse 7 miles south of Canterbury, 9 miles from the coast. Double and twin rooms, each with private facilities. Children welcome. B&B from £17.50.

N.J. ELLEN, CROCKSHARD FARMHOUSE, WINGHAM, CANTERBURY CT3 1NY (01227 720464; Fax: 01227 721125). Exceptionally attractive farmhouse. Ideally situated for visiting any part of Kent. Canterbury 15 mins, Dover 20, Folkestone 30. Terms from £17.50.

MR & MRS A. DIMECH, CLEVELAND GUEST HOUSE, 2 LAURESTON PLACE, OFF CASTLE HILL ROAD, DOVER CT16 1QX (01304 204622). 15 minutes by car from Channel Tunnel; within walking distance of Dover ferries. All rooms private/en suite facilities. Full English breakfast; early departures catered for.

AIRPORTS

GATWICK

MRS TOOKEY, POND FARM, PULLOXHILL, BEDFORDSHIRE MK45 5HA (01525 712316). Double, twin and family rooms with colour TV, washbasins, tea/coffee facilities. 3 miles from A6, 5 miles from M1 Junction 12. Ideal for touring. B&B from £14.

MRS GRETA MACLEAN, GORSE COTTAGE, 66 BALCOMBE ROAD, HORLEY RH6 9AY (Tel/Fax: 01293 784402). Comfortable detached accommodation. Two miles Gatwick Airport. Five minutes BR station. Pubs etc nearby; residential area. English Breakfast served.

CHALET GUEST HOUSE, 77 MASSETTS ROAD, HORLEY RH6 7EB (01293 821666). 5 minutes Gatwick Airport. Modern en suite facilities. Easy walk pubs and restaurants. Holiday car parking, £10 per week. AA, RAC, ETB 2 Crowns Commended. Bed and Breakfast from £21.

LYNWOOD GUEST HOUSE, 50 LONDON ROAD, REDHILL RH1 1LN (01737 766894). Conveniently situated near Redhill Station. Gatwick 10 mins by train or car. London 35 mins by train. Comfortable rooms with shower and colour TV. Car parking facilities. AA Listed.

BOOKHAM GRANGE HOTEL, LITTLE BOOKHAM COMMON, BOOKHAM, NEAR LEATHERHEAD KT23 3HS (01372 452742; Fax: 01372 450080). Country house hotel with gardens facing NT land. Excellent food and friendly service. Convenient for airports, sightseeing and business. BR station nearby. M25 four miles, A3 five miles.

STANTONS HALL FARM, BLINDLEY HEATH, LINGFIELD RH7 6LG (01342 832401). 18th century farmhouse. Family, double and single rooms. Most en suite. All with colour TV, CH, tea/coffee making. B&B from £16. Car parking facilities. Convenient for M25 and Gatwick.

MR & MRS P. CULPECK, FYFIELD HOUSE, 26 NEW STEINE, BRIGHTON, BN2 1PD (01273 602270). English/Swiss proprietors create central, clean home for you, overlooking sea. A MUST when in Brighton. Excellent food. Rooms from £16 to £27 per person per night.

MRS G. PRING, STAIRS FARMHOUSE AND TEAROOM, HIGH STREET, HARTFIELD TN7 4AB (01892 770793). Comfortable accommodation in 17th century farmhouse. All rooms colour TV and tea/coffee facilities. Countryside views. Gatwick/M25 30 mins. B&B from £19; EM by arrangement.

MR & MRS M. K. WAISTELL, JORDANS, CHURCH LANE. ARDINGLY RH17 6UP (01444 892681). Peaceful Victorian Listed Manor House in beautiful grounds on outskirts of village and within walking distance of Showground. 20 minutes from Gatwick Airport.

ROSEMEAD GUEST HOUSE, 19 CHURCH ROAD, HORLEY RH6 7EY (01293 784965 Fax: 01293 820438). Gatwick Airport 5 minutes. Small guest house. Car parking facilities. Single, standard, double or twin £35. En suite twin/double £42. En suite family £49. Tourist Board Commended, AA Listed.

"ROSEDEAN", 10 NORTH HEATH LANE, HORSHAM RH12 5AH (01403 218812). Modern house with delightful natural aspect. Good base for touring and London visits. One double, one twin, three single bedrooms, all with washbasins, TV and tea-making.

HEATHROW

MRS TOOKEY, POND FARM, PULLOXHILL, BEDFORDSHIRE MK45 5HA (01525 712316). Double, twin and family rooms with colour TV, washbasins, tea/coffee facilities. 3 miles from A6, 5 miles from M1 Junction 12. Ideal for touring. B&B from £14.

KAREN JACKSON & LYNETTE MOORE, TRINITY GUEST HOUSE, 18 TRINITY PLACE, WINDSOR SL4 3AT (01753 864186; Fax: 01753 862640). Comfortable guest house in the heart of Windsor. Close to Castle, river and stations. Run by traditional English family and Highly Recommended worldwide. ETB 2 Crowns.

CLARENCE HOTEL, 9 CLARENCE ROAD, WINDSOR SL4 5AE (01753 864436; Fax: 01753 857060). Clarence Hotel has a town centre location. All rooms en suite, TV, tea/coffee making facilities, radio alarms, hairdryers. Licensed bar. 25 minutes drive from Heathrow Airport.

CENTRAL HOTEL, 13-18 ARGYLE STREET, KING'S CROSS WC1H 8EQ (0171-278 8682/0171-837 9008). Family-run Hotel, newly renovated, convenient for all tourist attractions, close to railway/underground/coach stations. Bed and Breakfast. All rooms central heating, TV, washbasins etc. Recommended.

LINCOLN HOUSE HOTEL, 33 GLOUCESTER PLACE, LONDON W1H 3PD (0171-486 7630; Fax: 0171 486 0166). Centrally located, with easy access to motorways and airport. All rooms en suite. Double room from £49. Ideal for business, shopping or leisure.

GOWER HOTEL, 129 SUSSEX GARDENS, HYDE PARK, LONDON W2 2RX (0171-262 2262/3/4). Family run hotel centrally located, within easy reach of Paddington Station. Ideal base for exploring London. Easy access to airports. Single, double and family rooms, all en-suite.

FALCON HOTEL, 11 NORFOLK SQUARE, LONDON W2 1RU (0171-723 8603). Situated in central London, minutes from many attractions and shopping. All bedrooms have private facilities, TV and tea/coffee making. Within easy reach of airports.

PHILBEACH INN, 17 LONGRIDGE ROAD, LONDON SW5 9SB (0171-370 5213/5220; Fax: 0171-370 0734). Located near Exhibition Centre, 200 metres from Underground and 50 metres from bus stop. Most rooms with private bath/shower and toilet. Full English Breakfast. Singles £25, Doubles £35 (£40 en suite).

MRS. A WARWICK, THE CLOSE GUEST HOUSE, WITNEY ROAD, LONG HANBOROUGH OX8 8HF (01993 882485). Detached house close to Woodstock, Oxford, Cotswolds. All rooms en suite, TV, tea/coffee facilities. B&B from £15 per person. ETB 2 Crowns Commended, AA Listed.

JAMES L. LYNN, KINGSTON YMCA, 49 KINGSTON ROAD, SURBITON KT6 4NG (0181 390 0148). Superb budget hotel. 150 rooms: single, twin/double en suite. TV. Bed, Breakfast/Half Board. Two restaurants/bar. Health club. Beauty clinic, etc. Reasonable terms.

MRS J. MENZIES, VILLIERS LODGE, 1 CRANES PARK, SURBITON KT5 8AB (0181-399 6000). Comfortable accommodation in small guest house close to main line station to London. Easy reach of Heathrow, Gatwick and tourist attractions. Reasonable rates.

MRS JOAN SPITERI, BEECHTREE LODGE, 7 RYDENS AVENUE, WALTON-ON - THAMES KT12 3JB (01932 242738). Comfortable Edwardian home in quiet avenue; station 10 minutes' walk, Waterloo 25 minutes. Easy access Heathrow, Thorpe Park, Hampton Court etc. No smoking. B&B from £14; family rates available.

LUTON

PHIL AND JUDY TOOKEY, POND FARM, 7 HIGH STREET, PULLOXHILL MK45 5HA (01525 712316). Arable farm 11 miles from Luton Airport. Bedrooms with H&C, colour TV and tea/coffee facilities.Terms from £14. ETB Listed.

EASTLEIGH

TWYFORD LODGE GUEST HOUSE, 104 TWYFORD ROAD, EASTLEIGH SO5 4HN (01703 612245). Southampton (Eastleigh) Airport is only 10 minutes from our 15-bedroom Guest House. Early calls/Breakfast/taxis arranged when required.

MANCHESTER

MRS S. BRADSHAW, THE TEA COSY, PADDOCK LODGE, KETTLESHULME SK12 7RD (01663 732116). Lovely Grade II Listed building in Peak District village. Licensed. Car park. One double, two twin rooms, 15 minutes Manchester Airport. From £15 per person.

NEWCASTLE-UPON-TYNE

DENE HOTEL, 38-42 GROSVENOR ROAD, JESMOND, NEWCASTLE-UPON-TYNE NE2 2RP (0191-281 1502). Fully licensed hotel. All rooms with washbasins, tea/coffee facilities and colour TV. Most with en suite. Car park. Single rooms from £22.50, doubles from £39.

CARDIFF

WEST USK LIGHTHOUSE, ST BRIDES, NEAR NEWPORT NP1 9SF (01633 810126/815582). Unique 170-year-old Lighthouse converted to a superb Guest House. 3 miles Newport. 10 miles Cardiff. Exit Junction 28 M4. Bed and Breakfast from £18 nightly. WTB Two Crowns.

EDINBURGH

BEVERLEY HOTEL, 40 MURRAYFIELD AVENUE, EDINBURGH EH12 6AY (0131 337 1128). Small friendly hotel, close to station and airport on main route to the north. Excellent breakfast, CH. Parking. Restricted licence and en suite rooms.

RAEBURN HOUSE HOTEL, 112 RAEBURN PLACE, STOCKBRIDGE, EDINBURGH EH4 1HG (0131-332 2348; Fax: 0131-315 2381). Tourist Board registered Hotel, half a mile from Princes Street. Meals all day; lounge bar; beer garden. Children's facilities. Car parking. B&B from £19.

LUGTON'S B&B, 29 LEAMINGTON TERRACE, EDINBURGH EH10 4JS (0131-229 7033). Small friendly guesthouse offers value for money. Bedrooms have central heating, washbasins, tea/coffee facilities, hairdryer etc. Central situation, on main bus routes.

BRIG O'DOON GUEST HOUSE, 262 FERRY ROAD, EDINBURGH EH5 3AN (0131-552 3953). Close to city centre; parking. All rooms with washbasins, TV and tea/coffee facilities. B&B from £15, reductions for children sharing. View of castle; sorry no dogs. Non-smokers preferred.

SOUTHDOWN GUEST HOUSE, 20 CRAIGMILLAR PARK, EDINBURGH EH16 5PS (0131 667 2410). Just 10 minutes from Princes Street. All rooms with showers, tea/coffee making; colour satellite TV lounge. Open February to November. B&B from £17.50

MRS JEAN DANNAH, BRANXHOLME CASTLE, HAWICK TD9 OJT (01450 377253). Fully modernised wing of 11th century historic building set in its own grounds and parkland. Evening Meals available. Situated three miles south of Hawick on A7 Carlisle road.

GLASGOW

BROWN'S GUEST HOUSE, 2 ONSLOW DRIVE, DENNISTOUN, GLASGOW G31 (0141 554 6797). Family owned guest house near city centre and convenient for M8. Ideal for visiting Stirling and Edinburgh. B&B from £15 single, £13 twin/double.

MR & MRS BURNS, BEACHCLIFF, UNDERCLIFF ROAD, WEMYSS BAY PA18 6AN (01475 520955). Luxury accommodation, private beach, panoramic views, in tranquil situation. 10 minutes from trains and ferries, 30 minutes Glasgow Airport. Double room £30, single room £17.

FERRIES

The Continent, Isle of Wight, the Channel Islands, the Scillies

DOVER

MRS TOOKEY, POND FARM, PULLOXHILL, BEDFORDSHIRE MK45 5HA (01525 712316). Double, twin and family rooms with colour TV, washbasins, tea/coffee facilities. 3 miles from A6, 5 miles from M1 Junction 12. Ideal for touring. B&B from £14.

N. J. ELLEN, CROCKSHARD FARMHOUSE, WINGHAM, CANTERBURY CT3 1NY (01227 720464; Fax: 01227 721125). Exceptionally attractive farmhouse. Ideally situated for visiting any part of Kent. Canterbury 15 mins, Dover 20, Folkestone 30. Terms from £17.50.

ANNE AND NICK HUNT, BOWER FARMHOUSE, STELLING MINNIS, NEAR CANTERBURY CT4 6BB (01227 709430). Traditional farmhouse 7 miles south of Canterbury and 9 miles from coast. Double and twin room, each with private facilities. Children welcome. B&B from £17.50.

BLERIOT'S, 47 PARK AVENUE, DOVER CT16 1HE (01304 211394). Within easy reach of trains, bus station, town centre, Hoverport and docks. See main advertisement on page 64 for further details.

RESTOVER GUESTHOUSE, 69 FOLKESTONE ROAD, DOVER CT17 9RZ (01304 206031). A warm welcome awaits you at this family run establishment. Conveniently situated just 3 mins from ports and 10 mins from Channel Tunnel. All rooms with TV. ETB 1 Crown. B&B £13-£17pp.

ST ALBANS GUESTHOUSE, 71 FOLKESTONE ROAD, DOVER CT17 9RZ (01304 206308). Family run guest house situated 3 mins from docks and 10 mins from Channel Tunnel. Clean, comfortable rooms. ETB 1 Crown. B&B £13-£17pp.

CASTLE HOUSE, 10 CASTLE HILL ROAD, DOVER CT16 1QW (01304 201656; Fax; 01304 210197). For clean and comfortable accommodation minutes from all Dover's amenities and port. All rooms private shower and toilet, colour TV, tea-making facilities, central heating. ETB 3 Crowns, AA QQQ.

BRAKES COPPICE FARM, TELHAM LANE, BATTLE, EAST SUSSEX TN33 OSJ (01424 830347). Farmhouse modernised to high standard with three en suite bedrooms. Near large towns of Hastings and Eastbourne. No smoking. B&B single £25, double £39.50.

GREAT YARMOUTH

SPINDRIFT PRIVATE HOTEL, 36 WELLESLEY ROAD, GREAT YARMOUTH NR30 1EU (01493 858674). Small private hotel near seafront and leisure activities. All rooms with colour TV and tea/coffee making facilities. En suite available. Open all year. Double room, bed and breakfast from £25, en suite £30.

MRS J. M. WHITE, MILL HOUSE, WATER RUN, HITCHAM IP7 7LN (01449 740315). Detached house in 4 acres grounds. Room with colour TV, washbasins, tea/coffee; one en suite. On B1115 Stowmarket to Hadleigh Road. Prices from £12.50.

HARWICH

ROSE & CROWN HOTEL, EAST STREET, COLCHESTER CO1 2TZ (01206 866677; Fax 01206 866616). The oldest Inn in England's oldest recorded town, recently refurbished yet retaining its character. 30 en suite bedrooms. 40 miles Stansted, 20 miles Harwich. 4 Crowns Commended.

NEWCASTLE-UPON-TYNE

MRS MARGARET WEIGHTMAN, THE COURTYARD, MOUNT PLEASANT, SANDHOE, CORBRIDGE NE46 4LX (01434 606850). One hour drive west from North Sea terminal. Beautifully furnished country house, all rooms en suite with TV and heating. Supper by arrangement.

DENE HOTEL, 38-42 GROSVENOR ROAD, JESMOND, NEWCASTLE-UPON-TYNE NE2 2RP (0191-281 1502/8110). Fully licensed hotel. All rooms with washbasins, tea/coffee facilities and colour TV. Most with en suite. Car park. Single rooms from £22.50, doubles from £39.

NEWHAVEN

MRS P. BURNABY-DAVIES, BANKSIDE, RODMELL, LEWES BN7 3EZ (01273 477058). Family Bed and Breakfast, en suite, TV. Situated between historic Lewes and Newhaven Ferry. On Southdowns Way, close Glyndebourne. Delightful village once home of Virginia Woolf.

PENZANCE

PENALVA HOTEL, ALEXANDRA ROAD, PENZANCE TR18 4LZ (01736 69060). AA Approved QQQ. Non-smoking Hotel, immaculate interior, very good food. Convenient for airport, ferry and railway station. Highly recommended, warm welcome. ETB 3 Crowns.

GLORIA AND JOHN GOWER, TREVENTON GUEST HOUSE, ALEXANDRA PLACE PENZANCE TR18 4NE (01736 63521). En suite or standard rooms available. Full breakfast arranged for ALL sailings/flights. Bed and Breakfast from £13.00; Evening Meal optional. Highly recommended.

PLYMOUTH

MRS S. BUDZIAK, ALLINGTON HOUSE, 6 ST JAMES PLACE EAST, THE HOE, PLYMOUTH PL1 3AS (01752 221435). 5 minutes by car to ferry. Comfortable Guest House. All bedrooms have colour TV, washbasin, beverage facilities and central heating. Small and friendly.

MRS P. VANSTONE, THE OLD SMITHY, SLERRA HILLS, CLOVELLY, BIDEFORD EX39 5ST (01237 431202). Comfortable cottage accommodation within easy reach of Exmoor, Dartmoor and Cornwall. One en suite. Dogs allowed. Open all year. Telephone or SAE for details.

THE GLOBE INN, FROGMORE, NEAR KINGSBRIDGE TQ7 2NR (01548 531351). Friendly, owner-run 18th century village inn, close to Plymouth. Comfortable, well appointed accommodation. Good food. Parking.

MOOR VIEW HOTEL, VALE DOWN, LYDFORD EX20 4BB (0182 282 220). Small peaceful Victorian country house. En suite accommodation. English Breakfast, Dinner, reputation for good food and wine. No smoking. Midway Okehampton, Tavistock on A386. Open all year.

POOLE

SEACREST LODGE, 63 ALUM CHINE ROAD, BOURNEMOUTH BH4 8DU (01202 767438). A warm welcome awaits you whether on business or pleasure. Close to shops, restaurants, entertainments; within easy reach of New Forest and Poole Harbour. En suite rooms with colour TV. Ample parking.

MRS R. VINE, MANOR FARM COTTAGE, STUDLAND, NEAR SWANAGE BH19 3AT (0192 944 254). Bed and Breakfast. Lovely coastal and country walks. 5 minutes from beaches.

PORTSMOUTH

MRS TOOKEY, POND FARM, PULLOXHILLL, BEDFORDSHIRE MK45 5HA (01525 712316). Double, twin and family rooms with colour TV, washbasins, tea/coffee facilities. 3 miles from A6, 5 miles from M1 Junction 12. Ideal for touring. B&B from £14.

MRS B. WEST, "RIDGEFIELD", STATION ROAD, PETERSFIELD GU32 3DE (01730 261402). Follow A3(M) London signs. First town is Petersfield (20 minutes from Ferry). Take A272 Winchester slip road and follow Petersfield signs - we're on left before level crossing.

CRANBOURNE HOUSE, 6 HERBERT ROAD, SOUTHSEA, PORTSMOUTH PO4 0QA (01705 824981). En-suite accommodation just 10 minutes from Ferry Terminals and five minutes' walk from Seafront, in a QUIET area close to Theatre, Shops etc.

MRS S. TUBB "HAMILTON HOUSE", 95 VICTORIA ROAD NORTH, SOUTHSEA, PORTSMOUTH PO5 1PS (01705 823502). Family-run Guest House, 5 minutes by car from Ferryport. Breakfast served from 6.00 am. Colour TV and tea-making facilities, some en suite. Open all year. ETB 2 Crowns Commended, AA listed, RAC Acclaimed.

RAMSGATE

MRS JANET RHODES, YORK HOUSE, 7 AUGUSTA ROAD, RAMSGATE CT11 8JP (01843 596775). Homely Guest House near sea and shops. Bed and Breakfast from £11.00 per night each. Weekly rates. Good home cooking. Children, Senior Citizens welcome. Fire Certificate.

SPENCER COURT HOTEL, 37 SPENCER SQUARE, RAMSGATE CT11 9LD (01843 594582). Five minutes to Sally Line Ferry terminal at Ramsgate, five minutes to Manston Airport (Kent International). Overnight travellers most welcome. ETB 2 crowns Commended.

SOUTHAMPTON

MRS PAT WARD, ASHELEE LODGE, 36 ATHERLEY ROAD, SHIRLEY, SOUTHAMPTON SO1 5DQ (01703 222095). Guest House with friendly atmosphere, varied menus, TV lounge. Overseas guests very welcome. Near Docks for liners, ferries, Sealink, Stena. Brochure available.

WESTERN ISLES & CLYDE COAST

WEMYSS BAY

MR & MRS BURNS, BEACHCLIFF, UNDERCLIFF ROAD, WEMYSS BAY PA18 6AN (01475 520955). Luxury accommodation, private beach, panoramic views, in tranquil situation. 10 minutes from trains and ferries to Highlands and Islands: 30 minutes from Glasgow Airport.

IRELAND AND ISLE OF MAN

MILFORD HAVEN

MRS N. JONES, HIGHLAND GRANGE FARM, ROBESTON WATHEN, NARBERTH SA67 8EP (01834 860952). Lovely family home centrally situated on A40. Ideal for touring; extensive information and helpful host. Ground floor accommodation. Guest lounge. Country Inn 200 yards; beach 7 miles. Two Crowns.

ONE FOR YOUR FRIEND 1995

FHG Publications have a large range of attractive holiday accommodation guides for all kinds of holiday opportunities throughout Britain. They also make useful gifts at any time of year. Our guides are available in most bookshops and larger newsagents but we will be happy to post you a copy direct if you have any difficulty. We will also post abroad but have to charge separately for post or freight. The inclusive cost of posting and packing the guides to you or your friends in the UK is as follows:

Farm Holiday Guide ENGLAND, WALES and IRELAND
Board, Self-catering, Caravans/Camping, Activity Holidays. Over 400 pages. **£4.80**

Farm Holiday Guide SCOTLAND
All kinds of holiday accommodation. **£3.00**

SELF-CATERING & FURNISHED HOLIDAYS
Over 1000 addresses throughout for Self-catering and caravans in Britain. **£4.20**

BRITAIN'S BEST HOLIDAYS
A quick-reference general guide for all kinds of holidays. **£3.30**

The FHG Guide to CARAVAN & CAMPING HOLIDAYS
Caravans for hire, sites and holiday parks and centres. **£3.30**

BED AND BREAKFAST STOPS
Over 1000 friendly and comfortable overnight stops. Non-smoking, The Disabled and Special Diets Supplements. **£4.40**

CHILDREN WELCOME! FAMILY HOLIDAY GUIDE
Family holidays with details of amenities for children and babies. **£4.40**

Recommended SHORT BREAK HOLIDAYS IN BRITAIN
'Approved' accommodation for quality bargain breaks. Introduced by John Carter. **£4.20**

Recommended COUNTRY HOTELS OF BRITAIN
Including Country Houses, for the discriminating. **£4.20**

Recommended WAYSIDE INNS OF BRITAIN
Pubs, Inns and small hotels. **£4.20**

PGA GOLF GUIDE
Where to play and where to stay
Over 2000 golf courses in Britain with convenient accommodation. Endorsed by the PGA. Holiday Golf in France, Portugal, Spain and USA. **£9.50**

PETS WELCOME!
The unique guide for holidays for pet owners and their pets. **£4.60**

BED AND BREAKFAST IN BRITAIN
Over 1000 choices for touring and holidays throughout Britain. Airports and Ferries Supplement. **£3.30**

THE FRENCH FARM AND VILLAGE HOLIDAY GUIDE
The official guide to self-catering holidays in the 'Gîtes de France'. **£9.50**

Tick your choice and send your order and payment to FHG PUBLICATIONS, ABBEY MILL BUSINESS CENTRE, SEEDHILL, PAISLEY PA1 1TJ (TEL: 0141-887 0428. FAX: 0141-889 7204). **Deduct** 10% for 2/3 titles or copies; 20% for 4 or more.

Send to: NAME ....

ADDRESS ....

....

.... POST CODE ....

I enclose Cheque/Postal Order for £ ....

SIGNATURE .... DATE ....

Please complete the following to help us improve the service we provide. How did you find out about our guides:

☐ Press ☐ Magazines ☐ TV ☐ Radio ☐ Family/Friend ☐ Other.

MAP SECTION

The following seven pages of maps indicate the main cities, towns and holiday centres of Britain. Space obviously does not permit every location featured in this book to be included but the approximate position may be ascertained by using the distance indications quoted and the scale bars on the maps.

Map 1

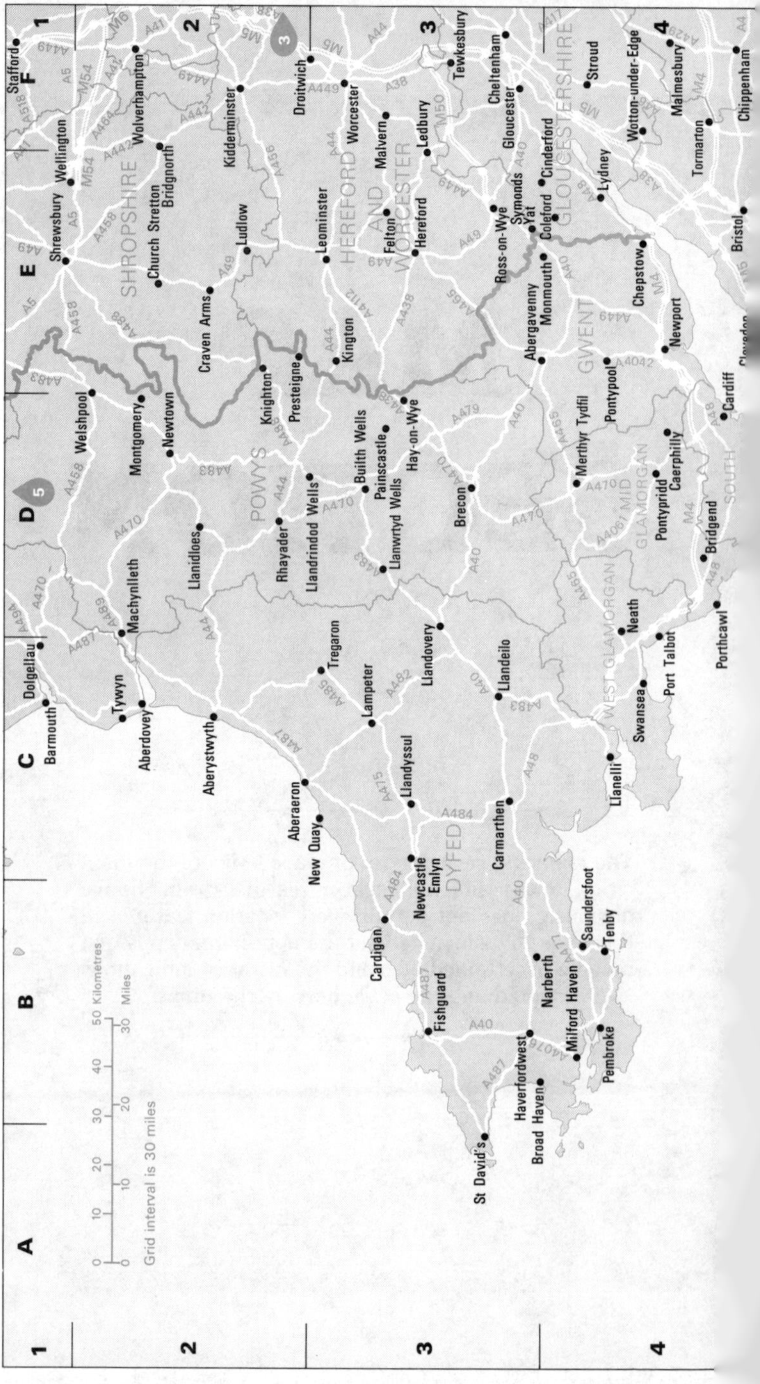

A
B
C
D
E
F
1
2
3
4
Grid interval is 30 miles
0 10 20 30 40 50 Kilometres
0 10 20 30 Miles
SHROPSHIRE
HEREFORD AND WORCESTER
GLOUCESTERSHIRE
POWYS
GWENT
MID GLAMORGAN
SOUTH
WEST GLAMORGAN
DYFED
Stafford
Wolverhampton
Wellington
Shrewsbury
Bridgnorth
Church Stretton
Kidderminster
Ludlow
Craven Arms
Droitwich
Worcester
Malvern
Leominster
Felton
Hereford
Ledbury
Tewkesbury
Cheltenham
Gloucester
Stroud
Wotton-under-Edge
Malmesbury
Tormarton
Chippenham
Cinderford
Lydney
Symonds Yat
Coleford
Ross-on-Wye
Monmouth
Chepstow
Bristol
Abergavenny
Newport
Pontypool
Cardiff
Caerphilly
Pontypridd
Merthyr Tydfil
Bridgend
Porthcawl
Neath
Port Talbot
Swansea
Llanelli
Kington
Presteigne
Knighton
Welshpool
Montgomery
Newtown
Llanidloes
Rhayader
Llandrindod Wells
Builth Wells
Painscastle
Hay-on-Wye
Brecon
Llanwrtyd Wells
Llandovery
Llandeilo
Machynlleth
Dolgellau
Barmouth
Tywyn
Aberdovey
Aberystwyth
Tregaron
Lampeter
Aberaeron
New Quay
Llandyssul
Carmarthen
Newcastle Emlyn
Cardigan
Fishguard
Narberth
Saundersfoot
Tenby
Haverfordwest
Milford Haven
Pembroke
Broad Haven
St David's
M5
M6
M54
M50
M4
A5
A38
A40
A44
A48
A49
A449
A458
A470
A483
A487
A484
A465

Map 2

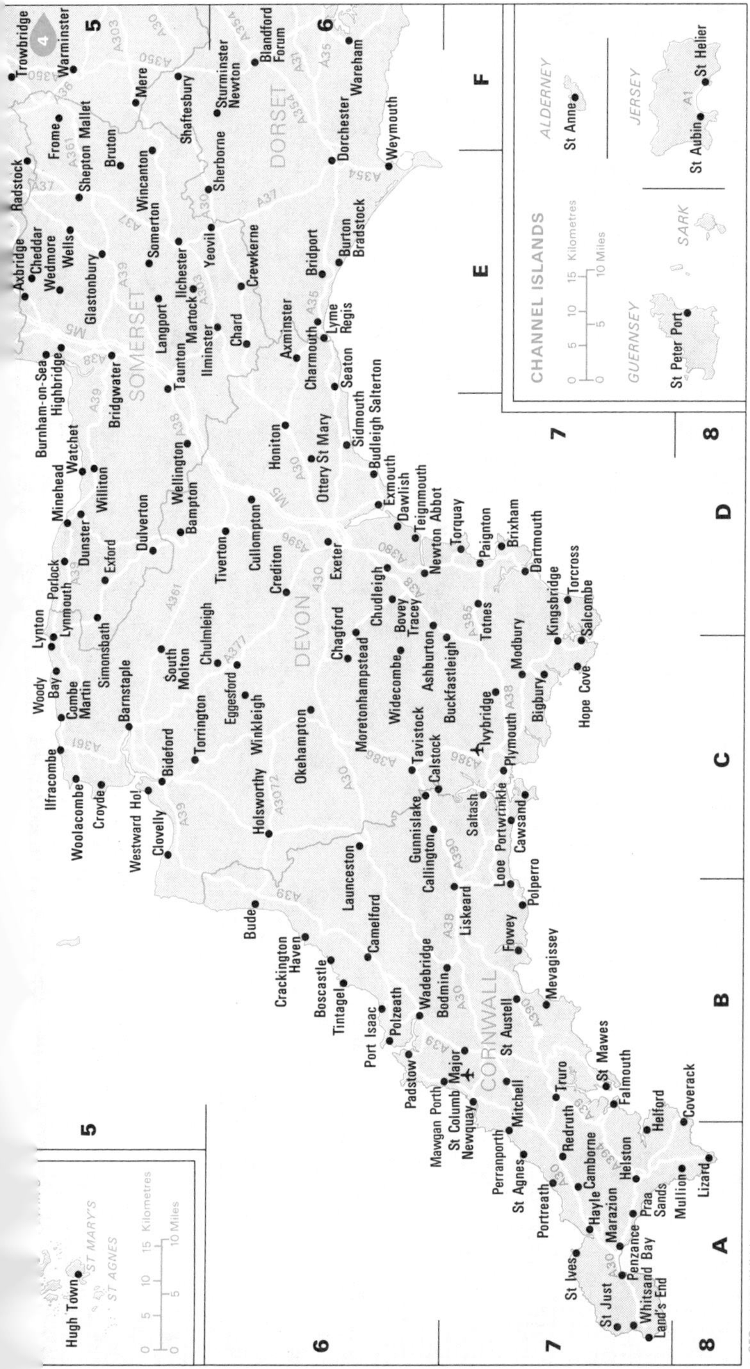

SOMERSET
DEVON
CORNWALL
DORSET
CHANNEL ISLANDS
ALDERNEY
St Anne
JERSEY
St Helier
St Aubin
SARK
GUERNSEY
St Peter Port
Kilometres
Miles
ST MARY'S
ST AGNES
Hugh Town
Trowbridge
Warminster
Frome
Shepton Mallet
Radstock
Axbridge
Cheddar
Wedmore
Wells
Glastonbury
Bruton
Wincanton
Mere
Shaftesbury
Sturminster Newton
Blandford Forum
Wareham
Dorchester
Weymouth
Sherborne
Yeovil
Somerton
Ilchester
Martock
Langport
Crewkerne
Bridport
Burton Bradstock
Lyme Regis
Axminster
Charmouth
Chard
Ilminster
Taunton
Bridgwater
Burnham-on-Sea
Highbridge
Watchet
Minehead
Williton
Wellington
Seaton
Honiton
Ottery St Mary
Sidmouth
Budleigh Salterton
Exmouth
Dawlish
Teignmouth
Newton Abbot
Torquay
Paignton
Brixham
Dartmouth
Kingsbridge
Torcross
Salcombe
Hope Cove
Bigbury
Modbury
Totnes
Ivybridge
Plymouth
Buckfastleigh
Ashburton
Bovey Tracey
Chudleigh
Exeter
Crediton
Cullompton
Tiverton
Bampton
Dulverton
Exford
Dunster
Porlock
Lynmouth
Lynton
Simonsbath
Woody Bay
Combe Martin
Ilfracombe
Woolacombe
Croyde
Barnstaple
South Molton
Chulmleigh
Eggesford
Winkleigh
Chagford
Moretonhampstead
Widecombe
Okehampton
Tavistock
Calstock
Gunnislake
Callington
Saltash
Portwrinkle
Cawsand
Looe
Polperro
Fowey
Mevagissey
St Austell
Liskeard
Launceston
Holsworthy
Torrington
Bideford
Westward Ho!
Clovelly
Bude
Crackington Haven
Boscastle
Tintagel
Camelford
Wadebridge
Bodmin
Port Isaac
Polzeath
Padstow
St Columb Major
Mawgan Porth
Newquay
Mitchell
Truro
St Mawes
Falmouth
Perranporth
St Agnes
Redruth
Camborne
Portreath
Hayle
St Ives
St Just
Penzance
Marazion
Praa Sands
Helston
Helford
Coverack
Mullion
Lizard
Whitsand Bay
Land's End
A B C D E F
5 6 7 8

Map 3

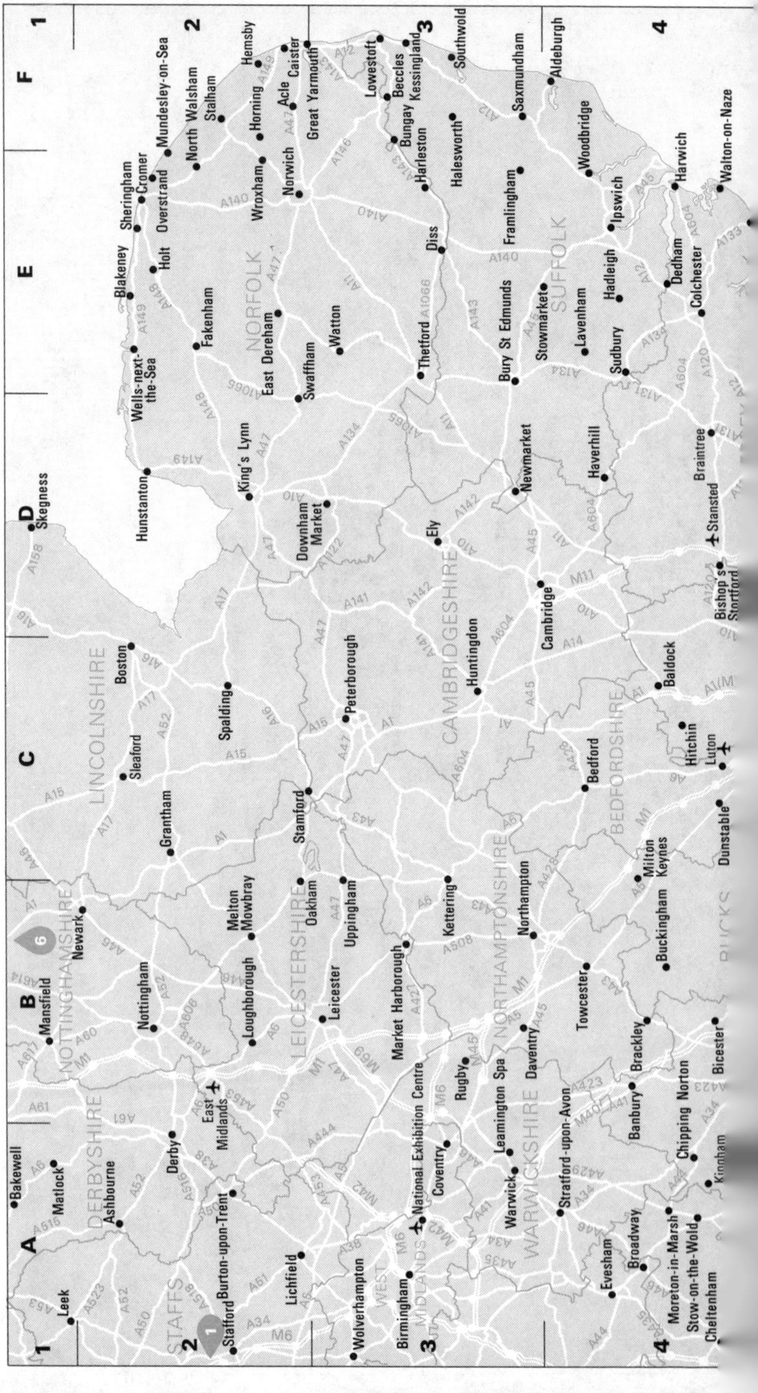

LINCOLNSHIRE
NOTTINGHAMSHIRE
DERBYSHIRE
STAFFS
LEICESTERSHIRE
WEST MIDLANDS
WARWICKSHIRE
NORTHAMPTONSHIRE
CAMBRIDGESHIRE
BEDFORDSHIRE
NORFOLK
SUFFOLK
BUCKS
Leek
Bakewell
Matlock
Ashbourne
Derby
Burton-upon-Trent
Stafford
Lichfield
Wolverhampton
Birmingham
National Exhibition Centre
Coventry
Warwick
Leamington Spa
Stratford-upon-Avon
Evesham
Broadway
Moreton-in-Marsh
Stow-on-the-Wold
Cheltenham
Kingham
Chipping Norton
Banbury
Bicester
Brackley
Towcester
Daventry
Rugby
Market Harborough
Leicester
Loughborough
East Midlands
Nottingham
Mansfield
Newark
Melton Mowbray
Oakham
Uppingham
Kettering
Northampton
Buckingham
Milton Keynes
Dunstable
Luton
Hitchin
Baldock
Bedford
Huntingdon
Cambridge
Bishop's Stortford
Stansted
Braintree
Colchester
Dedham
Harwich
Walton-on-Naze
Ipswich
Hadleigh
Sudbury
Lavenham
Haverhill
Newmarket
Ely
Peterborough
Stamford
Grantham
Sleaford
Boston
Spalding
Skegness
Hunstanton
King's Lynn
Downham Market
Swaffham
Watton
Thetford
Bury St Edmunds
Stowmarket
Framlingham
Woodbridge
Saxmundham
Aldeburgh
Halesworth
Southwold
Diss
Harleston
Bungay
Beccles
Kessingland
Lowestoft
Great Yarmouth
Caister
Acle
Norwich
Wroxham
Horning
Hemsby
Stalham
North Walsham
Mundesley-on-Sea
Overstrand
Cromer
Sheringham
Holt
Blakeney
Wells-next-the-Sea
Fakenham
East Dereham
M1
M6
M11
M42
M40
M45
M69
A1
A1(M)
A6
A5
A12
A14
A17
A47
A11
A10
A45
A140
A134
A143
A146
A149
A148
A604
A15
A16
A52
A60
A61
A50
A38
A34
A46
A43
A428
A508

Map 4

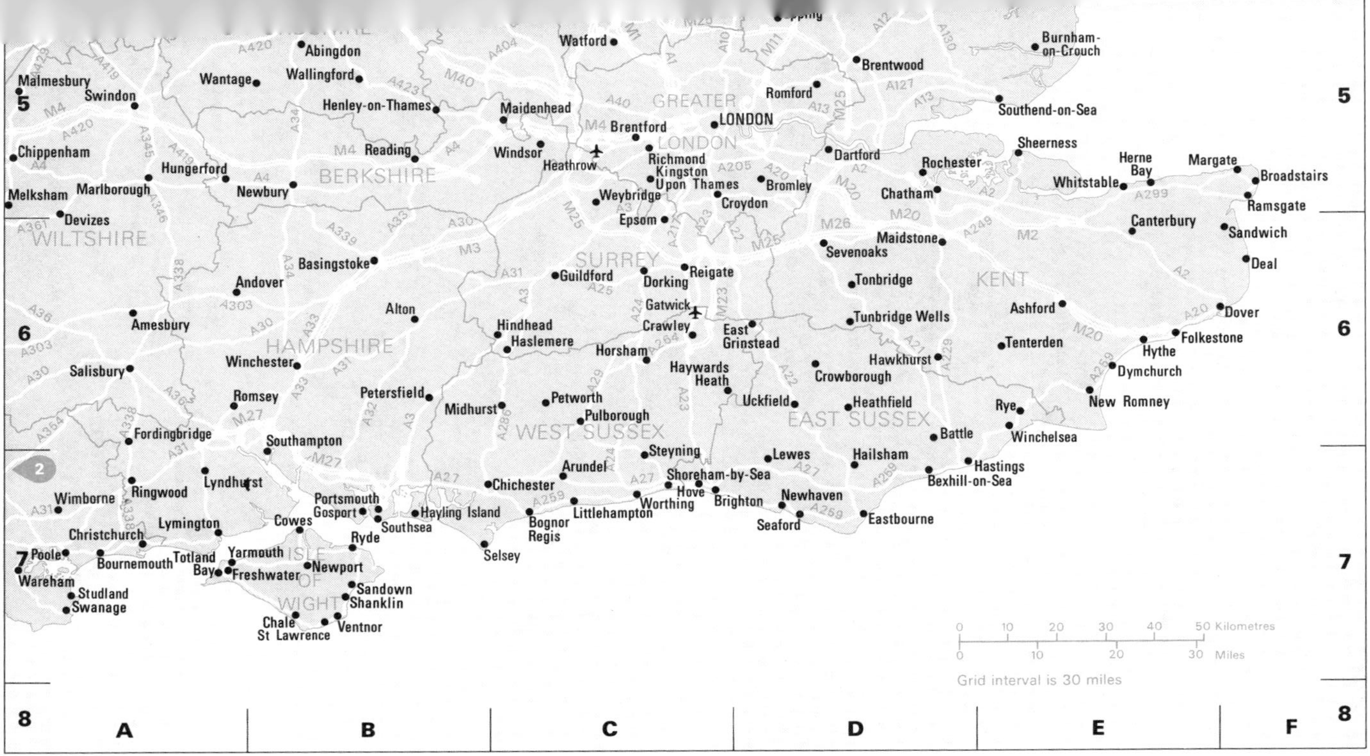
Watford
Burnham-on-Crouch
Abingdon
Brentwood
Malmesbury
Wantage
Wallingford
Swindon
Romford
Henley-on-Thames
Maidenhead
GREATER LONDON
LONDON
Southend-on-Sea
Brentford
Chippenham
Reading
Windsor
Heathrow
Sheerness
Dartford
Rochester
Hungerford
BERKSHIRE
Richmond
Kingston Upon Thames
Bromley
Herne Bay
Margate
Broadstairs
Melksham
Marlborough
Newbury
Weybridge
Croydon
Chatham
Whitstable
Ramsgate
Devizes
Epsom
WILTSHIRE
Canterbury
Sandwich
Maidstone
Sevenoaks
Basingstoke
SURREY
Guildford
Dorking
Reigate
Deal
Andover
Tonbridge
KENT
Gatwick
Ashford
Dover
Alton
Hindhead
Amesbury
Crawley
East Grinstead
Tunbridge Wells
HAMPSHIRE
Haslemere
Horsham
Tenterden
Folkestone
Hythe
Salisbury
Winchester
Hawkhurst
Haywards Heath
Crowborough
Dymchurch
Romsey
Petersfield
Petworth
Midhurst
Uckfield
Heathfield
New Romney
Pulborough
Rye
EAST SUSSEX
WEST SUSSEX
Fordingbridge
Battle
Southampton
Winchelsea
Steyning
Lewes
Hailsham
Arundel
Hastings
Ringwood
Lyndhurst
Shoreham-by-Sea
Bexhill-on-Sea
Chichester
Hove
Wimborne
Portsmouth
Brighton
Newhaven
Gosport
Worthing
Hayling Island
Littlehampton
Eastbourne
Lymington
Cowes
Southsea
Bognor Regis
Seaford
Christchurch
Ryde
Selsey
Poole
Bournemouth
Totland Bay
Yarmouth
ISLE OF WIGHT
Newport
Wareham
Freshwater
Sandown
Studland
Shanklin
Swanage
Chale
St Lawrence
Ventnor
0 10 20 30 40 50 Kilometres
0 10 20 30 Miles
Grid interval is 30 miles
5
6
7
8
A
B
C
D
E
F
2

Map 5

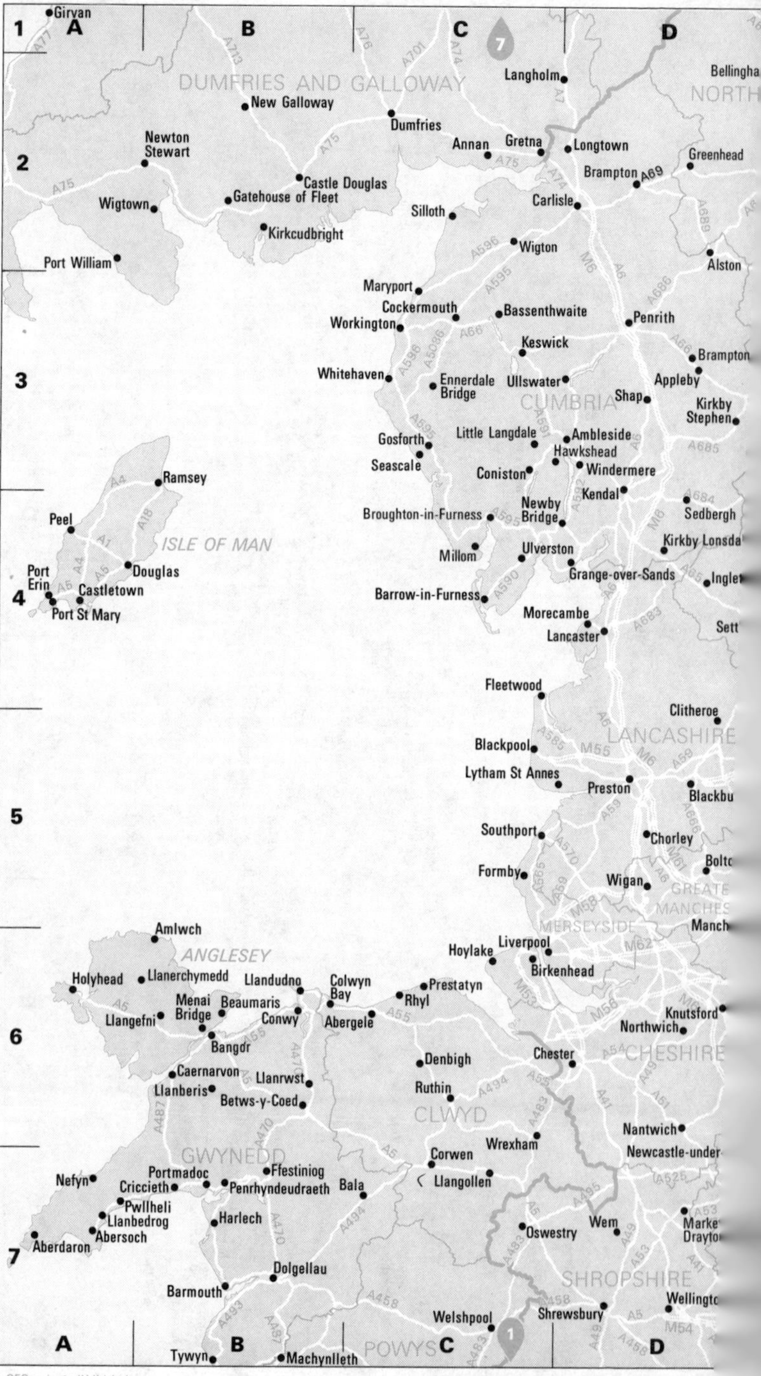

DUMFRIES AND GALLOWAY
Girvan
New Galloway
Dumfries
Langholm
Newton Stewart
Annan
Gretna
Longtown
Castle Douglas
Gatehouse of Fleet
Wigtown
Kirkcudbright
Port William
Silloth
Carlisle
Brampton
Greenhead
Wigton
Alston
Maryport
Cockermouth
Bassenthwaite
Workington
Penrith
Keswick
Whitehaven
Ennerdale Bridge
Ullswater
Appleby
Brampton
Shap
CUMBRIA
Kirkby Stephen
Gosforth
Little Langdale
Ambleside
Hawkshead
Seascale
Coniston
Windermere
Kendal
Sedbergh
Broughton-in-Furness
Newby Bridge
Millom
Ulverston
Grange-over-Sands
Barrow-in-Furness
Morecambe
Lancaster
Ramsey
Peel
ISLE OF MAN
Douglas
Port Erin
Castletown
Port St Mary
Fleetwood
Clitheroe
LANCASHIRE
Blackpool
Lytham St Annes
Preston
Southport
Chorley
Formby
Wigan
MERSEYSIDE
Amlwch
ANGLESEY
Hoylake
Liverpool
Birkenhead
Holyhead
Llanerchymedd
Llandudno
Colwyn Bay
Prestatyn
Rhyl
Menai Bridge
Beaumaris
Llangefni
Conwy
Abergele
Bangor
Knutsford
Northwich
CHESHIRE
Chester
Denbigh
Caernarvon
Llanrwst
Llanberis
Ruthin
Betws-y-Coed
CLWYD
Nantwich
Wrexham
GWYNEDD
Corwen
Ffestiniog
Nefyn
Portmadoc
Criccieth
Penrhyndeudraeth
Bala
Llangollen
Pwllheli
Llanbedrog
Harlech
Abersoch
Aberdaron
Oswestry
Wem
Dolgellau
SHROPSHIRE
Barmouth
Welshpool
Shrewsbury
POWYS
Tywyn
Machynlleth

Map 6

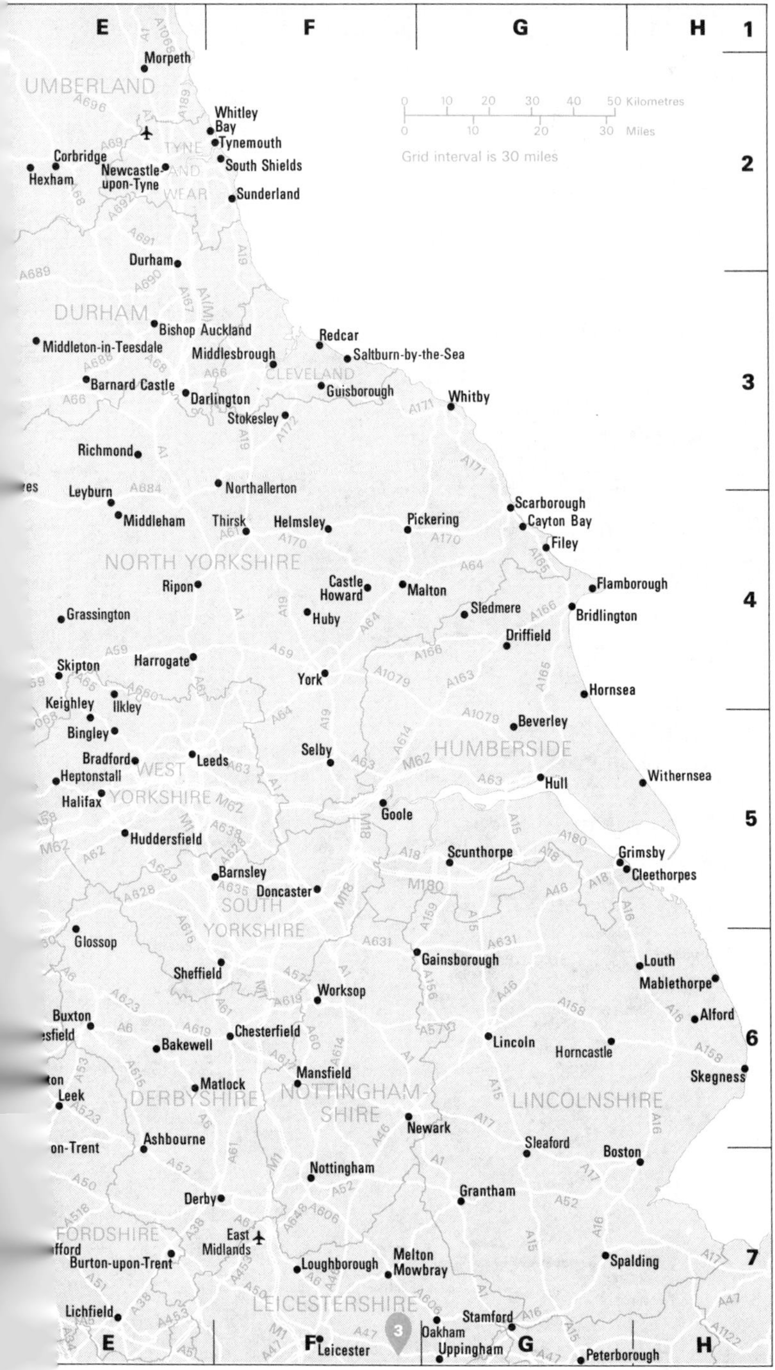
E
F
G
H
1
2
3
4
5
6
7
0 10 20 30 40 50 Kilometres
0 10 20 30 Miles
Grid interval is 30 miles
Morpeth
UMBERLAND
Whitley Bay
Tynemouth
Corbridge
Hexham
Newcastle-upon-Tyne
TYNE AND WEAR
South Shields
Sunderland
Durham
DURHAM
Bishop Auckland
Middleton-in-Teesdale
Middlesbrough
Redcar
Saltburn-by-the-Sea
CLEVELAND
Guisborough
Barnard Castle
Darlington
Stokesley
Whitby
Richmond
Northallerton
Leyburn
Middleham
Thirsk
Helmsley
Pickering
Scarborough
Cayton Bay
Filey
NORTH YORKSHIRE
Ripon
Castle Howard
Malton
Flamborough
Sledmere
Bridlington
Grassington
Huby
Driffield
Skipton
Harrogate
York
Hornsea
Keighley
Ilkley
Bingley
Beverley
Bradford
Leeds
Selby
HUMBERSIDE
Heptonstall
WEST YORKSHIRE
Halifax
Hull
Withernsea
Goole
Huddersfield
Scunthorpe
Grimsby
Cleethorpes
Barnsley
Doncaster
SOUTH YORKSHIRE
Glossop
Sheffield
Gainsborough
Louth
Mablethorpe
Worksop
Buxton
Alford
Bakewell
Chesterfield
Lincoln
Horncastle
Skegness
Mansfield
Matlock
Leek
DERBYSHIRE
NOTTINGHAM-SHIRE
LINCOLNSHIRE
Newark
Ashbourne
Sleaford
Boston
Nottingham
Grantham
Derby
East Midlands
Burton-upon-Trent
Loughborough
Melton Mowbray
Spalding
LEICESTERSHIRE
Lichfield
Stamford
Oakham
Leicester
Uppingham
Peterborough
3

Map 7
0 10 20 30 40 50 Kilometres
0 10 20 30 Miles
Grid interval is 30 miles
A
B
C
D
E
F
G
1
2
3
4
5
6
7
8
9
10
11
SHETLAND ISLANDS
YELL
MAINLAND
Lerwick
Sumburgh
ORKNEY
MAINLAND
HOY
Kirkwall
Stromness
John o'Groats
Thurso
Durness
Bettyhill
Tongue
Wick
Scourie
LEWIS
WESTERN ISLES
Lochinver
Lairg
Helmsdale
Golspie
Ullapool
Bonar Bridge
Dornoch
Tain
Gairloch
Poolewe
Cullen
Banff
Fraserburgh
Dingwall
Rosemarkie
Elgin
Fochabers
HIGHLAND
Fortrose
Nairn
Forres
Keith
Turriff
Peterhead
Beauly
Inverness
Daviot
Huntly
Portree
RAASAY
SKYE
Kyle of Lochalsh
Dornie
Kyleakin
Broadford
Grantown-on-Spey
Carrbridge
Tomintoul
GRAMPIAN
Inverurie
Aviemore
Fort Augustus
Kingussie
Aberdeen
INNER HEBRIDES
Mallaig
Braemar
Banchory
Stonehaven
Fort William
Kinlochleven
Kinloch Rannoch
Pitlochry
Brechin
Montrose
Ballachulish
Glencoe
Tobermory
Aberfeldy
TAYSIDE
Forfar
Dunkeld
Blairgowrie
Arbroath
MULL
Oban
Taynuilt
Killin
Dundee
Carnoustie
Monifieth
Dalmally
Crianlarich
Lochearnhead
Perth
Crieff
Cupar
St Andrews
Inveraray
Callander
Auchterarder
FIFE
Arrochar
Tarbet
Aberfoyle
CENTRAL
Kinross
Stirling
Dunfermline
Kirkcaldy
JURA
Lochgilphead
Luss
Drymen
North Berwick
Ardrishaig
Dunoon
Gourock
Balloch
Dumbarton
EDINBURGH
Dunbar
Greenock
Tarbert
Glasgow
Dalkeith
Haddington
Eyemouth
ISLAY
Rothesay
Paisley
LOTHIAN
Chirnside
Largs
Berwick upon
STRATHCLYDE
Hamilton
Duns
Lauder
Ardrossan
Kilmarnock
Lanark
Peebles
Coldstream
Cornhill-on-Tweed
KINTYRE
Brodick
Irvine
Troon
Lamlash
Prestwick
Biggar
Galashiels
Kelso
Wooler
Selkirk
BORDERS
Jedburgh
Campbeltown
ARRAN
Ayr
Abington
New Cumnock
Hawick
Alnwick
Maybole
Moffat
Beattock
Girvan
NORTHUMBERLAND
Langholm
Bellingham
DUMFRIES & GALLOWAY
New Galloway
Dumfries
Gretna
Longtown
Newton Stewart
Castle Douglas
Annan
Newcastle-upon-Tyne
Stranraer
Greenhead
Hexham
Corbridge
Gatehouse of Fleet
Carlisle
Portpatrick
Wigtown
Kirkcudbright
Silloth
CUMBRIA
Alston
Port William
Bassenthwaite
Penrith
5
6
A9
A836
A838
A895
A837
A835
A832
A890
A96
A98
A95
A82
A87
A939
A93
A92
A830
A86
A94
A85
A816
A83
A91
A915
A8
M9
M8
M74
A73
A71
A77
A70
A76
A702
A703
A68
A1
A697
A7
A74
A701
A713
A75
A69
A689
A6
M6